This book presents Edwardian entertainment and the Edwardian entertainment industry as parts of a vital but troubled era whose preoccupations and paranoias mirror those of our own age. Responding to the Edwardian stage as a social, economic and cultural phenomenon, it takes as its province broad patterns of theatrical production and consumption, focussing upon the economics of theatre management, the creation of new audiences, the politics of playgoing and the emergence of popular forms of entertainment such as variety theatre, sensation melodrama, the stage musical and the cinema. Employing new methodologies from allied disciplines contributors offer fresh insights into topics as diverse as music hall cross-dressing, the rise of musical comedy and the vexed relationship between theatre practice and suffrage politics. The book, with illustrations from the period, will be of interest to students and scholars of theatre and performance history, social history, cultural studies, women's studies and English literature, as well as to general readers.

THE EDWARDIAN THEATRE

THE EDWARDIAN THEATRE

Essays on performance and the stage

EDITED BY

MICHAEL R. BOOTH

JOEL H. KAPLAN

CAMBRIDGE
UNIVERSITY PRESS

Published by the Press Syndicate of the University of Cambridge
The Pitt Building, Trumpington Street, Cambridge CB2 1RP
40 West 20th Street, New York, NY 10011–4211, USA
10 Stamford Road, Oakleigh, Melbourne 3166, Australia

First published 1996

Printed in Great Britain at the University Press, Cambridge

A catalogue record for this book is available from the British Library

Library of Congress cataloguing in publication data

The Edwardian theatre: essays on performance and the stage / edited
by Michael R. Booth, Joel H. Kaplan.
p.   cm.
Includes index.
ISBN 0 521 45375 5 (hardback)
1. Theater – Great Britain – History – 20th century.   2. Music-halls
(Variety-theaters, cabarets, etc.) – Great Britain – History – 20th
century.   1. Booth, Michael R.   II. Kaplan, Joel H.
PN2595.E35   1996
792′.0941′09041 – dc20   95-18271   CIP

ISBN 0 521 45375 5 hardback

Contents

Illustrations

Contributors

EDITORS

MICHAEL R. BOOTH teaches theatre history at the University of Victoria. He is author of *English Melodrama* (1965), *Victorian Spectacular Theatre 1850–1910* (1981), and *Theatre in the Victorian Age* (1991). He has also edited *Hiss the Villain* (1964), *Eighteenth Century Tragedy* (1965), *English Plays of the Nineteenth Century* (1969–76), and *The Lights o' London and Other Victorian Plays* (1995).

JOEL H. KAPLAN is Professor of Drama and Chair of the Department of Drama and Theatre Arts at the University of Birmingham. He is co-author of *Theatre and Fashion: Oscar Wilde to the Suffragettes* (1994), and the forthcoming *Wilde on Stage: A Cultural and Performance History*.

CONTRIBUTORS

PETER BAILEY teaches social history and cultural studies at the University of Manitoba. He is editor of *Music Hall: The Business of Pleasure* (1986) and author of *Leisure and Class in Victorian England* (2nd edn 1987), and *Champagne Charlie Meets the Barmaid*, a forthcoming collection of essays on the popular culture of the period.

J. S. BRATTON is Professor of Theatre and Cultural History at Royal Holloway, University of London. Her publications include a theatre history edition of *King Lear*, and co-authorship of *Acts of Supremacy: The British Empire and the Stage* (1991) and *Melodrama: Stage/Picture/Screen* (1994).

JIM DAVIS is Head of the School of Theatre and Film Studies at the University of New South Wales. His publications include *John*

Liston, Comedian (1985), an edition of plays by H.J. Byron, and *The Britannia Diaries* (1992).

TRACY C. DAVIS teaches in the Departments of Theatre, English, and Performance Studies at Northwestern University. She is author of *Actresses as Working Women: Their Social Identity in Victorian Culture* (1991), *George Bernard Shaw and the Socialist Theatre* (1994), and articles on feminist theatre, gender history, and historiography.

JOSEPH DONOHUE, Professor of English at the University of Massachusetts, is author of *Dramatic Character in the English Romantic Age* (1970) and *Theatre in the Age of Kean* (1975). He is editor of *Nineteenth Century Theatre* and general editor of *The London Stage 1800–1900: A Documentary Record and Calendar of Performances*.

VICTOR EMELJANOW is Professor of Drama at the University of Newcastle, Australia. He is author of *Chekov: The Critical Heritage* (1981) and *Victorian Popular Dramatists* (1987). He is also a contributing editor to the Cambridge University Press Theatre in Europe series.

DENNIS KENNEDY holds the Samuel Beckett Chair of Drama and Theatre Studies at Trinity College, Dublin. His books include *Granville Barker and the Dream of Theatre* (1985), an edition of Barker's plays, *Looking at Shakespeare* (1993), and *Foreign Shakespeare* (1993). He is also a playwright and dramaturg.

DAVID MAYER is Professor of Drama at the University of Manchester, director of the Victorian and Edwardian Stage on Film Project, and consultant to The American Memory Program at the US Library of Congress. He is author of *Harlequin in His Element* (1969) and editor of *Henry Irving and The Bells* (1980). His most recent book is *Playing Out the Empire: Ben Hur and Other Toga Plays and Films* (1994).

DAVE RUSSELL is Senior Lecturer in the Department of Historical and Critical Studies at the University of Central Lancashire. He is author of *Popular Music in England 1840–1914: A Social History* (1987) and has published a number of articles and papers on the history of popular music and popular culture.

JOHN STOKES is Reader in English at the University of Warwick. He is author of *Resistible Theatres* (1972) and *In the Nineties* (1989), and editor of *Fin-de-siècle/Fin du Globe: Fears and Fantasies of the Late Nineteenth-Century* (1992).

SHEILA STOWELL is Senior Research Fellow in the Department of Drama and Theatre Arts at the University of Birmingham. She is author of *A Stage of Their Own: Feminist Playwrights of the Suffrage Era* (1992), and co-author of *Theatre and Fashion: Oscar Wilde to the Suffragettes* (1994).

Acknowledgements

Eight of the following papers were first presented at 'The Edwardian Stage', an international conference held at Dunsmuir Lodge, Vancouver Island, Canada, in September 1992. We would like to thank the University of Victoria and the University of British Columbia for co-hosting that event, and the Social Sciences and Humanities Research Council of Canada for generous financial support.

Two papers initially offered at the Dunsmuir Lodge conference, George Rowell's 'The Battle of Waterloo Road: The Old Vic 1901–1914' and Joel Kaplan and Sheila Stowell's 'The Red Mouth of a Venomous Flower: Edwardian London's Millinery Theatres' have since been subsumed in other publications. Readers are directed to the relevant sections of George Rowell's *The Old Vic Theatre: A History* (Cambridge University Press 1993), pp. 59–96, and Joel Kaplan and Sheila Stowell's *Theatre and Fashion: Oscar Wilde to the Suffragettes* (Cambridge University Press 1994), pp. 115–51.

M.R.B.
J.H.K.

Introduction

Joel H. Kaplan

Two decades ago, in what is still our most compact guide to the drama of the period, J. C. Trewin likened the Edwardian stage to a house, its principal rooms chambers for compartmentalizing that era's theatrical experience. In its dining room, Trewin tells us, we can sample the culinary fare of Pinero and Jones, in its study the intellectual wares of Shaw, Galsworthy, and Granville Barker. A conservatory is provided for the verse dramas of Stephen Phillips, and a playroom for the musical comedies of George Edwardes (*The Edwardian Theatre* 25–6). If, however, Trewin's structure neatly echoes the rich variety of Edwardian theatre, its subdivisions do little to suggest the interplay of forms or genres that seems, to late twentieth-century eyes, one of the most remarkable features of pre-war entertainment. To be sure, Trewin's conceit was in 1977 both a response to and corrective of an image that W. Macqueen-Pope, that 'wistful remembrancer', had used some three decades earlier. In *Carriages at Eleven: the Story of the Edwardian Theatre* (1947) Macqueen-Pope had compared Edwardian playgoing to a series of domestic visitations, hosted by that era's leading actor-managers: 'you always knew where your friend, the actor-manager, lived ... Provided you had executed that little formality at the box office or paybox, you were equally his honoured guests no matter where you sat' (9–10). Play attendance was, for Macqueen-Pope, a round of commercial at-homes, in which one called upon one's 'friends' at their respective playhouses. Yet while Trewin's house substitutes diversity for the gentility of Macqueen-Pope's houses, both participate in a view of the Edwardian stage that has come to seem increasingly untenable. In part this has been the result of a larger shift of attitudes towards the Edwardians and their world. The past quarter-century, in particular, has seen 'the old Edwardian brigade' mocked by John Osborne's Jimmy Porter, but reinforced by popular novels (and more popular films) like *The Go-Between* and *The Shooting Party* – 'All home-made cakes and croquet, bright ideas, bright uniforms' – yield to images of mid-channel nausea meant to catch the sensibilities of an era social historian Samuel Hynes has likened to 'a narrow place made turbulent by the thrust and tumble of two powerful opposing tides' (*The Edwardian Turn of Mind* vii). Recent exhibitions such as the Barbican Art Gallery's 'The Edwardian Era' (1987–8) and the Museum of London's 'Suffragettes in London' (1992–3) have insisted upon such turbulence, registered in anxieties about gender, class, and race, and bodied forth in a series of increasingly violent street demonstrations, as emblematic of an age that had become both theatrical about its politics and political about its theatre. Viewed within this context, the Edwardian stage, one house or many, seems in need of major refurbishment.

The eleven essays that make up the present volume attempt such reconstruction. Indeed, their subject-matter alone is indicative of some of the ways in which theatre and performance studies have themselves been reshaped since Trewin's initial work. Twenty years ago it would have been unthinkable to offer a book on the Edwardian stage without substantial consideration of the dramas of Bernard Shaw, the managements of Granville Barker, or the theatre journalism of Max Beerbohm. All appear in the present volume, but obliquely as parts of a larger, more comprehensive cultural enquiry. Instead of retracing the not inconsiderable achievement of individual authors, directors, or drama critics, the present work takes as its province broader patterns of theatrical production and consumption, focussing upon the economics of Edwardian management, the creation of new audiences, the politics of playgoing, and the emergence of popular, distinctly un-literary forms of entertainment, including variety theatre, East End melodrama, musical comedy, and the cinema. In an introductory essay, Joseph Donohue stakes out the perimeters of this altered landscape, commenting upon problems of approach and access that have hitherto hindered disinterested discussion. Donohue's initial concern is one of definition. Yet in attempting to fix boundaries, and establish an appropriate degree of scholarly distance from a subject that has endured more than its share of uncritical nostalgia, he proposes 'a manageable group of qualities or attributes' helpful in distinguishing the Edwardian stage from both its late Victorian forbears and early modern descendants. Among Donohue's categories are a number of topics that assume the status of leitmotifs in the essays that follow. The new puritanism Donohue associates with much of the period's progressive drama, for example, brings in its wake the larger question of Edwardian eroticism and its place in both coterie and popular theatre. It is a theme sounded by Peter Bailey in his enquiry into the rise of musical comedy, and J. S. Bratton in her account of male impersonators and music hall cross-dressing. The quest for new kinds of audiences, raised by Donohue in a discussion of the period's repertory movement, returns, not only where one might expect it, in Dennis Kennedy's reassessment of avant-garde spectators, but in Dave Russell's account of a newly gentrified music hall and Jim Davis's survey of East End neighbourhood playhouses. The social and moral earnestness Donohue finds in much of the era's political drama is likewise explored in Sheila Stowell's study of suffrage theatre agitation, and in Victor Emeljanow's account of the professional fraternities that helped to define the agendas of mainstream drama criticism. In each case attempts at rigorous localization are used to provide a fresh context for reassessing texts both familiar and now marginalized.

Donohue's challenge to see Edwardian entertainment as both an object in its own right and part of a larger cultural matrix is taken up by a number of contributors who bring new critical methodologies to bear upon popular forms of theatre and performance art. In the 1890s William Archer observed, not without misgivings, that the new century's 'real New Drama' would not be the theatre of Ibsen, Maeterlinck, or Shaw, but the sex-and-shopping musicals already attracting attention at George Edwardes's Gaiety Theatre. In '"Naughty but nice": musical comedy and the rhetoric of the girl', Peter Bailey seeks to account for the enormous success of this most Edwardian of genres. Drawing parallels with the Hollywood musical as that form has been reseen by post-modern film critics, Bailey shows 'how familiar and apparently unproblematical forms can reveal much of social and ideological significance'. Central to this concern, and introducing a theme that resonates through the volume, is the figure of the girl-heroine and her implications for understanding Edwardian formulations of sexuality and gender. Indeed, the celebration of woman as 'girl' in a succession of stage musicals like *A Gaiety Girl*, *The Sunshine Girl*, *The Shop Girl*, *The Girl from Kays*, and *The Girl Behind the Counter*, enables Bailey to explore in tandem the stage persona of the Gaiety heroine and the professional status of the Gaiety Girls who impersonated her. Proposing both military and industrial models for the production-line techniques of musical comedy, Bailey invites a comparison of the regime of impresario George Edwardes – 'Svengali, martinet, snooper , and sugar daddy' – with both older paternalistic modes of authority and newer patterns of industrial production, a convergence of forces nicely caught in his reproduction of a Gaiety Girl punching a time clock. Such focus upon the Edwardian stage as a large-scale cultural industry, an emphasis echoed in Dave Russell's study of variety theatre, and Tracy C. Davis's essay on the economics of Edwardian theatre management, allows Bailey to link actual conditions of employment to the representation of work and workers on the musical stage. Here what Bailey calls the 'brokered sexuality' of Edwardes's musicals, conveyed to spectators through an acknowledged system of codified gestures and an infusion of music hall 'knowingness', takes its place within an emerging consumer culture, whose centre was the already theatricalised glamour of the purpose-built department store. In pieces like *Our Miss Gibbs*, *The Girl Behind the Counter*, and *This Way Madam*, all set in identifiable replicas of actual stores, a reactionary patriarchy on both sides of the footlights sought to define its own New Woman. What remained to be seen was whether, in the end, a female workforce would submit to such control, or oppose to it what Bailey terms 'a more independent sense of self'.

What Bailey does for musical comedy, Dave Russell and J. S. Bratton do for the equally problematic form of Edwardian music hall. In 'Varieties of life: the making of the Edwardian music hall', Russell challenges a conventional scenario which casts early twentieth-century variety theatre in the role of syndicate-controlled villain, appropriating and finally silencing earlier, more 'authentic' Victorian voices. Identifying the origins of such a tale in Edwardian debates about the 'soullessness' of mass entertainment, Russell proposes an alternative narrative in which Edwardian music hall re-emerges as a resilient response to new business practices and altered patterns of audience attendance, triggering the transformation of an institution dominated by comic song into one characterized by a rich collection of hybrid acts. Russell's emphasis falls, accordingly, on the success of Edwardian variety in constructing new constituencies, its courting of respectability in an attempt to make peace with Temperance opponents and municipal licensing boards, and its role in helping to shape the iconography of a democratic or popular monarchy, an effort that culminated in the attendance of George V at a Command Performance at London's Palace Theatre of Varieties in 1912. M_intaining that definitive readings of individual performers or acts are, at this distance, neither possible nor desirable, Russell focusses upon the ways in which Edwardian variety functioned as a social barometer, registering economic, political, and moral disturbances, before resolving them in the interests of its increasingly genteel clientele. In 'Beating the bounds: gender play and role reversal in the Edwardian music hall', J. S. Bratton presents us with just such an instance. Taking as her starting point a collection of pin-up postcards of cross-dressed Edwardian women, Bratton asks what variety artists like Hetty King or Bessie Wentworth thought they were doing when they blacked-up, dressed as men, and delivered themselves of music hall set-pieces like 'Looking for a Coon Like Me'. Approaching such acts through a sequence of carnival tropes, and citing gender theorist Judith Butler on the relationship of cross-dressing to specific periods of cultural crisis, Bratton explores the manner in which variety transvestism (and Bailey's music hall 'knowingness') may be seen as a response to the fierce misogyny of the halls themselves. Read as burlesques of the masculine, such performances take their place as parts of a larger process in which popular entertainment contributed a space for the testing and contesting of gender. The vilification of independent women – the need, especially, to punish in stage sketches assertive suffragettes – taken together with the appeal of a figure Bratton identifies as the 'disarming androgyne' allows us to see in luminous detail some of the tensions between oppositional image-making and the policing of traditional boundaries that Russell identifies as one of the hallmarks of Edwardian variety.

The new forms of entertainment surveyed by Bailey, Russell, and Bratton have their counterparts in the new management structures and audiences examined, in turn, by Tracy C. Davis and Dennis Kennedy. For Davis, in 'Edwardian management and the structures of industrial capitalism', the shifts of sensibility recorded by Bailey and Russell are less the result of new repertoires or dramatic forms than of Edwardian innovations in industrial organization. Indeed, the centralized brokering of talent that both Bailey and Russell discuss as a feature of Edwardian popular entertainment is seen here as a concomitant of a larger push that saw theatre ownership and management pass at the century's close from limited liability partnerships to large publicly owned corporations. In seeking to understand such organizations, the financial environment in which they flourished, and the consequences of both for women in managerial positions, Davis urges a refinement of critical vocabulary, spelling out with precision some of the differences between manager, lessee, entrepreneur, and impresario. It is an exercise that allows us to see how the emergence of integrated organizations for the large-scale production and distribution of entertainment effectively shut women out of financially significant ventures, an economic perspective that helps to explain both the 'girl' heroines of musical comedy and the suffrage grotesques of the halls. As an attempt to understand the Edwardian stage as a function of its commercial imperatives, Davis's piece is complemented by Dennis Kennedy's study of the demographics of Edwardian playgoing. In 'The New Drama and the new audience', Kennedy sets attempts by English theatre managers to reform their spectators within the wider context of European modernism. Beginning with the paradoxical role audiences played in the rise of an avant garde, he enumerates the strategies by which organizations like the Independent Theatre and Stage Society helped to lay the groundwork for the Court Theatre's management of its spectators. Attempts to regulate audience behaviour, including the reshaping of attitudes towards applause, curtain calls, and theatre dress are seen as parts of a modernist desire to control the nature of aesthetic perception. Even the Court's sustained campaign against the wearing of matinée hats is shown to have been a political act with cultural implications. The problem with such reforming agendas, Kennedy concludes, was that in the absence of any kind of state subsidy (readily available to Antoine in Paris and Brahm in Berlin) Edwardian London's progressive drama had to survive within a larger theatre community that quite patently did not want to be reformed. The result was a series of uneasy and in the end disastrous compromises – Granville Barker at the St James's, with Shaw's portrait on the programme opposite an advertisement for the International Fur Store – that helped to promote the new theatre's 'loathing' of its audience.

If Kennedy's concern is with efforts to build new constituencies for a new drama, the trio of essays by Victor Emeljanow, Sheila Stowell, and John Stokes direct attention to the appearance in the period of a new kind, or kinds, of theatre critic. In 'Towards an ideal spectator: theatregoing and the Edwardian critic', Emeljanow traces the trajectory of mainstream theatre journalism from the formation of the Society of Dramatic Critics in 1906–7 to its replacement, some half a decade later, by the more narrowly defined Critics' Circle. In considering the shift from the 'amateur gentlemen' of the former organization – a group that included A. B. Walkley, William Archer, and J. T. Grein – to the 'professional players' of its more journalistic successor, Emeljanow is able to show how the language of theatre criticism was reshaped by a professional fraternity seeking to grapple with an irreparable breach between 'the art of the theatre' and a more commercially minded 'theatre industry'. In 'Suffrage critics and political action: a feminist agenda', Sheila Stowell argues that, for all their internal disputes and quarrels, the institutions anatomized by Emeljanow were (literally) male clubs. To their collective voices she adds those of Edwardian feminists for whom the stage was a place for political activity. Observing that prominent leaders of the suffrage cause, such as Christabel Pankhurst, Emmeline Pethick Lawrence, and Charlotte Despard, wrote theatre columns for an oppositional press that included *Votes for Women*, *The Suffragette*, *The Vote*, and *Common Cause*, Stowell seeks to identify the principles upon which individual performances were attended and reviewed, as well as those issues upon which feminist critics closed ranks against male colleagues. A concluding section reviews the militant theatre demonstrations of 1912–14, in which suffrage critics, articulating their cause, disrupted stage performances with a 'living drama' of their own. John Stokes, in sharp contrast, calls attention to the theatre writings of a single figure. In 'A woman of genius: Rebecca West at the theatre', he brings together the observations of a remarkable woman who determined to take an active role in the theatre of her time as a feminist-socialist drama critic. Using as a control the theatre journalism of West's compatriot Christina Walshe, Stokes underscores the sensitivities of an idiosyncratic personality who scorned the plays of suffrage activists, had major reservations about Shaw, neatly placed, along with Wells, Galsworthy, and Arnold Bennett, as one of the era's 'four uncles', and, above all, grasped with some prescience both the real modernity of Granville Barker ('He went thinking as other people go hunting') and the charged relationship between Edwardian performance, sex, and a newly theatricalized consumerism that set West End patrons ogling scantily clad dummies in the display windows of Regent Street shops.

The volume's concluding essays extend its frame of reference both spatially and temporally. Jim Davis's survey of London's East End cautions us against identifying Edwardian theatre exclusively with the amusements of Mayfair or the more high-minded enterprises at the Royal Court or Duke of York's. Reminding us that East London in the pre-war years contained a twentieth part of the population of Britain, Davis traces a vigorous record of theatrical life and theatrical change, one that witnessed the disappearance of large neighbourhood playhouses like the City of London, the Grecian, and the Garrick, and saw a variety of strategies adopted by those theatres that wished to resist the seemingly inevitable transformation into music halls, or (later) cinemas. For the Whitechapel Pavilion survival meant turning to an increasingly Jewish constituency to become the home of England's Yiddish theatre, while the Standard in Shoreditch aligned itself with the 'wicked woman' melodramas of the brothers Melville, popular potboilers like *The Girl Who Lost Her Character*, *The Girl Who Took the Wrong Turning*, and *The Girl Who Wrecked His Home* that developed a 'rhetoric of the girl' as potent and influential as that Bailey describes in their Gaiety counterparts. The Standard's attempt to instruct and reform its suburban audiences, similarly, presents us with an alternative to the repertory techniques enumerated by Kennedy. While progressive managements were proclaiming that formal dress was no longer obligatory even at the fashionable St James's, East End theatres in a push towards respectability began to insist upon the wearing of collars and ties. The cinema, that together with the music hall offered the most formidable threat to the existence of such venues, is the subject of David Mayer's 'Changing horses in mid-ocean: *The Whip* in Britain and America'. Mayer, however, is less concerned with the emergence of film, by 1914, as the most significant art form of the new century, than he is with the interstices between stage and film. Using as a test case Henry Hamilton and Cecil Raleigh's 1909 Drury Lane melodrama *The Whip* and Maurice Tourneur's 1916 cinematic adaptation, Mayer considers some of the ways in which early cinematographers paused in the development of their own craft to record for posterity the legitimate drama of the period. The end products, Mayer concedes, may represent a backsliding for filmmaking as an art, but largely for this reason preserve for later viewers the stage languages of their era. Asking why sensation cinema eventually replaced Drury Lane drama, Mayer challenges the conclusions of film historians like A. N. Vardac, suggesting that it was less a matter of inadequate stage illusion than of the economic advantages of being able to print and circulate multiple copies of a single performance. According to such lights, Tourneur's war-time film, like the theatre it documents, may be said to celebrate an Edwardian penchant for the stage pose and extravagant gesture.

Taken together the essays that make up the present work offer Edwardian entertainment and the Edwardian entertainment industry as parts of a vital but troubled era whose preoccupations and paranoias anticipate those of our own age. Responding to the Edwardian stage as a social, economic, and intellectual phenomenon, the volume's contributors take up Donohue's challenge to approach their common subject as a field 'for sustained comprehensive inquiry'. Employing a variety of methodologies, they not only suggest new lines of investigation and directions for research, but show some of the insights to be gained by submitting Edwardian performance, in all its multiplicity, to broad cultural analysis and interdisciplinary debate.

CHAPTER I

What is the Edwardian theatre?

Joseph Donohue

The image of Albert Edward, the cigar-smoking, pleasure-loving sportsman, playgoer, and first gentleman of Europe who succeeded his mother Queen Victoria as King Edward VII in 1901, looms over the decade he dominated in characteristic but problematic ways. Sixty years of age when he ascended the throne, Edward was an old man with less than ten years to live. Remarkably and unexpectedly, he conferred an energy and a sense of fresh beginnings on that brief period that endowed it with significant new life. Never all things to all men, he opened up new political vistas in Europe through his own personal diplomacy but remained at the same time neglectful of domestic problems, social unrest, and the increasing gap between rich and poor.[1] His activities at home and abroad were assiduously followed by the rapidly developing illustrated English press, so much so that his complex identity as monarch, statesman, and high liver was perhaps better defined in the popular mind than that of any previous monarch. And yet, paradoxically, during the decade itself and after, he symbolized a simple life of unhurried, unworried indolence. That symbol, reified and reinterpreted in a thousand ways then and later, typically emphasized the 'peculiar glamour' of all that was 'Edwardian'.[2] Other, more recent misperceptions include an image of a never-never land of 'high summer, the long days in the sun, slim volumes of verse, crisp linen, the smell of starch', comprising the 'brief little world' inhabited by the 'old Edwardian Brigade' vilified by the disaffected Jimmy Porter in John Osborne's *Look Back in Anger*.[3] Perhaps the most persistent bias of all has been a view of the Edwardian years as innocently but ironically moving forward into the deepening shadows of the cataclysm to come, the First World War.

These and other retrospective fallacies occur, early and late, even in the very attempt to establish the term used to designate the period itself and the span of years it encompasses. The author of the unsigned

obituary published in the *English Review* in June 1910, shortly after
Edward's death, observed that Britain mourned 'more than the man,
the symbol, the King: we mourn an epoch'.[4] Later, in an essay called
'The Edwardian Decade' published in 1933, the historian G. B.
Gooch described what he called the 'Edwardian era' as spanning the
time from the death of Victoria to the outbreak of the First World
War; for while Edward himself died in 1910, England 'continued
without change till the call to arms turned the world upside down'.[5]
The popular social historian and self-styled 'hopeless Edwardian'
Percy Colson, 29 when Victoria died, was of like mind but extended
his limits even further back, entitling his book on the subject *Close of an
Era 1887–1914*. In a foreword his friend Thomas Moore praised
Colson's 'delicate art ... of creating a nostalgic longing for a way of
life which the majority of his readers have never experienced',
offering 'a dignity, a graciousness, a beauty, all of which it is no doubt
stupid to regret in these days of mechanical progress'.[6] Nostalgia is
apparent in the title itself of the theatre historian W. Macqueen-Pope's
atmospheric study *Carriages at Eleven: The Story of the Edwardian
Theatre*, an account devoted to the days when London was 'a city of
smiles, the habitation of wealth, of peace, of security, and of power', a
city 'conscious that it was the centre of the whole world...'.
Edwardian days, Macqueen-Pope explains, actually began in 1897,
the year of Victoria's Diamond Jubilee, and extended 'with very little
difference' after Edward's death and the accession of his son, George
V, right up to the beginning of the war in 1914, 'when the whole
world changed'.[7]

The question of the duration of the Edwardian period quickly joins
with another question having to do with the nature and distance from
the subject of our own vantage point. In one of the best studies of its
kind, Samuel Hynes's *The Edwardian Turn of Mind* – a book linking
literary, political, social, and cultural issues in useful and suggestive
ways – the author generally identifies the period called Edwardian as
'the years just before the First World War', having roots in the 1890s
and ending in August 1914:

That time stands in an odd pivotal position between the nineteenth century
and the twentieth: it was not quite Victorian, though conservatives tried to
make it so, nor was it altogether modern, though it contained the beginnings
of many ideas that we recognize as our own. It was a brief stretch of history,
but a troubled and dramatic one – like the English Channel, a narrow place
made turbulent by the thrust and tumble of two powerful opposing tides.

That turbulent meeting of old and new makes the Edwardian period both interesting and important, for out of the turmoil contemporary England was made.[8]

The period highlighted yet not perfectly circumscribed by Edward's reign and brought to an end suddenly and catastrophically by a political assassination in the Balkans may well feel to us either alarmingly analogous to our own or, more likely, a period seemingly so brief and fleeting, and followed shortly after by such world-shattering events, that the entire decade can appear to be a kind of historical footnote to Victoria's much longer and more perspicuous reign. Hynes's clearsighted view of the relevance of the period to later twentieth-century life is therefore a salutary one. All the same, approaches toward understanding the theatre in the time of Edward have too often reflected a tendency toward over-generalization or inadequate differentiation. Scholars have been basically oriented toward the previous century and its characteristic 'Victorian' culture or else so forward-looking that the first decade of the century is judged important largely for what it gave way to, not for what it was.

A prominent example of the latter, forward-looking historian lies in the unlikely person of Allardyce Nicoll, the subtitle of whose history *English Drama 1900–1930* is *The Beginnings of the Modern Period*. In his preface, the historian and bibliographer of the 240 years of post-Restoration English drama to 1900 explains his view that the world of the modern English theatre, although 'anticipated vaguely' in the last years of the Victorian period, was 'essentially a creation of the twentieth century' and that the three decades from 1900 to 1930 'had been possessed by a spirit characteristically its own'. Nicoll cites the particulars combining in the new spirit he has discovered: the growth of Shaw, Barrie, and Galsworthy as dramatists led to a sense of 'greatness in the air'; and yet it was not simply individual achievement that created the new spirit, for there was equal moment in the rise of innumerable play-producing societies, many invigorated by novel aims. The 'collective effort' of ubiquitous play production and dense concentration of great playwrights together resulted in a newly introduced 'sense of endeavour' in the thirty years of Nicoll's coverage and an even more significant 'confident hope such as barely can be discerned in earlier times'.[9] Supporting his perception of a swift, perceptible departure from the theatre of the end of the century, Nicoll begins by citing and endorsing St John Ervine's categorical declaration that the theatre's 'revolutionary change' in character occurred immediately after Victoria's death in 1901.[10] For all his authoritativeness, however, one senses in Nicoll's argument a kind of double bias. He is surprisingly neglectful of the theatrical and dramatic continuities streaming into the Edwardian age, and he is oddly disinclined to acknowledge that the qualities constituting the new spirit he finds in the theatre of the first thirty years of our century all come to the fore during the brief but highly energized decade of Edward's reign itself.

No doubt, that ten-year period must be approached with wariness and no little scepticism. We must carefully give what is new its proper due without necessarily over-valuing it for what it would later become, or give way to, at the same time taking care to chart exactly the common ground that the Edwardian theatre shares with the Victorian. Avoiding any hint of retrospective fallacy, we must likewise avoid its inverse corollary – what might be called, to borrow a term from linguistics, the back-formation fallacy. In this case, certain ideas, techniques, preoccupations, or other characteristics of a major writer whose working life spans a considerable period are identified as fully articulated in major works of that writer's maturity; and then, by way of some illogical sleight-of-hand, the seeds of those same full-blossomed features are re-sown back in the pliant but less well-defined ground of the author's earlier works. William Butler Yeats's development of a poetic theatre modelled partly on the Japanese Noh play is a good example. It is all too easy to envision the germs of that seemingly apolitical art form sprouting promisingly in more overtly political early works such as *Cathleen ni Houlihan* – an Edwardian play produced in Dublin by the Fay brothers in 1902 – a play Yeats himself at times vigorously denied had any essential connection with contemporary politics.[11]

Another act of fallacious back-formation even closer to home is one committed by Bernard Shaw himself. In the 'Author's Apology' to the two-volume publication in 1907 of *Dramatic Opinions and Essays*, Shaw said his reviews were not a series of impartial judgements but 'a siege laid to the theatre of the XIXth Century by an author who had to cut his own way into it at the point of the pen'. True enough, but one wonders at the extreme clear-sightedness that in the next sentence Shaw imputes to his younger self: 'I postulated as desirable a certain kind of play in which I was destined ten years later to make my mark as a playwright (as I very well foreknew in the depth of my own unconsciousness); and I brought everybody, authors, actors, managers, to the one test: were they coming my way or staying in the old grooves?'[12] One discerns in Shaw's remarks more than a hint of spurious, self-serving prescience that hardly does justice to the exhilarating variety and scope and the sharp-tongued critical judgement of the essays and reviews collected in the three volumes of *Our Theatres in the Nineties*. Shaw's retrospective self-reconstruction grossly over-simplifies the authentic tone those essays and reviews convey of a writer instinctively if brilliantly feeling his way along, relying on the spur-of-the-moment insight, disarmingly acknowledging prejudice, jettisoning one newly espoused principle in favour of still another, and providing overall one of the most engaging accounts of first-hand theatrical experience by any critic who ever lived. The idea of possessing foreknown knowledge in the depth of one's unconscious is, of course, unproved and unprovable. However important it may have been to Shaw to see himself as a boy who was father to the man, the theatregoing public of the early 1890s cared not at all for psycho-biography in the making, any more than they did for what a masterly biographer writing nearly half a century after Shaw's death might make of the connection between the boy and the man.[13] What they cared about were the plays they had seen, or might see, on the basis of what the irrepressibly ebullient and eagle-eyed critic for the *Saturday Review* would say about them.

Finally, then, the decade of the Edwardian period must be taken fully on its own. At the same time, we cannot ask the question 'What is the Edwardian theatre?' without an awareness that our very methods and assumptions determine the conclusions we reach and also, in a prior way, even affect the documentation that we seek to assemble.[14] Given these premises, and the complicated situation of scholarship at the present moment, how may we proceed toward an answer?

Deferring theoretical questions to another time, I propose simply to scrutinize a manageable group of qualities or attributes that, by broad consent, characterize the theatre of Edwardian times, at the same time identifying some telling examples. The following five characteristics may usefully combine to describe the Edwardian theatre and drama.

First, a new realism: not simply the apotheosis of nineteenth-century verisimilitude in settings, costumes, and decor, but a newer, moral realism that prizes truthfulness even at the cost of pleasantness of subject or tidiness of dramatic construction. Included in this characteristic is a concomitant sense of earnestness, thoroughly Victorian and yet more discriminating, self-conscious, and sceptical than Victorian middle-class morality ever was. Also present is a sense of the importance of adducing a definitive social environment for events and human actions. In short, this is a realism that views society simultaneously in social and moral aspects as a matrix of moving and shifting values, rather than as an essentially monolithic conglomeration of persons and classes all with fixed attributes. This new realism thus appears as the product of an insistent, restless drive to see things for what they really are, name them accordingly, and set them in meaningful contexts.

Related to this new realism is a second, yet quite different quality: an enthusiastic idealism that vents itself, among other ways, in visions of a new theatre and even a new audience. Beyond that, it occasionally envisions a new, or improved, society, in many cases endowing the hoped-for changes with an historical dimension that can be identified as an idea of progress. Closely related to that sense of progress is a sense of departure, of new directions. A feeling that emerges with the death of Victoria and the advent of Edward, it carries a quality of strong *re*-orientation toward the future; connected with this new-found sense of direction comes a quasi-teleological sense of progress toward a goal (whatever it might be).

Also related in complex ways to both the new realism and the burgeoning idealism is a third characteristic, a new Puritanism, which appears to emerge in both vulgar and more intellectual forms. Shaw's series entitled *Three Plays for Puritans* (comprising *The Devil's Disciple*, *Caesar and Cleopatra*, and *Captain Brassbound's Conversion*), published in 1900, lays down a challenge that the Edwardian decade proceeded to take up, in a variety of guises. Shaw himself sounded something of a keynote in his preface to the series, where he tied together the problematic question of eroticism in the theatre and the seemingly unrelated question of true religious instinct.[15] The term 'puritan' itself would undergo considerable redefinition – and distortion – in the period, only partly as a sociolinguistic manifestation of the feminist and suffrage movements.

A fourth characteristic emerges in a continuing love of fantasy, perhaps the most obvious heritage bequeathed by the Victorian theatre to the Edwardians but redefined by them, to some extent unconsciously, in more personal, even idiosyncratic ways. Related to this quality is a heightened appreciation of and appetite for pleasure – hedonistic, intellectual, innocent, or guilty, as the case may be.

Finally, there emerges in the Edwardian theatre and its ambiance a fifth characteristic, a notable quality of leisure, paradoxically coexistent with persistent, indefatigable energy and industriousness. Although seemingly not much different from qualities observable in the Edwardians' Victorian predecessors, in this later time these energies and attitudes are more often channelled toward the accomplishment of idealistic goals and less often toward achieving that hobgoblin of Victorian minds, increased respectability. A prominent exception to this generalization is the tendency toward a greater gentility in the music hall. This tremendous gathering of resources in the first years of the new century, an indication of the freshly energized and newly channelled industriousness of the age, is exemplified in the number of new theatres constructed or rebuilt during the ten years following the death of Victoria, carrying on the momentum of theatre building begun in the 1890s.[16]

Some important attributes of the first characteristic Edwardian quality, realism, may be identified by examining two critical books by one of the ubiquitous presences in this age, as in the period that preceded it, William Archer. Archer's revaluative account of western drama, *The Old Drama and the New*, published in 1923, and an earlier treatise on dramatic craftsmanship, *Play-making*, dating from 1912, together offer useful instruction in what was happening to the notion of realism in the first decade of this century.

In *The Old Drama and the New*, Archer sought in the long process of dramatic development since the ancient Greeks a 'guiding principle of evolution', and found it in the rise of the drama out of two sources, as he saw them, *imitation* and *passion*. The first term was, he thought, too obvious to need definition. By *passion* he meant 'the exaggerated, intensified – in brief, the lyrical or rhetorical – expression of feeling'.[17] The two tendencies were essentially antithetical, he believed, and could be seen throughout history warring between themselves for dominance. Arbitrarily singling out two works from the great multi-millennial residue of dramatic art, Archer takes from his shelves at random John Vanbrugh's post-Restoration comedy *The Provok'd Wife* and contrasts it with John Galsworthy's Royal Court play of 1906, *The Silver Box*. He concludes that the realistic art of the modern play is 'incalculably more faithful, more subtle and more highly developed than that of the late seventeenth-century comedy' (p. 24). History has come down on the side of imitation, casting out the 'lyrical element' and raising to a triumphant place 'the mimetic instinct'. Archer's rationalist prejudice has led him to champion modern realistic drama as 'a pure and logical art-form' representing the culmination of a long, slow process of development. His lack of historical imagination is evident in his condemnation of the ancient Greeks' 'curious adherence' to the use of masks and the association of drama with religion, practices that 'prevented them from inventing that indispensable instrument of realism, the small or moderate-sized theatre' (p. 14). And Archer's bias is similarly evident in his observation that antiquity 'never rose (I say deliberately, rose, not sank) to anything like the sober, unexaggerated portrayal of contemporary character on the stage' (p. 11).

One of the most important figures in the late Victorian and Edwardian theatre, this indefatigable playgoer, critic, scholar, and fast friend remains an unavoidable reference point in it.[18] It is precisely because of Archer's evident limitations as an historical critic that his assumptions about realism make him so broadly informative about the predilections of his time and thus so representative of the age of Galsworthy and his contemporaries. For his writings often betray in lucid ways certain prejudices, assumptions, and values that help considerably to define the true contours and substance of the Edwardian, and late Victorian, theatre.

That profile of the theatre of the age comes even more clear when set in the nearer perspective of Archer's *Play-making*. In chapter XXI, entitled 'The Full Close', an investigation of the way some playwrights maintain suspense to the very end, Archer relates the ending of Pinero's *Mid-Channel* (1909) to ideas of tragedy and specifically to 'the artistic use and abuse of suicide'.[19] Archer admonishes the would-be playwright to build the causes for climactic self-immolation deeply into the fabric of the play. The question of suicide turns, however, on the deeper point of the play of chance in the world at large and in the drama itself. To illustrate, Archer turns to *Mid-Channel*, which ends with Zoe Blundell's 'leap to nothingness' (p. 236). Although he makes a good case for a convincing inevitability in Zoe's suicide, the workings of chance in Pinero's concluding action still nag at Archer's consciousness. A defensive tone creeps into his commentary. Chance, he maintains, 'is a constant factor in life, now aiding, now thwarting, the will . . .'; and yet 'it is only when the playwright so manipulates and reduplicates chance as to make it seem no longer chance, but purposeful arrangement, that we have the right to protest' (p. 237). The real issue, Archer implies, is not chance but the playwright's creation of the illusion of plausibility – a more subjective matter altogether and, finally, we ourselves might argue, a culturally determined quality. For the play of chance in fictive art has, as we know, links with complex matters relating to style, theatrical effects, generic characteristics, audience expectations, and other factors as well, which combine to establish the felt plausibility of a dramatic action. Archer's defensiveness on behalf of Pinero suggests that the Edwardian audience's own sense of plausibility is in crisis and undergoing a series of painful tests. Considering the formal and stylistic differences between, say, Granville Barker's *The Voysey Inheritance* (1905) and his *The Madras House* (1910), we can see the strain being placed, in this period, on an audience's sense of causative event. Even more strain occurs in the case of another Barker play, *Waste*. Archer thought it a 'grave flaw' that this play 'should open with a long discussion, by people whom we scarcely know, of other people whom we do not know at all, whose names we may or may not have noted on the playbill'.[20] Barker's departure from dramaturgical norms speaks of a deepening rift between what the commercial playwright can ask his audience to accept and the unconventional, rough-edged moral truth that Barker insists on telling – and, moreover, in the face of a hostile and ultimately repressive censorship.

Archer's *Play-making* is the most articulate and comprehensive defence of the English well-made play ever written. That is at once its chief feature and most signal limitation. For Archer could not really see, from his foreshortened perspective, that the changes occurring in English society during the years of Edward's reign had an increasing force and moment that would eventually make the term *well-made play* itself one of universal disapprobation. The very fact that Archer feels called upon to defend a play, no matter how well crafted, against charges of implausibility indicates pretty clearly that the game is already up. In fact, the game was up by the end of the 1890s, and even more manifestly so in the ten years of serious drama that followed. To avert increasing scrutiny of its plausibility, a play had to be written with such immense skill that nothing sufficiently life-like as random coincidence could be allowed to ripple its mirrored surface. And so the well-made play would appear to be perfecting itself out of existence, retreating to an ever smaller drawing-room of perfect plausibility ever more remote from the roughness, randomness, and heterogeneity of actual life.

One wants to look at evidence and counter-evidence for such an assertion. Pinero's *The Thunderbolt* (1908) exemplifies the perfection of the well-made play, and Barker's *The Madras House* indicates the tendency toward apparent formlessness. For good measure, Galsworthy's *Justice* (1910) uneasily straddles the barrier between coherent tragic action and a reform-oriented social action drama.[21] We can attempt to link the specific phenomenon of a changing sense of what is plausible and convincing on the stage to larger cultural and socio-literary currents, but we should bear in mind that change may have come more slowly to the theatre of the Edwardian age than to its fiction, poetry, and other imaginative writing.[22] This would have been the case because of the inherent conservatism of the commercial theatre, the baneful activity of the Examiner of Plays, a disinclination on the part of the audiences to do any thinking, as Mario Borsa, a contemporary Italian historian of the theatre, maintained – the 'intellectual apathy' of the 'great British public' was, he asserted, 'the secret of its social force'[23] – and because of other factors, such as the continuing domination of the actor-manager.

Our sense of the forces, social and otherwise, in the Edwardian theatre resistant to change may be all the more strong because we can see so clearly a strain of idealism present in spite of them that characterizes the efforts of certain men and women of the theatre. Let us proceed to the second of the five characteristics of the Edwardian theatre under discussion. Is it merely coincidence that the same year of 1904 saw the founding of the Royal Court Theatre enterprise by John Vedrenne and Harley Granville Barker and the reclamation of an old morgue in Abbey Street, Dublin, as the venue of a new Irish national theatre? We would be right, I think, to associate the Vedrenne–Barker venture, short-lived though it was, with parallel schemes for a national theatre in London and Dublin and to view them collectively as reflecting a strong idealism emergent in the theatre of the age.

Barker and his business-like colleague Vedrenne put together a non-commercial theatre operation that was, paradoxically, commercially viable, at least marginally. Now, commercial viability was an important part of the rationale behind an idea of a national theatre gaining momentum at this time. In 1910 Barker looked back, in a lecture published as 'The Theatre: The Next Phase', at a decade of theatrical progress and concluded there could be no doubt that 'we are fairly launched upon a striking development of the Theatre', a development evident also for some years on the continent and even in

America. The time was still right for a national theatre, Barker pointed out. The Irish National Theatre had been an accomplished fact for some years, and movements for citizens' theatres had surfaced in Glasgow and elsewhere; these developments followed an older 'Secessionist Movement', dating from the time of J. T. Grein's Independent Theatre, whose influence in turn was spread by the Stage Society. Essentially, Barker thought, the movement comprised an assertion that 'the dignity of our drama should be a recognised part of our national dignity'.[24] In a later retrospective assessment Barker was still convinced of the need and the rightness of the project. The British Library copy of Archer and Barker's *A National Theatre: Scheme & Estimates* (1907) – Barker's own copy – has been heavily annotated by him at some later date. In Section XII Barker and Archer had insisted that the proposed theatre building be 'provided free of rent, taxes, insurance premium, and cost of upkeep' and that a Guarantee Fund should in addition be raised to assure for a certain period the solvency of the institution. In a retrospective marginal note Barker comments that 'in the strictest sense of the phrase' the theatre should be self-supporting, but that 'rent, rates, taxes, and competitive advertisement are too onerous a charge upon art done solely for art's sake'; these costs should therefore be covered by the endowment, 'and the theatre still be *morally self supporting*'.[25]

It is interesting, and ironic, to see how Barker obfuscates the notion of commercial viability through recourse to an idealism that substitutes a moral imperative for an economic one and gives precedence to the former. The failure of that scheme in Barker's own day is the essential fact of its pre-war history. Barker's moral ideal has, it seems, at last been realized in the form of the annual government grants now given to the imposing edifice on the South Bank. Two world wars occurred, however, and two foundation stones were laid futilely before his and his contemporaries' dream became concrete, and Barker himself did not live to see the day. Idealism, then and at other times, remained a commodity purchased at considerable cost.

Connected in various ways to that burgeoning but in so many ways short-lived Edwardian idealism, of which the movement for a national theatre is only one example, is what I have called a 'new Puritanism', being the third characteristic of Edwardian theatre. In his reiterated call for a national theatre in the 1910 essay 'The Theatre: The Next Phase', Barker had argued that the realization of the enterprise would confer an enormous moral benefit on the impressionable 17–30 age group, and it was vital for them, he thought, that the theatre 'should be of good report, clean, wholesome, making for righteousness'.[26] Elsewhere in the essay Barker defines this theatre as a 'Normal Theatre', consisting of 'normal plays about and for normal people, capable of normal success under normal conditions' (p. 638). How define that troublesome term 'normal'? Barker asks. J. M. Barrie's distinction between a 'sincerely unconventional play' and 'a meretricious piece of riskiness' – namely, that 'you could always tell whether a thing was well meant or not' – is much to the point. Consequently, by 'cultivating an artistic as well as a moral conscience' one can soon distinguish between 'a normal work of art and an abnormal'. Barker states his conviction that the Normal Drama is notable for its Puritan spirit – 'for the fact that, good-naturedly, portentously, industriously, or light-heartedly, it somehow makes for righteousness'. The obvious test is whether this drama presents 'an undistorted view' of life; and implicit in the call for a morally righteous drama is the rejection of stage censorship, since otherwise the Normal Drama cannot be truly free (pp. 640, 643).

Barker's Puritanism is clearly not of a squeamish kind; he takes the Speaker of the House of Commons to task for testifying at the recent parliamentary enquiry that theatrical censorship did not keep 'any healthy-minded author with a wholesome plot' from writing. 'Why', Barker asks rhetorically, 'will men worry about unhealthy and disgusting things?' (p. 643). Four years earlier, in 1906, St John Hankin made a similar point in his essay 'Puritanism and the English Stage', advocating the abolition of censorship as a step toward a national drama because it is impossible to have 'a national drama of serious intellectual interest if you cut it off from all the most vital and inspiring subjects'.[27]

Barker's, and Hankin's, idealization of truth-telling is notable here. As a theatre artist and a dramatist Barker conscientiously embraces the imperative of dealing with what Shaw, in publishing his first collection of plays in 1898, had called 'unpleasant' subjects.[28] The debate over the place and treatment of human sexuality on the stage appears to have raged on and off over the whole Edwardian period. As early as 1900, in his Preface to *Three Plays for Puritans*, Shaw described the dilemma of the theatre manager: convinced that plays depend for dramatic force 'on appeals to the sex instinct', the manager nonetheless must make sure that what appear on his stage be 'perfectly genteel plays' (p. 22). Out of that dilemma arose the old romantic play, Shaw explains, in which 'love is carefully kept off the stage' while being alleged 'as the motive of all the actions presented to the audience' (p. 23). This leads Shaw to define his own Puritan attitude toward art: he was as fond of 'fine music and handsome building' as Milton or Cromwell or Bunyan, but if he discovered that they were turning into 'the instruments of a systematic idolatry of sensuousness', he would consider it necessary to blow up the cathedral, organ and all; for 'the substitution of sensuous ecstasy for intellectual activity and honesty is the very devil' (pp. 27–8).

In his foreword to Shaw's *Dramatic Opinions and Essays* of 1907, James Huneker identified Shaw as a Puritan, although he perhaps overstated, or mis-stated, the case. 'He finds in our art and literature', Huneker said, 'that sexual passion plays far too important a rôle', and 'the slimy sentimentalities of the popular play are too much for his nerves' (pp. xiii–xiv). Others took a different view. In an essay of 1910 called 'The Dramatic Sense', Gilbert Cannan (who served as secretary to J. M. Barrie's campaign to abolish the censor and whose adultery with Barrie's wife Mary caused the breakdown of that marriage[29]) condemned Shaw, and Barker as well, for their 'unhealthy and unwholesome preoccupation with the sexual relationship of men and women'. The world of Philip Madras, he said, quoting Barker himself, was a 'farmyard world of sex'.[30] The obituarist of King Edward, writing in the same issue of the *English Review*, was premature, it seems, in concluding that Edward had 'pricked the bladder of Puritanical flummery'.[31] Cannan's is a vulgar puritanism, with a small 'p', and is cynical and hypocritical as well. And yet persons as avowedly intellectual as Shaw's friend and fellow Fabian Beatrice Webb were also deeply offended by what Webb described in her diary in March 1910 as the obsession of Shaw, and Barker, with 'the rabbit-warren aspect of human society'. Webb's objections went even deeper. Both Barker and Shaw, she noted, 'harp on the mere physical attractions of men to women, and women to men, coupled with the insignificance of the female for any other purpose but sex attraction...'. That world', she added, 'is not the world I live in.'[32]

In a real sense Shaw comes into his own as an Edwardian dramatist, dominating not only the Vedrenne–Barker Court Theatre enterprise itself but the play of ideas over the entire decade, from *Man and Superman* (written 1901–3) through *John Bull's Other Island* (1904) and *Major Barbara* (1905) to *Misalliance* (1910).[33] He inspired, said Desmond MacCarthy, 'an admiration for courage and intellectual honesty, and for a kind of spontaneity of character which is a blending of both'.[34] Yet, notwithstanding his success, Shaw remained a controversial and often misunderstood writer who ironically went to extreme lengths to explain himself, in play, preface, and essay, as well as innumerable letters, but who was constantly caught by the conflict he himself perceived between entertainment and edification.

Beatrice Webb's hostile response to the dramaturgical efforts of Shaw and Barker may be placed in broader moral and political contexts that include the long line of late Victorian and Edwardian protesters in the Social Purity Alliance, the burgeoning feminism of the new century, the contemporary suffrage movement, and their various reflections in the new drama of the time.[35] That the same complex issues of sexuality link a suffrage play such as Elizabeth Robins's *Votes for Women!*, produced with close supervision and advice by Barker early in 1907 at the Royal Court, and Barker's own ill-fated drama *Waste*, dating from later the same year – the link in the case of these two plays being the strikingly specific one of illegal abortion – suggests how extensively intertwined and various are the subjects and issues that are grouped here, for convenience' sake, under the rubric of 'a new Puritanism'.

Subjects such as the Royal Court venture and suffragism in the drama naturally attract the attention of scholars, by habit intellectually inclined and by training and interest alive to the social contexts in which theatrical performance takes place. In focussing on topics that could be rated 'Mature Adult', however, we may easily neglect the more popular, sometimes childlike attractions in the theatres of the age of Edward VII that drew far more playgoers to Shaftesbury Avenue and its environs than even Bernard Shaw did to the experimental theatre in Sloane Square. Let us turn to the fourth characteristic of the Edwardian theatre, fantasy and its attendant pleasures. 'For a hundred persons who go to *As You Like It*', St John Hankin observed in his 1906 *Fortnightly Review* essay 'Puritanism and the English Stage', 'for one who goes to *The Wild Duck*, ten thousand go to the Empire or *The Girl from A's*'.[36] In his essay 'J. M. Barrie as a Dramatist', written at the end of the decade, Barker said he thought he was the only playgoer in London who had not seen *Peter Pan* (p. 14).[37] Two months later a revised version of the play opened on Boxing Day, the day of its first production in 1904, at its original venue, Charles Frohman's Duke of York's.[38] Boxing Day seems the most appropriate opening date in the year for this play and its challenging spectacular and pantomime-like production requirements. A curious amalgam of dramatic genres combined in a delightful story about a 'boy who wouldn't grow up', *Peter Pan* represented the kind of fantasy that annually in the Christmas season captured the imaginations of the young and not-so-young – fantasy that was the stock-in-trade of the traditional English pantomime.

By Edwardian times pantomime had developed considerably from its eighteenth-century form, whose origins lay in the Italian *commedia dell'arte*, but it remained a characteristically indigenous entertainment. J. C. Trewin's description of the perennial attraction as 'a holiday gallimaufry, a music-hall in disguise, a spectacle for parents as much as their children'[39] captures an up-to-date sense of its general nature and appeal for Edwardian audiences as a hodgepodge of spectacular and idiosyncratic elements, some traditional, others recently imported from musical comedy and the music hall; but Trewin slights its highly conventionalized format. That format had itself gradually undergone considerable change, away from an emphasis on the harlequinade, which by Edwardian times had declined or fallen away altogether, towards an ever-increasing development of the opening and an ever-greater reliance on spectacle. Probably the single most powerful influence on the development of pantomime in the last decades of Victoria's reign was Augustus Harris's production of a long series of highly spectacular Christmas entertainments at Drury Lane beginning in the 1880s. Under Harris and his Edwardian successor Arthur Collins, a flexible format evolved which allowed for the forward movement of a story-line while still affording room for musical comedy and music hall stars, notably Dan Leno and Herbert Campbell, to display their inimitable talents and idiosyncratic personalities, as well as scope for ever more opulent scenic and special effects.[40] In fact, by Edwardian times the term *pantomime* had attained its current broad and vague generic signification of extravagant, colourful holiday entertainment.[41]

From a managerial point of view, the persistence and ever greater lavishness of the Christmas pantomime through the late Victorian and Edwardian period are easily explained by its highly lucrative results. From the vantage point of audiences who flocked to this immensely attractive seasonal entertainment, not only in London itself but in suburbs and provinces, in England, Scotland, and Ireland, its success at the box office was a product of the unique pleasure and satisfaction it brought, and not just to the eye itself. In some ways similar to farce in its representation of a chaotic and menacing world full of traps for the unwary and the overconfident, pantomime organized a release of inhibitions of the sort traditionally associated with the idea of holiday itself. And, like farce, it allowed its audiences opportunity for vicarious indulgence in irregular or forbidden activity, comforted by the certain knowledge that all would be restored to rule and order at the end. The typical resolution of pantomime, however, raised life from the humdrum world of everyday reality characteristic of the denouement of farce to a more ideal, blissful plane. In the end – as indeed throughout the performance – sheer fantasy prevailed. Meanwhile, under the semi-transparent guise of innocent, even childish entertainment, unburdened by tragic themes or even the commonplace cares of adult life, pantomime offered the onlooker a sustained glimpse of a hostile world gone delightfully awry – invariably, to the ultimate benefit of the well-deserving. Little wonder that the Christmas pantomime was the annual resort of hordes of adults, who ostensibly went along to treat their children to children's pleasures. In 1899 Max Beerbohm complained that the pantomime offered pale, idealized imitations of children tailored to adult tastes instead of what children themselves really wanted, 'a show with plenty of monsters, demons, noise, and buffoonery'.[42] Although such things could be found at Drury Lane, they were never unalloyed, and Beerbohm complained largely in vain.

Drury Lane continued its dominance as a purveyor of fantasy into the Edwardian period, although challenged in 1907 by a series of pantomimes undertaken at the Lyceum and, earlier, by the phenomenal success of *Peter Pan*.[43] Barker thought the theatrical strength of Barrie's plays generally derived from his 'power of completely envisaging his effects'. The more particular power and pleasure of *Peter Pan* accrue, Barker implied, from the fact that Barrie 'never loses and never lets his audience lose the exciting hovering of the mind between make-believe and reality which so endears the theatre to a child'. But there was something else about the play that also caught Barker's attention, a quality that may be instructive for latter-day historians. He discerns in Barrie's plays a 'half-dread of reality'; a weakness in other plays, this quality lends 'an obvious strength to *Peter Pan*'.[44] Andrew Birkin, Barrie's biographer, notes that it has become the fashion to dismiss him 'as sentimental or "whimsical"', but asserts that neither adjective is fully descriptive.[45] For those who have been reading too much William Archer and who see the popular theatre of the Edwardian period as over-indulgent in fantasy and shirking the sobering issues of reality insistently thrust upon the stage by cynical Royal Court dramatists, a re-reading of Barrie may prove a useful corrective. It may uncover resonances that help to draw together the popular theatre of the period – the fantasy, the spectacle, the pantomime, the musical comedy – and the progressive or otherwise serious 'realistic' drama of the age in some more meaningful connection. In a review of the Steven Spielberg film *Hook*, Tom Shippey identifies various scenes in the film 'all based on but extrapolating from features which Barrie himself [in writing *Peter Pan*] could not cope with'. Someone engaged in the production of the film 'has thought deeply', Shippey concludes, 'about what Barrie's fable means, and about what it refuses to face'.[46] Interesting, in this connection, is Barker's suggestion that Barrie's turn-of-the-century play *The Wedding Guest* (1900) showed the author's growing interest in experimenting with 'how far pathology is justified in the theatre'.[47] For, finally, there is something pathological about a child who will not grow up, a man-child who thinks of death as an awfully big adventure. One does not wonder, Max Beerbohm pointed out in his review of the first production of *Peter Pan*, that Barrie's preoccupation with children 'endears him to the community. The strange thing is the preoccupation itself. It forces me to suppose that Mr. Barrie has, after all, to some extent, grown up.'[48]

A perceptive man, Max Beerbohm; the irony and paradox of Barrie's personal situation does not escape him. A suggestive extension of the point Beerbohm raises is provided by Pinero's widely useful St James's play *Mid-Channel*, whose suicidal heroine Zoe Blundell comes face to face with the disastrous consequences of growing up and, in middle age, facing mortality. In Act One she tells her young friend Ethel Pierpont and Ethel's mother about her frequent theatregoing. The new play at the St Martin's is 'all about children – kiddies. There are the sweetest little tots in it. Two especially – a tiny, round-eyed boy and a mite of a girl with straw-colored hair – you feel you must clamber on to the stage and hug them.' Ethel says she has been reading the story of the play to her mother. Zoe goes on: 'The man who wrote the thing must be awfully fond of children. I wonder whether he has any little 'uns. If he hasn't, it's of no consequence to him; he can imagine them.'[49] The biographical accuracy of the comment suggests some inside knowledge of Barrie on Pinero's part, unless the story of Barrie's deep affection for the orphaned sons of

Arthur and Sylvia Llewelyn Davies, known in some circles, had by
this time become public knowledge. The friendship of Irene Vanbrugh,
the creator of the role of the childless Zoe Blundell, with Barrie is also
a contextual case in point.[50]

It is interesting to speculate to what extent these nuances would
have been accessible to the St James's audience. Some would
undoubtedly connect Ethel's reading of the story of Peter Pan to her
mother to the chapters about Peter in Barrie's earlier Edwardian
book *The Little White Bird* (1902), or to the re-publication of those
chapters in 1906 as *Peter Pan in Kensington Gardens*, with illustrations by
Arthur Rackham. In any case, the reference itself to Barrie's play, a
huge success on the London stage since its opening in 1904, could
hardly be missed by any London playgoer. A kind of intertextuality of
the stage is operating here, linking two disparate and seemingly
unconnected plays, and two wholly different theatregoing experiences,
in ways that define the Edwardian audience as a complex subculture
of its own. We gain some insight here into the myriad strands of the
connectedness of social life, and of individual emotional life as well, of
which this (or any) age is made up. The reference to Barrie's
lighthearted fantasy early in Pinero's realistic tragedy is a dramaturgical
device, a 'finger-post' (to use Archer's term[51]) erected by this skilful,
confident master of the well-made form and meant to point to a place
much later in the play, to Zoe's last conversation with her husband
Theo in which she expresses her deep regret for their decision not to
have children: 'If there had been "brats of children" at home, it
would have made a different woman of me, Theo; such a different
woman of me – and a different man of you.'[52] Pinero's object here is a
pathos arising in response to the character's painful feelings of loss,
anguish, and self-accusation – a concentration of emotion intended to
prepare for Zoe's despairing leap from the balcony a few moments
later. The larger concentric circles, beyond the confines of the theatre
auditorium, in which a performed play makes its impact felt are on
view in this example of subtle but telling connectedness.

Behind connections of this kind, and indeed behind everything else
pertaining to the subject of the Edwardian theatre, lies the ubiquitous
presence of a great and ever-growing theatre audience. Space does
not allow for even a partial listing of books on the Edwardian theatre
and drama that are badly needed, but one may be mentioned: the big
book on the Victorian and Edwardian audience that has yet to be
written. No doubt it would be in many ways different, and perhaps

more comprehensive, than James J. Lynch's helpful survey, now some 40 years old, of the eighteenth-century audience, *Box Pit and Gallery*, and different as well from J. C. Trewin's balanced and useful but too brief and too narrowly conceived *The Edwardian Theatre*.[53] By indirections we have arrived at the fifth, and last, characteristic of the theatre and drama of the age. Something that any historian of the nineteenth- and early twentieth-century theatre audience cannot fail to notice is the tremendous sense of leisure possessed by audiences toward the latter end of this period. Contemporary observers remark on the almost overwhelming presence of people out in town after dark. 'Night after night we crowd the playhouses', George R. Sims said in his article 'In London Theatre-Land', a contribution in his own multi-volume compilation *Living London*, published at the beginning of the Edwardian period.[54] And as the theatres empty around 10.30 pm, Sims's fellow contributor A. St John Adcock observed, pandemonium – but 'a very respectable pandemonium, and very good-tempered' – reigns.[55] When Edward ascended the throne, the cinema was still in its infancy, and the theatre – especially if we extend the term (as we should) to include its musical forms and the varied entertainment available in the music hall – was the central, and most comprehensive, mode of contemporary entertainment. No wonder that this era is one of the important ages of theatre building; no wonder also that the English theatre, and most especially the London theatre, had an unrivalled reputation for catering to the comfort of its audiences, for whom theatregoing was, as the contemporary French historian Georges Bourdon observed, 'a luxurious pleasure, a premeditated distraction'.[56] In the audiences themselves we perceive a luxurious sense of self-gratifying time at their disposal; in those authors, producers, and other professional theatre persons who cater to that ubiquitous popular demand to fill the time pleasurably, we feel a persistent sense of energy, not frantic or compulsive so much as emphatic and well-directed. They too, in their own ways, have the time available for multiple pursuits. List the activities and accomplishments over the decade of a Beatrice Webb or a Bernard Shaw (an unusually prodigious example), a Gordon Craig, an Elizabeth Robins, or a George Edwardes, and one is left mentally breathless. The sheer variousness and substance of accomplishment are staggering.

Can we find a centre in it – if indeed some centrally important factor or phenomenon needs to be found? A way of thinking about the

Edwardian theatre that concentrates on the nature of the theatrical experience itself may be identified by adducing a passage from Bourdon's important but rarely cited book, *Les Théâtres anglais*. Bourdon helpfully links the several characteristics of the Edwardian theatre described in the present essay by summing up the particular nature of the Edwardian theatrical experience itself:

It is sometimes claimed that their [the theatres'] managers are the realists of the theatre. This does not say enough. They are that, and something else as well. What they try to achieve in the *mise en scène* is not so much the representation, in a form as precise as possible, of material objects that will confer value as a sign of art. They are preoccupied less with establishing a decor that will constitute a faithful image of nature than with giving adequate symbolic expression to the nature of the characters who inhabit it. The job of painters and carpenters is not to restore nature itself: they evoke environments, they create 'atmosphere', they confer thought and a voice on decor, they make of it a living, speaking character, they impose it on the spectator's mind, they send across the auditorium the soul of the work itself, elusive but still present.[57]

Scrutiny of the disparate phenomena that make up the Edwardian theatre suggests, then, that ultimately it is its own thing more for the changes and developments that took place in its own time than for its continuity with the previous period or its effect on future times. 'That prosperous age', said Lascelles Abercrombie, writing on the literature of Edwardian England in 1933, 'so rich in its inheritance, so stable in its possessions, had nevertheless a strong inclination to go forward: it was not only progressive, it was even adventurous – but all the same it meant to keep what it had.'[58] It is a theatre remarkable more for practical experimentation than for theoretical concern; and yet it witnesses the emergence of Gordon Craig as an exciting and sometimes baffling or infuriating voice describing, and to an extent implementing, a kind of theatre never before seen. Witness also the emergence in Ireland of a theory of a theatre that would speak in some definitive, truth-telling way to a nation hungry for something it could not define for itself – a nation that would, ironically, then proceed to rise up in obstreperous rebellion, as it did in the cases of plays by both William Butler Yeats and John Millington Synge, against unpalatable images of itself presented by those same offensive, idealistic truth-tellers.[59] The seasons at the Royal Court Theatre organized by Barker and Vedrenne from 1904 to 1907 represent important examples of new notions of stagecraft and *mise en scène* – witness the stage-filling dining

table in the second act of *The Voysey Inheritance* – but they also
exemplify new ideas about the nature of theatre and theatrical
performance itself emerging at this time. The dominance of Shaw's
plays at the Court not only signals the further development of a major
dramatic voice but frames, in this age of the self-serving actor-manager,
the complex relationship between the theatre and the individual
playwright. Dramatists now are more public figures, engaging
readers as well as playgoers and sometimes doing futile battle with an
ever-present censorship still endorsed by the theatrical establishment
itself. Although women, more than may easily be named, wrote plays
for the Victorian stage, women playwrights emerge on the Edwardian
stage in more visible ways, sometimes urging on their audiences the
most pressing issues of the day; one thinks first, inevitably, of
Elizabeth Robins's *Votes for Women!*, but there are many more.[60]
Internationally known dramatists (Ibsen, Chekhov, Maeterlinck),
who had only a slim foothold or none at all in the theatre of the 1890s,
begin more forcibly to break down parochial barriers. And all over
the country production groups begin to emerge, some ambitious
enough to attempt even the most difficult of Shakespeare's plays,[61]
capturing and enhancing a contagious national enthusiasm for things
theatrical that had never been higher and would perhaps never again
rise so high. At the same time, audiences continue to be pleased and
nourished by traditional fare, melodramatic, fantastic, and increasingly
spectacular, provided by authors old and new. The time-honoured
pantomime survives and flourishes; the music hall expands and
becomes still more genteel. Reputations catch fire (Barrie's), develop
further (Pinero's), or are rehabilitated (Wilde's).

The remarkable range, variety, and, above all, vitality of the
theatre of the period would appear to be evident wherever we turn
our gaze. 'What is the Edwardian theatre?' we are asking ourselves.
Whatever it is, it is not the same as the Edwardian drama – if by
'drama' we mean merely to identify and characterize those dramatic
texts whose publication has made them available to us down through
the decades since Victoria died and her son Edward ascended the
throne. Rather, it is the *theatre*, alive in its time, in its moment, and
comprehensive of the authors who wrote for it, the players who
performed in it, the artists, technicians, and administrators who
produced it, and the audiences who witnessed it – or, in a few cases,
who failed to perform, produce, or witness it because of the actions of
a certain functionary in the Lord Chamberlain's office (actions

endorsed, however, by consensus of the theatrical community itself[62]): that is our essential concern. So it may be said, at least. And yet, to ask 'What is the Edwardian theatre?' today is simultaneously to ask a question about the nature, methods, and goals of theatre study. The same question would be raised if the subject were the Elizabethan theatre, or the Balinese theatre, or any other, but the difference would be that, unlike the theatre of those other periods and cultures, which we might argue calls for *re*definition in light of freshly perceived critical, theoretical, and historical exigencies, our sense of the Edwardian theatre must be that it has never really been the subject of sustained, comprehensive enquiry.

The time has now arrived when that enquiry needs to be made. The task will inevitably reflect our ongoing concerns with theatre as a cultural, social, and in certain ways intellectual phenomenon, susceptible of placement in as many contexts as our professional preparation, developing interests, changing tastes, and ineluctable biases may supply. A fresh review and re-examination of the Edwardian theatre should be a prime object for theatre scholars and, beyond them, for students of social, cultural, and intellectual history as well. We may, indeed, all find ourselves joining that same large camp, if we are not in it already. It is time to make common cause in our common interest.

NOTES

1 In a speech at Leicester in September 1909, Churchill described contemporary society as poised at a crossroads, 'the richer classes ever growing in wealth and in number, and ever declining in responsibility, the very poor remaining plunged or plunging even deeper into helpless, hopeless misery' (quoted in Paul Thompson, *The Edwardians: The Remaking of British Society*, 2nd edn (London, 1992), p. 236).

2 A. E. Wilson, *Edwardian Theatre* (London, 1951), pp. 10–11. For a characterization of Edward set in the political currents of his decade, see Barbara W. Tuchman's description of his funeral in *The Guns of August* (New York, 1962).

3 John Osborne, *Look Back in Anger*, 1956 (New York, 1982), p. 17.

4 'The King', *English Review*, 5 (June 1910), p. 414.

5 G. B. Gooch, 'The Edwardian Decade', in *Edwardian England A.D. 1901–1910*, ed. F. J. C. Hearnshaw (London, 1933), p. 9.

6 Percy Colson, *Close of an Era 1887–1914* (London, [1945]), pp. 9, 7.

7 W. Macqueen-Pope, *Carriages at Eleven: The Story of the Edwardian Theatre*, 1947 (rpt. Port Washington, NY, 1970), pp. 7–8. Challenges of the

sufficiency of the term have continued unabated, as in Jane Beckett and Deborah Cherry's recent comment, 'To call the years 1901 to 1910 the Edwardian era is misleading, mediating the complexity and discordancy of this decade through a single patriarchal figure' (*The Edwardian Era*, ed. J. Beckett and D. Cherry (London, 1987), p. 15).

8 Samuel Hynes, *The Edwardian Turn of Mind* (Princeton, 1968), p. vii.

9 Allardyce Nicoll, *English Drama 1900–1930: The Beginnings of the Modern Period* (Cambridge, 1973), p. viii.

10 St John Ervine, foreword to Rex Pogson, *Miss Horniman and the Gaiety Theatre, Manchester* (1952), p. vi, quoted in Nicoll, *English Drama 1900–1930*, p. 1.

11 See Maria Tymoczko, 'Amateur Political Theatricals, *Tableaux Vivants*, and *Cathleen ni Houlihan*', *Yeats Annual*, no. 10 (Houndmills, Basingstoke, 1993), pp. 33–64.

12 Bernard Shaw, *Dramatic Opinions and Essays with an Apology by Bernard Shaw* (London, 1907), vol. I, p. xxi.

13 I refer to volume 1 of Michael Holroyd's biography *Bernard Shaw: 1856–1898: The Search for Love* (New York, 1988).

14 For a systematic discussion of these questions see Thomas Postlewait, 'Historiography and the Theatrical Event: A Primer with Twelve Cruxes', *Theatre Journal*, 43 (May 1991), pp. 157–78; and Joseph Donohue, 'Evidence and Documentation', in *Interpreting the Theatrical Past: Essays in the Historiography of Performance*, ed. Thomas Postlewait and Bruce McConachie (Iowa City, IA, 1989), pp. 177–97.

15 George Bernard Shaw, *Three Plays for Puritans* (1900), in *The Bodley Head Bernard Shaw*, ed. Dan H. Laurence, vol. II (London, 1971), pp. 11–48.

16 No definitive list exists, but at least eight new theatres appeared during the Edwardian decade and at least seven others were rebuilt; see the helpful brief account of major constructions and reconstructions in Wilson, *Edwardian Theatre*, pp. 36–7. An even greater number of new structures emerged in the previous ten years; the most complete information, from which data for either decade may be compiled, is provided in Diana Howard, *London Theatres and Music Halls 1850–1950* (London, 1970).

17 William Archer, *The Old Drama and the New: An Essay in Re-valuation* (London, 1923), p. 4.

18 See Thomas Postlewait, *Prophet of the New Drama: William Archer and the Ibsen Campaign* (Westport, CT, 1986).

19 William Archer, *Play-making: A Manual of Craftsmanship*, 1912 (New York, 1960), p. 235.

20 Archer, *Play-making*, p. 81.

21 See Gary J. Scrimgeour, 'Naturalist Drama and Galsworthy', *Modern Drama* (May 1964), pp. 65–78.

22 For a broad study of subjective changes occurring in the literary production of the Edwardian era, see John A. Lester, Jr, *Journey Through*

Despair 1880–1914: Transformations in Literary Culture (Princeton, 1968).

23 Mario Borsa, *The English Stage of To-day*, trans. Selwyn Brinton (London, 1908), pp. 44–5.

24 Harley Granville Barker, 'The Theatre: The Next Phase. A Lecture given on June 9, 1910', *English Review*, 5 (July 1910), p. 631.

25 William Archer and H. Granville Barker, *A National Theatre: Scheme & Estimates* (London, 1907), British Library copy, p. 112 and marg. note.

26 Barker, 'The Theatre: The Next Phase', p. 637.

27 St John Hankin, 'Puritanism and the English Stage', *Fortnightly Review* (December 1906), p. 138.

28 See the first volume of Shaw's *Plays Pleasant and Unpleasant*, first published in 1898.

29 Andrew Birkin, *J. M. Barrie & the Lost Boys: The Love Story that Gave Birth to Peter Pan* (New York, 1979), p. 168.

30 Gilbert Cannan, 'The Dramatic Sense', *English Review*, 5 (June 1910), pp. 481, 483.

31 'The King', *English Review*, 5, p. 420.

32 Beatrice Webb, *Our Partnership*, p. 447, quoted in Hynes, *Edwardian Turn of Mind*, p. 129.

33 Shaw puns on the term 'play of ideas' in the Preface to *Three Plays for Puritans*, where he explains that the wealthy English consumer typically prefers 'politics and church-going' to the theatre, and when he wants sensuality practises it himself. 'From the play of ideas – and the drama can never be anything more – he demands edification, and will not pay for anything else in that arena', Shaw asserts. Consequently, the theatre will never exert serious influence on society until it turns 'from the drama of romance and sensuality to the drama of edification', p. 14.

34 *Desmond MacCarthy's The Court Theatre 1904–1907: A Commentary and Criticism*, ed. Stanley Weintraub, Books of the Theatre Series, no. 6 (Coral Gables, FL, 1966), p. 101. Gerald Weales has provided one of the most thoughtful assessments of Shaw in this period in 'The Edwardian Theatre and the Shadow of Shaw', *Edwardians and Late Victorians*, English Institute Essays 1959, ed. Richard Ellmann (New York, 1960), pp. 160–87.

35 See, for example, Sheila Stowell, *A Stage of Their Own: Feminist Playwrights of the Suffrage Era* (Ann Arbor, MI, 1992).

36 Hankin, 'Puritanism and the English Stage', p. 135.

37 Harley Granville Barker, 'J. M. Barrie as a Dramatist', *Bookman*, 39 (October 1910), p. 14.

38 See J. P. Wearing, *The London Stage 1900–1909: A Calendar of Plays and Players*, 2 vols. (Metuchen, NJ, 1981), entry 4.265.

39 J. C. Trewin, *The Edwardian Theatre* (Oxford, 1976), p. 163.

40 Among various accounts, many anecdotal, see especially Michael R. Booth's historical overview of pantomime in *English Plays of the Nineteenth Century*, vol. v, *Pantomimes, Extravaganzas and Burlesques* (Oxford, 1976), pp. 1–63, and the topically organized study by Gerald Frow, *"Oh, Yes It*

Is!": *A History of Pantomime* (London, 1985), pp. 181–2.

41 Studies of pantomime that note its apparent decline in Edward's time overlook the diffusion of the term into whimsical or other quasi-generic descriptions reflecting the increasing disequilibrium of the form itself. In the 1909 season in the West End, for example, one could find three instances of a 'Fairy Play' (Maeterlinck's *The Blue Bird*, Graham Robertson's *Pinkie and the Fairies*, and an inevitable *Cinderella*; *Peter Pan* was, ironically, billed simply as a 'Play'), along with a 'Fantasy', an 'Opera', and a 'Musical Play'; only the rival Lyceum and Drury Lane productions of *Aladdin* were actually billed as a 'Pantomime' or 'Children's Pantomime' (see Wearing, *The London Stage 1900–1909*, 9.356, 9.358, 9.362, 9.367, 9.369, 9.371, 9.374, 9.375, and 9.378). Meanwhile, dozens of pantomimes were produced outside the West End, in greater London and the provinces (see, for example, statistics for the 1900–1 Christmas season published in *The Stage*, n.d., cited in Raymond Mander and Joe Mitchenson, *Pantomime: A Story in Pictures* (New York, 1973), pp. 40–1).

42 *Saturday Review*, vol. 88 (30 Dec. 1899), quoted in Booth, *English Plays of the Nineteenth Century*, vol. V, p. 55n.

43 See Wearing, *London Stage 1900–1909*, entries 7.370, 8.349, and 9.371. The 1909 offering at the Lyceum, *Aladdin*, was evidently mounted as a direct challenge to Drury Lane's pantomime of the same title (9.375). After its long initial run of 150 performances in 1904, *Peter Pan; or, The Boy Who Wouldn't Grow Up*, billed usually as a 'Fairy Play', continued to draw large audiences annually through the Edwardian period, achieving more than 100 performances in 1905, 1906, and 1907 and more than 80 in 1908 and 1909 (see Wearing, 4.265, 5.310, 6.310, 7.364, 8.348, and 9.369).

44 Barker, 'Barrie as a Dramatist', pp. 15, 14.

45 Birkin, *Barrie & the Lost Boys*, p. ix.

46 Tom Shippey, 'Darling Children', *The Times Literary Supplement*, 17 April 1992, p. 18.

47 Barker, 'Barrie as a Dramatist', p. 14.

48 Max Beerbohm, 'The Child Barrie', 7 January 1905, *Around Theatres* (London, 1953), p. 360.

49 Arthur Wing Pinero, *Mid-Channel*, in *Contemporary Drama: European, English and Irish, American Plays*, ed. E. Bradlee Watson and Benfield Pressey (New York, 1941), p. 595.

50 I am indebted for some details of this discussion to Birkin, *Barrie & the Lost Boys*.

51 Archer, *Play-making*, p. 131.

52 Pinero, *Mid-Channel*, in *Contemporary Drama*, ed. Watson and Pressey, p. 631.

53 See James J. Lynch, *Box Pit and Gallery: Stage and Society in Johnson's London*, 1953 (New York, 1971), and J. C. Trewin, *The Edwardian Theatre* (Oxford, 1976). Ian Clarke's *Edwardian Drama: A Critical Study* (London,

1989), though providing surveys of such major dramatists as Galsworthy and Barker, begs the question of its subject, since the author spends so much time on the Victorian plays of Jones, Pinero, and Shaw and fails to distinguish their characteristics from those written and produced in the Edwardian period. See, in contrast, Joel Kaplan, 'Edwardian Pinero', *Nineteenth Century Theatre*, 17 (1989), pp. 20–49; and Penny Griffin, *Arthur Wing Pinero and Henry Arthur Jones* (New York, 1991).

54 George R. Sims, ed., *Living London: Its Work and its Play: Its Humour and its Pathos: Its Sights and its Scenes*, 3 vols. (London, 1901), vol. I, p. 248.

55 A. St John Adcock, 'Leaving the London Theatres', in *Living London*, vol. II, p. 10.

56 Georges Bourdon, *Les Théâtres anglais*, pref. by Edwin O. Sachs (Paris, 1903), p. 8; translations here and below are my own.

57 *Les Théâtres anglais*, pp. 12–13.

58 Lascelles Abercrombie, 'Literature', in *Edwardian England A.D. 1901–1910*, ed. F. J. C. Hearnshaw (London, 1933), pp. 186–7.

59 Among recent studies of the Irish dramatic renaissance and the Abbey Theatre, see especially Adrian Frazier, *Behind the Scenes: Yeats, Horniman, and the Struggle for the Abbey Theatre* (Berkeley, 1990).

60 See Stowell, *A Stage of Their Own*, and the earlier study by Julie Holledge, *Innocent Flowers: Women in the Edwardian Theatre* (London, 1981). A list of Victorian women dramatists may be found in *English Drama of the Nineteenth Century: An Index and Finding Guide*, comp. and ed. James Ellis, asst. Joseph Donohue (New Canaan, CT, 1985), Appendix A, pp. 301–2.

61 See, for example, Barker's description of the Stockport Garrick Society's amateur productions of Shakespeare, Sheridan, Ibsen, Shaw, and other British and continental dramatists, in 'The Theatre: The Next Phase', p. 632.

62 See John Russell Stephens, *The Censorship of English Drama 1824–1901* (Cambridge, 1980).

'Naughty but nice': musical comedy and the rhetoric of the girl, 1892–1914

Peter Bailey

Musical comedy – the forerunner of today's stage and film musical – has received scant scholarly attention as a significant cultural form. Recollections of its spectacular debut in the 1890s talk of it only in idealized terms as 'the theatre of enchantment', set in a world of jingling hansoms, champagne suppers and velvet nights. Today's theatre historians remain preoccupied with the social problem plays of the era in the New Drama of Wilde, Ibsen, and Shaw, while their attention to the popular stage focusses on melodrama rather than the upstart new genre. Nor do recent cultural histories of the period have much to say, one noting only that musical comedy was indeed 'wildly popular . . . [but] breathtakingly vacuous'.[1]

Perhaps this is all musical comedy deserves – sentimental indulgence, critical disparagement, or silence. (The last two responses are memorably wedded in Kenneth Tynan's heading for his review of *The Sound of Music* – 'The Case for Trappism.'[2]) Yet the Hollywood musical, as a latterday variant of musical comedy, has received serious critical scrutiny in film studies, and cultural studies generally have shown how familiar and apparently unproblematical forms can reveal much of social and ideological significance.[3] Certainly some contemporaries thought the new genre was significant. 'This is the real New Drama', wrote William Archer in 1894, later calculating that its popularity outstripped all other theatre forms, including melodrama. It was, he said, 'a form to be reckoned with, a form that has come to stay'. 'One day', he maintained, its history 'will form a curious study'.[4]

The study on offer here speaks as yet to a selective curiosity. Though there is plainly need for a comprehensive history of musical comedy (including its two-way traffic across the Atlantic), my concern is with its representations of gender and sexuality as embodied in the girl-heroine who featured so heavily in its productions, from her collective role as newly modernized chorus girl to that of the female lead starring as the young working woman adventuring in the big city. At the same time, I want to put this in the context of everyday life in the period, get behind the present dismissive evaluations, and begin to explain rather than merely register the enormous popularity of this new genre.[5]

But first, it will be helpful to review the received account of musical comedy and its provenance.[6] As a popular compound of song, dance, and romantic narrative, the genre is said to derive primarily from the Victorian (English) burlesque, an eclectic form based on the parody of some well-known historic episode, legend, play, or book.[7] Written in verse and set to existing melodies, burlesque was a costume drama, featuring transvestite roles for women, actresses in tights, and a numerous female corps de ballet. Over the period, burlesque's characteristic element of often erudite pastiche yielded increasingly to topical allusions, and it was by virtue of its more direct attention to contemporary life that musical comedy came to supplant the older form. While still a confection of song, dance, and romantic story-line (very loosely constructed), the new genre was written in everyday speech, and played in everyday settings. Burlesque's love affair with the pun gave way to the pursuit of the catchphrase, and each of the new shows came with an original musical score aimed at generating its own self-referential hit songs. Where burlesque had been enamoured of the grotesque and the eccentric, the new production style was lavish and spectacular, its sophistications punctuated only by the ribaldry of comic turns imported from the music hall. If its manners were modern, musical comedy's use of the vernacular was nonetheless very selective, constituting a distinctly stylized form of naturalism. Thus its resort to modern dress heavily favoured high fashion, as part of its intense glamorization of women, both as stars and members of a reconfigured dance chorus.

By most accounts, the first show in the new style was *In Town*, staged by George Edwardes at the Prince of Wales Theatre in London in 1892. A stopgap production, it was so successful that Edwardes commissioned a more considered follow-up of his ad hoc invention. This was *A Gaiety Girl*, written by Sidney Jones and Owen Hall, the first work to be termed 'musical comedy', and the definitive hit of the new form. Running from 1894 to 1896, the show celebrated the modern chorus girl and her most famous home. Musical comedy and the Gaiety Theatre became synonymous, and contributed mightily to the theatre boom of the 1890s and the consolidation of the West End as the prime site for theatregoing and the big night out. The success of long-run productions on the London stage was duplicated by touring companies in the provinces and abroad, notably in America. To export was added import, when the first indigenous American musical, *The Belle of New York*, played in London in 1898. There was also a trade in light opera, brought in from the continent and served up under the new label.

At the centre of this highly profitable phenomenon stood the legendary George Edwardes – businessman, theatre and music hall manager, and impresario. Learning his trade at the Savoy (a reminder of musical comedy's further debt to Gilbert and Sullivan), Edwardes took over the managership of the Gaiety from John Hollingshead in 1886 while it was still a burlesque and variety house. After the successful introduction of musical comedy, he remained in charge of this 'theatre of enchantment', together with its satellites (notably Daly's), and the touring companies. Musical comedy was a collaborative form, but its writers and composers have received little acknowledgement compared to that awarded George Edwardes, 'the Guv'nor'. Was it his ghost, his mother, or a former mistress who wrote his entry in the *Oxford Companion to the Theatre*, with its congratulatory note of a man at once magical, businesslike, and benign?

He had an extraordinary flair for knowing what the public wanted and spared no cost in providing it, with a meticulous care for detail. He was rewarded by crowded houses and the trust and affection of the public and the profession alike.[8]

This was the man most responsible for the exaltation of the woman as girl. The girl who was celebrated in an endless string of show titles: *A Gaiety Girl*, *The Sunshine Girl*, *The Shop Girl*, *The Girl Behind the Counter*, *The Girl from Kays*, *The Girl in the Taxi*, etc. The girl who was naughty but nice...

There are several categories within which the musical comedy girl can be understood – as working woman, stage persona, public image, and private person – though they constantly intersect and elide. I concentrate here on the first two.

As working women, both actresses and chorus girls in musical comedy seem to have enjoyed higher status and higher salaries than was general within their profession. Certainly the musical comedy chorus played a more prominent role than the conventional female stage auxiliary, and enjoyed something of a collective star status. This was notably so for that model of the new order, the Gaiety Girls, which had its own internal differential, paying its tallest and most imposing members – the Big Eight – three to four times more than the regular chorus.[9]

But the experience of the Gaiety Girls also demonstrates the social cost of such rewards in their submission to close male managerial control under George Edwardes. Edwardes employed tutors to teach his girls both stage and social skills – song and dance, but also speech, carriage, and dress. Thus groomed and instructed, the girls became ladies and were encouraged to frequent fashionable restaurants and parade themselves at Ascot. Their off-stage conduct was closely monitored. Head waiters reported back to the Guv'nor on the girls and their escorts, and in a stage take-off of Edwardes, his double was made to say '(Cunningly) I see you all far oftener than you suspect.'[10] All-too-short stage careers could be more abruptly foreshortened: if his girls grew too fat or too thin, became pregnant or ceased to smile, they were sacked. In his youth Edwardes had narrowly failed to qualify as an army officer, remarking later 'That's why I'm commanding regiments of chorus singers instead of soldiers.' The Guv'nor's military alter ego was masked by the more manipulative style of the chivalrous chauvinist. He could be generous with presents, solicitous in his attentions, and adept at smothering dissent with a mix of concern and implicit threats: 'You look tired and ill . . . you are not taking care ... (handing out pills) ... now you mustn't lose your looks...'[11] Variously Svengali, martinet, snooper and sugar daddy, George Edwardes is a more complex and darker figure than standard accounts allow, alerting us to the often hazardous off-stage sexual politics that went with the relatively advantaged position of women working in this sector.

Edwardes's extensive investments as a businessman invite an industrial as well as a military analogy for the stage operations of musical comedy and its working relationships. Thus the general phenomenon of the modern chorus line can be read as duplicating the more intensified and routinized production regimes of the late Victorian factory. Compared to the eccentric or balletic styles of dance in burlesque and music hall, the musical comedy chorus was more mechanical, performing repetitious, standardized operations in a more closely supervised workplace. Its members were among a numerous, interchangeable, and readily replaceable category of semi-skilled workers, employed in long production runs in a large-scale culture industry of global scope. The Gaiety Girls may be the exception here, since they were reported to pose as much as dance, emphasizing perhaps a superior, metropolitan sophistication, but the model of the modern production line fits well for the Manchester-based Tiller Girls, whose troupes staffed Edwardes's touring companies and were employed world wide.

The original troupe was founded in 1890 by John Tiller, the favoured nephew of a rich cotton manufacturer.[12] 'Mr John' thought the Gaiety Girls undisciplined compared to his own, who were graduates of stern instruction in the Tiller Method. A man of explosive temper, his autocratic discipline extended to the off-stage life of his predominantly working-class charges. They recalled him as 'very strict but kind' and talked, a little wryly, of being 'Tillerized' by the system, a fitting echo of contemporary industrialists who advocated 'Taylorizing' factory production according to the teachings of F. W. Taylor, the American pioneer of scientific management. Thus older paternalist modes of authority combined with the newer patterns of industrial production, while the military ideal of well-drilled preparedness reflected the additional priorities of an imperial age. 'In matters of discipline', says the male shopwalker inspecting the finger nails of his assistants in The Shop Girl (1894), 'General Wolseley and myself entertain views precisely the same.'[13]

The correspondence of life in the chorus line with that of the modern worker was most obvious in The Sunshine Girl (1912), set in a soap factory plainly based on the Lever Brothers model industrial plant on Merseyside, where the chorus sings 'You've got to get a move on / Your ways you must improve on.' The Sketch delighted in reproducing a photograph from New York showing a lady of the chorus punching a time-clock to register her arrival at the theatre (plate 1).[14] In revealing such features of operation to the public and their continuity with life outside the theatre, the press reinforced the message of women under control and grounded the theatrical dream world in the new routines of modernity.

The musical comedy girl was not only a worker in her own profession, but was commonly cast as a worker on stage. Dramatists drew their typical heroines from young working women in the burgeoning new service sector of the economy, those who held court from behind a counter in telegraph offices, bars, teashops and, most prominently, department stores. The writer for The Shop Girl (1894)

1 The Chorus Girl as Disciplined Modern Worker. (*Sketch*, 13 January 1909)

claimed to have spent long hours in research in Whiteley's and the Army and Navy, to meet what he discerned as the new public appetite for 'the local and the real ... the life of today'.[15] The large shop or department store would indeed have been familiar to metropolitan and big city audiences. Many of them may have gone straight from shopping to the show – *This Way Madam* (1913) at the Queen's Theatre was set in an almost exact replica of the Swan & Edgar store that was its next-door neighbour on London's Regent Street. Others in the audience would have known department stores and similar settings as workers in the labour-intensive retail industry. Not that the social realism of the new genre was much concerned with the oppressive actualities of shop work, with its long hours, petty subordinations, and austere living-in conditions.[16] Rather, the department store recommended itself to writers as a locus of everyday life that was already highly theatricalized by its emphasis on glamour and display. Here too was a new social space that facilitated romantic encounter, for the transactions of shopping allowed and yet regularized a relatively easy and unmediated public exchange between the sexes and the classes that elsewhere might have seemed either lowering or impertinent. Certainly the shop was a less hazardous or compromising site than the street.[17]

The setting of the store also emphasized the pleasures of shopping and consumption in an avidly consumerist era.[18] Indeed, there was a direct link between stage and commerce as musical comedy was recruited to the promotional battles between the big stores slugging it out for domination of London's West End. The heroine of *Our Miss Gibbs* (1909) staffs the counter at 'Garrods', a luxurious replica of the Knightsbridge Harrods which was locked into a shopping war with the new Selfridge's, the Americanized upstart on Oxford Street. Shopping at 'Garrods' was said to be 'Paradise', but one which was open to all, for musical comedy often featured a 'shop till you drop' number where the working girl broke out from behind the counter to claim her other identity as the lady consumer (plate 2):

> In and out and round about,
> Hardly ever stopping,
> Buying this and buying that and leaving me to pay –
> Won't you come out shopping, shopping, shopping for the day?

Women so bent on consumption were expensive, but shopping in turn consumed them, absorbing energies that might otherwise be put to more threatening ends. In Sidney Grundy's didactic hit play on the straight stage, *The New Woman* (1894), three angry feminists pass from attacks on 'Man the Betrayer' to teatime chatter about dresses on sale in Peter Robinson's and other London stores. If at times

2 'Lady Clients at Garrod's Stores.' The Opening Chorus of *Our Miss Gibbs, or The Girl at the Stores.* Gaiety 1909. (*Play Pictorial,* 1909)

somewhat alarmingly open-ended, shopping was nonetheless a form of control in a well-controlled setting.

Of course, the shop girl – any girl – might be sprung from the worthy routine of her working life through romance and marriage to a rich, well-born male, a motif much beloved of the period and celebrated in another hit *The Earl and Girl* (1903).[19] Musical comedy sometimes played safe in the traditional convention of the heroine who qualifies for the honour through the discovery of her own genteel birth, lost but now recovered. Yet its more typical apotheosis of the working girl represents marriage above her station as the due reward for her own inherent virtues. Thus she surmounts the barriers of class by a natural gentility which, though it may require a little pardonable artifice, is available to all. As the chorus sings in *A Gaiety Girl*, 'everyone's a lady who behaves herself as such'. The show girls maintain this proposition in the face of the hauteur of the young titled women with whom they now compete for male attention, concluding triumphantly: 'We would rather be ladies by nature / Than mere Upper Ten nomenclature.'

Musical comedy was thus both highly caste conscious yet staunchly egalitarian, maintaining its soundly democratic principles by the simple exclusion of all those who were most obviously unequal. Few proletarians appear on its stage, in an era when 75 to 80 per cent of the population came from the manual labouring class. In the factory setting of *The Sunshine Girl*, choruses of workmen and working girls sing briskly about the labour that goes into a bar of soap – 'the toilin' work, the boilin' work ... the killin' work, the grillin' work' – but the heroine works in the perfume department. In other settings where working people feature as a class, they are also suitably sanitized. As Max Beerbohm noted of 'Gaietyland', 'the mingling of the classes was on the easiest of terms ... [with] never a crude word or gesture'. There was, he observed, 'nothing to choose between the classes, for all the characters are refined, though not', he added, 'in the least like in actual life ... they have a school, a higher school of their own'.[20] Thus musical comedy's claim to social realism seems pitched in the idiom of a highly contrived bourgeois populism, in which, with few exceptions, the ordinary and everyday are irreducibly middle class, a flattering state of self-election for us all. But then, as one of its everyday charming characters puts it, in a rare surfacing of the subtext: 'It is stupid to be poor.'

It is also stupid to be ugly. Thus in musical comedy, the working girl – its ordinary girl – was also invariably pretty. While this was a traditional prerequisite of the heroines of popular stage romance, musical comedy glamorized its women in a more calculated and spectacular fashion, juxtaposing and interfusing the ordinary and the extraordinary to construct its erotic milieu. 'The first sensation', of *The Shop Girl* (1896), wrote one reviewer, was the entry of its 'stage beauties in such costume as they might wear in the street'; in the second act, however, the old Gaiety traditions asserted themselves with 'shapely women in a frou frou of scant but delicate drapery'.[21] To judge from the playscript, the latter were girls from the Frivolity Theatre, introduced into the store's charity bazaar as the occasion for a show within a show, their actress role sanctioning their burlesque semi-nudity. But both sets of women, shop assistants and actresses, were glamorously lit and presented, their very separate social identities elided in their common representation as women on show – 'show girls', everyone of them, to use a coinage of the era. Seaside settings gave further cause for show in glamorous un-dress, as with *The Girl from Kays* (1902) whose chorus paraded 'in red and orange bathing garb'.[22] It became common to musical comedy formula to shift the second act away from such enclosed settings as the store to a freer milieu such as the seaside or the exhibition or fairground, exploiting the sense of greater licence in dress and behaviour.[23]

Thus musical comedy's stock in trade was, as Beerbohm further noted, 'of a wholly sexual order'. Yet we may well fail to register fully its more intensely eroticized stage discourse, unless we understand the disarming rhetoric within which its female bearer was positioned. This was the rhetoric of the musical comedy woman as girl, which framed its subject as 'naughty but nice', or, in another formulaic phrase, 'not too good and not too bad'. These ambiguous apologetics served both to sensationalize and contain sexual expression in a manageable form – parasexuality – that was central to the musical comedy aesthetic.[24]

The boundaries marking off a disabling excess of goodness were plainest drawn, as in the much-mocked image of the saintly 'Old Fashioned Girl' and 'the extremely maiden aunt' caricatured in *The Shop Girl*'s hit song 'Her Golden Hair Was Hanging Down Her Back'. If 'old' was out, so also was too radical a formulation of the new, as in the over-intellectualized and sexually neutered New Women. Also much too good for the musical comedy girl were the Salvation Army lasses pilloried in several shows. When the shop girls from Kays are invited to an Army meeting to learn 'how to resist temptation' they subvert the occasion by deriding its 'Goody Goody Girls' and proclaiming their own determination to 'Frolic, flirt and spoon'. As another musical comedy lyric maintained, 'It was silly to be chilly'.

It was, of course, in the limits to be set to the opposite pole of freedom and licence that musical comedy was more self-consciously circumspect. Yet here, in language that seems to us ludicrously coy and minimalist, is evidence of that sexual freighting that needs taking more seriously, as in the prime case of 'naughty', the sign that both licensed and contained badness, and gave its arch yet potent imprimatur to the decade that fathered musical comedy. We should listen to Margaret Schlegel in *Howard's End*, 'who hated naughtiness more than sin'.[25] Now defined as 'mildly indecent or titillating', naughty spoke to contemporaries in the language of the brothel and the nursery. A naughty house was nineteenth-century slang for brothel and the word could be part of the prostitute's typical address to her client – 'Who's a naughty boy, then?' – at once an invitation, a challenge, and an indulgent semi-reproach. In combination with the vocabulary of the boy and the girl, the term sanctions sexual adventure as no more than childish mischief, to be understood and condoned by nurse or nanny, fond authorities in the middle-class male psyche nourishing strong fantasies of sexual initiation, emotional dependence, and pleasurable guilt. Within this powerful regressive interpellation of the bawdy and the infantile, the 'girl' could be unproblematically co-opted as the fellow (*sic*) conspirator and playmate. That the girl in this case was also an actress no doubt fuelled the sense of complicit delinquency, for while much has been made of the increasing respectability of the profession in this period, the actress was still cast as an inherently promiscuous figure in the public eye, not least because the circumstances of her work – on show, nocturnal, co-sexual – echoed those of the prostitute.[26]

It was the prostitute who was the irrevocably naughty girl, ostensibly beyond the respectable outer limits of musical comedy's sexometer, yet her too, too bad-ness suggestively haunts its texts. The shop girl as milliner pursued an occupation that had throughout the century been regarded as a cover for casual prostitution, an association both distanced and acknowledged when one of the girls from Kays observes that her room is situated 'at the virtuous end of Regent Street', the resort of the daytime prostitute. Implications of prostitution or some kind of sexual buccaneering may help to account for the huge success of the hit song 'And Her Golden Hair Was Hanging Down Her Back' that helped *The Shop Girl* to run nearly 600 performances in 1894–5. It is a conventional enough tale of 'artless Flo', a country girl who comes up to London, learns the way of the world and returns home 'With a naughty little twinkle in her eye'. The tag line, 'And her golden hair was streaming/hanging down her back' sung at the conclusion of each verse, carries a ready message of her freeness of manner, together with symbolic associations of sexual power and, in its goldenness, its translation into money. There were other topical allusions that gave the song its risqué appeal and Archer registered its corrupt underside by describing it as 'better fitted for Hogarth than Hicks' – Seymour Hicks, that is, the popular light comedian who co-authored and sang the song, and enjoyed a long career in musical comedy, advising thus on the necessary style for stage success: 'Your manner must be ever alert, your twinkle perpetual, and your gaiety a thing to be envied.'[27]

Twinkles, of course, came in the eye and, as in the case of Flo, were invariably naughty, if only little. Yet it was this littleness or minimalism that endlessly enlivened and refined the otherwise modest scale within which musical comedy's sexuality was bracketed. Thus a song from *The Sunshine Girl* provided instruction on the tactics of erotic display in cosmetics and dress:

> Just a little touch
> Will often be enough,
> A touch of powder puff
> Will be enough, puff, puff.
> Just a little teeny teeny tiny touch,
> Not a bit too little,
> Not a bit too much
>
> And above the ankle
> Let a little something show,
> A little frill or so.
> What they see of you
> Will frill them frou and frou
> If it's only just a tiny touch.

The same show offered other modulations of littleness by importing Marie Lloyd's notorious music hall hit, 'Every Little Movement Has a Meaning of Its Own', no doubt with its distinctive code of gesture and body language, for it was in performance as much as its writing that musical comedy exploited the minimal to maximum effect.

Crucial here was the genre's extensive use of 'knowingness', the technique of hints and silences that left the audience to fill in the gaps and complete the circuits of meaning, thus flattering them in the sense of their own informed and superior worldliness. Archer noted 'the common knowingness' that focussed on matters of the day and reinforced musical comedy's concern with being 'smart and modern', but also he noted how much its attentions were exercised in sexual matters. 'In this playful gambolling on the verge of indecency', observed Archer, 'lies half the art of the "up to date" librettist.' The other half of the art lay in its performance, particularly in the role of the comedian, a regular feature of musical comedy and usually an import from the music halls where sexual knowingness was a highly developed second language. Crossover artists from the halls readily broke the frame of dramatic formality with their ad libs and direct address to the audience.[28] This infusion of music hall style not only gave musical comedy a greater spontaneity and rapport with its audience than other forms of popular or music drama, but more sharply exploited the knowingness specific to the West End. Here theatres co-existed with a sub-rosa world of pornography, prostitution, and assignation that reached right up to the stage door and produced a popular mentality that continued to cast the actress as its ready accomplice.[29]

Knowingness not only sexualized musical comedy as discourse, but elasticated its imagined limits, for in the alchemy of performance a little could be made to signify a lot, not only in a diffuse sense, but in that of the fullest discharge of sexual desire – in male terms, of intercourse and orgasm, the lot. The double message is plainest in the contradictions invested in 'Tararaboomdeay', the greatest hit song of the nineties that commentators saw as emblematic of the era's popular culture.[30] George Edwardes poached the song and its tempestuous singer-dancer, Lottie Collins, for the Gaiety in early 1892. Derived from an American popular song, possibly of brothel origins, 'Tararaboomdeay' was rewritten for Collins, who was an established performer both on the halls and musical comedy stage. The accompanying dance was supposedly of her own devising, though it borrowed from the can-can and corresponded closely to the vernacular skirt dance then popular in America. Significantly, Collins would begin her performance in diffident fashion, building to a frenzied climax of high kicking and whirling petticoats, affording the hopeful glimpses of the red (Liberty's silk) drawers underneath.[31] The erotic abandon of the dance offers an extravagant contrast to the measured qualifications of the lyrics.

> A smart and stylish girl you see,
> The Belle of High Society,
> Fond of fun as fun can be
> When its on the strict QT.
> Not too young and not too old,
> Not too timid, not too bold,
> Though free as air, I'm never rude,
> I'm not too bad, and not too good.
> Tararaboomdeay etc.

The emphasis on discretion and moderation may seem no more than a disarming and disingenuous gesture, lost in the transport of the dance, yet the artist was at pains to articulate the message of the words:

Just as soon as I find myself getting a little too free on a word, I immediately tone myself down on the words that follow. My idea of the song is that it represents a young woman who is really not as bad as she seems to be, but who takes advantage of the absence of her elders to have a harmlessly lively time by herself. You will notice that I throw a good deal of emphasis on the assertion 'I'm not too good and not too bad' and the audience has to accept that.[32]

Even so, the corrective emphasis Collins was at pains to impart in her delivery of the lyrics hardly seems well served by 'the little knowing shake of the head' reported in her performance, signalling as it did her complicity in a liberal interpretation of the song, a liberality manifest in the abandon of the dance itself which always left her physically and emotionally spent.[33] In many perceptions, no doubt, the language of littleness preserved a saving innocence and moderation, but 'Tararaboomdeay' provided the fullest expression of the genre's persistent metonymy that a little might mean the lot, a message that could thus be knowingly read into the many more muted inflections of its code, signifying a sexual plenty even as they prescribed its proper containment.

How were 'girls' to navigate these tricky waters? The songs suggest that whatever the prescribed limits of sexual expression, these were negotiable. Thus to 'flirt, frolic, and spoon' was not always just a tactic of romantic arousal to the conventional end of landing a man in marriage, but a careful deployment of sexual power in the achievement of a woman's independence that stopped short of marriage or other consummation. This constitutes both an opportunity and a dilemma, as the hit song 'The Bonnet Shop' from *The Girl from Kay's* reveals:

> When a girl of common sense
> Wants to make a competence
> It's a theme for thought intense
> How she is to make it;
> If she happens to prefer
> Starting as a milliner
> There's a bonnet shop for her –
> She has but to take it.
> But what has she to do for it,
>   to do for it, to do for it?
> She has to snare a millionaire
> A Christian or a Jew for it,
> To smile and say, 'Perhaps some day,'
> And then of course to stop –
> Oh, it takes a lot before you've got
>   your little bonnet shop.
>
> But remember where you are,
> Do not flatter him too far,
> For you cannot trust these money making chaps;
> Take his presents if you will
> But be sure to tell him still
> You may like him with a very big 'perhaps'.

This is sex on the instalment plan with no guarantee on either side of final payment. For the woman it involves a kind of sexual brinkwomanship but can be nervously exhausting, suggesting new freedoms yet reinforcing the claims of marriage as the safer career (though marriage did not get a uniformly good press in musical comedy, and as one song proclaimed, 'I fear we shall be naughty / Till we're getting on for forty.')

In musical comedy the bidding and dealing in sexual favours echo the speculative transactions of the market and the risks and rewards of the business deal. Thus sex itself is a resource or commodity like the nitrates, the oil, soap or pork that generated the spectacular new wealth of the era. The new business girl – the 'Well Regulated Girl', in the knowing phrase of popular humour[34] – seemed well set to negotiate her share, yet this bold agenda was unsettling both for its actors and society at large, as Pinero's comedy drama of 1912, *The 'Mind the Paint' Girl*, suggests.[35]

Pinero's play was set in the off-stage world of musical comedy. The title is that of the hit song, 'Mind the Paint', that has taken the heroine Lily Paradell from plebeian obscurity to fashionable stardom. Her surname suggests some glamorized brand-name product – 'Paradell Pampers Your Parts!'? – or the lily gilded, and the theme of cosmetic, fetishized and thus distanced beauty is reinforced in the song. This tells of the heroine's house – 'a very charming dwelling' – that stands in for herself and her body as a glossily finished construct that invites approach but denies contact or entry:

> When you pay my house a visit,
> You may scrutinise or quiz it
> But you mustn't touch the paint!
> > Brand new paint!
> Once you smear it or you scratch it
> It's impossible to match it;
> so take care, please, of the paint,
> > Of the paint!
>
> And I'll cry out for assistance,
> Should you fail to keep your distance;
> Goodness gracious, mind the paint!
> > Mind the paint!
> Chorus:
> Mind the paint! Mind the paint!
> A girl is not a sinner, just because she's not a saint!
> But my heart shall hold you dearer –
> You may come a little nearer –
> If you'll only mind the paint!
> > Mind the paint!

The idea of women's sexuality as an attractive yet carefully controlled commodity is carried through elsewhere in the play. Two girls from the chorus line are shown in negotiation with wealthy admirers over presents of motor cars and trips to the continent. They express their dissatisfaction with the returns to Lionel Roper, an avuncular devotee of Lily who tries to shelter her from undesirable liaisons and, as a City man, also looks after her financial interests. 'It's a shame of you, that's what it is', grumbles one of the girls to Roper; 'You went and put Lily Paradell into rubber and enabled her to make a bit.' Playing off the metaphor of the paint as second skin and protective shield, this could be read as a displaced allusion to the contraceptive, both as further protection and as an accessory to a controlled and profitable intimacy.[36] As it turns out, Lily did

handsomely out of rubber, putting the returns into decorating her
house. 'Mind the paint! Mind the paint! A girl is not a sinner just
because she's not a saint...'

The suggestion of a brokered sexuality is reinforced in Pinero's
caricature of George Edwardes as the impresario Carlton Smythe.
There are various hints in the text that Smythe – 'with his half-closed
eyes' – was something of a pimp and a pander, and contemporaries
took the play to be an attack on the musical comedy world. Defenders
of 'the Guv'nor' and his interests were sufficiently disturbed to mount
a first-night protest.[37]

Yet while the career of George Edwardes demonstrates the male
power that controlled musical comedy and its representation of
women, the male characters who appeared on his stages were in
general a debilitated lot – faceless manikins immobilized in their
adoration of the girl and unfitted for any other work than the
transactions of the stock market, an ambiguous milieu celebrated as
the fount of new fortunes, but sniped at as a less than manly
occupation. The male shopwalker in *Our Miss Gibbs* is a Mr Toplady,
suggesting the further failings of effeminacy and worse. Marriage
partners for the girl are mostly sturdy chaps, but the enfeeblement of
the supporting male cast does echo contemporary anxieties at racial
degeneration and the sense of masculinity in crisis. What is less easy to
read is the extent to which such representations express the more
particular and displaced self-contempt of the writers and composers
of musical comedy, as marginalized members of mainstream bourgeois
culture engaged in a profitable yet professionally déclassé work. The
prolific librettist Adrian Ross used this pseudonym to disguise his
identity as a one-time Fellow of King's, author of a history of the
Merovingian dynasty, and a serious poet. Among other writers was
the young P. G. Wodehouse, who wrote endlessly about witless young
Englishmen, but chose to do so from his preferred new home in America.

There is space here for only the briefest attention to the other two
categories under which the musical comedy girl can be read, those of
public image and private life. Certainly, leading female players were
the subject of heavy media attention. The genre itself played up the
importance of publicity and self-advertisement, as with Mrs Farquahar,
the maverick widow in *Our Miss Gibbs*, who sings of 'Paragraphs and
Pictures' and the need to make the Sunday papers. The chorus in *A
Gaiety Girl* proclaimed their pictorial potential: 'Don't we look
extremely fetching, / Subjects fit for artists' sketching.' This was a nice

reminder of Dudley Hardy's striking posters for the show which covered the front of the theatre and, together with his programme illustrations, achieved their own celebrity. Bold in line and colour, Hardy's images of the girl were widely employed in other advertisements, denoting the close association of commerce and art in which musical comedy was an unabashed partner.[38] Together with regular press reviews of the plays there was increasing use of the featured interview with the star, and a clutch of glossy weeklies devoted to the stage provided illustrations of productions and players. Fashion columns gave special attention to costume, discussing not only specially designed couturier gowns but the dresses that could be had ready-made in listed department stores. Boxes of chocolate and other confectionery bore prominent pictures of the musical comedy girl. More extensive visual currency came with the picture postcard, most opportunely freed from its original General Post Office monopoly in 1894 (a year after the opening of *A Gaiety Girl*). This cheap popular medium featured tinted photos of actress stars 'looking soulful under rose covered trellises'.[39] In sub-rosa counterpoint to these sentimentalized images were other pictures of 'so-called chorus girls ... in a wide range of publications', that Archer denounced as 'a canker of the commonwealth' and 'the journalistic counterpart of the comedian's leer'.[40] Journalistic knowingness no doubt added spice to speculative items of chat about actresses' private lives. Interviews were invariably respectful, though a slightly mocking hyperbole and extensive use of reported speech also suggests a mix of resentment and condescension on the part of (male) interviewers unable or unwilling to see much beyond predictable responses to predictable questions about stage careers (wonderful), motorcars (wonderful), and marriages (more mutedly wonderful). Yet we may conjecture that the overall tone of reverent confidentiality gave readers still new to the formula a sense of privileged access to the star, thus adding significantly to her other multiple projections as actress and musical comedy girl.

These then were some of the factors that helped make this new theatrical form 'wildly popular'. But wildly popular with whom? One authority speaks of musical comedy as 'a polite and highly fashionable form of entertainment' which suggests a predominantly middle-class audience.[41] This was certainly an important element, but the centre of gravity probably lay further down the social scale. At the Duke of York's Theatre one Saturday night in 1896, Archer judged the 'great majority' of his fellow patrons to be 'young men and women who worked hard for their living at the desk or behind the counter . . . the people to whom this sort of thing was really addressed'. 'We were simply good, honest, respectable, kindly lower middle class lads and lasses [i.e. boys and girls], enjoying an entertainment exactly suited to our taste and comprehension.'[42] The stage-door johnny lying in wait for the female star was most often represented as a besotted member of the upper classes, but came from a surprising social range – it was the Sultan of Zanzibar who tried to buy Madge Saunders, but it was a rubbish collector who spent his life savings following Violet Lloyd all over the country.[43] Women performers also commanded a substantial following among their own sex, witness the millgirls devoted to Mabel Russell and the servant girls who wrote to Ada Reeve.[44] With its extensive provincial hinterland and wide media exposure, musical comedy commanded an audience that made it broadly as well as wildly popular.[45] It was indeed a bourgeois construct, but one whose middlebrow formula spoke to a new mass market.

What might be said of the further social impact of musical comedy and its reception in popular and gender consciousness? Certainly it spoke specifically to male desires in its representation of women. Its more intense techniques of glamorization enhanced the mystique of the woman as object of the male gaze, as star, and secular goddess. At the same time its naturalized stage settings and action collapsed the allure of the distant and spectacular into the routines of a stylized but familiar version of everyday life, encouraging hopes of access in its plausible mix of the fantastic and the mundane. The rhetoric of the girl worked further wonders, generating a welcome androgyny that converted the girl into the playmate or one of the boys, transforming the stilted exchanges of conventional social address between the sexes into the chummy discourse of men relaxing with other men. Through the running allusions to the actress behind the stage persona and her implication in the freely imagined world of assignations and quasi-prostitution, the easy address of boy and girl could generate fantasies of consummation and promiscuity in a licensed naughtiness that elasticated while it did not quite break the bounds of respectability. One telling male testimony to this effect was that of Beerbohm, who talked of the Gaiety's 'innocent libertinism', speaking perhaps less as the critic than as a man who had himself been heavily girl-struck in his younger years.[46]

What was the appeal of musical comedy for women and how might it have affected their lives and relationships with men? Women's adulation of women as stars suggests a ready response to newly fashioned consumerist ideals of feminine beauty and success which reinvigorated traditional motifs of social mobility and happiness. In playing out its eroticized urban fairy-tale, musical comedy cast women as active and competent adventurers, which delighted them as an audience, for on Archer's evidence they were as flattered as the men in assuming the worldly identity conferred by knowingness.[47] At the same time, the new genre privileged rewards over risks in its reassurance that you can have your cake and eat it – in this case, that a woman can entertain desire without inviting disgrace – while encouraging a greater sexual competitiveness in women's bid for men's favour. All of this can be read as a male construction of femininity – reactionary men defining their own ideal New Woman – yet however compromised, musical comedy did canvass more enterprising roles for women and may well have contributed to their growing cultural assertiveness as registered in other contemporary evidence.

Novels of the 1890s, for example, suggest that while for men jobs in offices and shops were invariably represented as stifling and narrow, for women they were more often seen as a means of escape from the even more restrictive confines of domestic bondage.[48] Although both in its own internal regime and its writing musical comedy reproduced the subordination of women that prevailed in the shops and stores it favoured for its setting, the prominence of shop girls and other women workers as its spirited heroines may have reinforced women's appreciation of such occupations as avenues of freedom and opportunity. In New York young working women of the period were exploiting one of its favourite tropes to turn the tables on men, by being naughty but not particularly nice – *and* getting away with it, though there is nothing as yet to tie this phenomenon to the parallel success of musical comedy in America.[49] That such exploits seemed only realizable through modes of dress and self-presentation that spoke to male ideals and the further subjections of consumerism may make any claims for advance inadmissible. Yet within a generation the evidence of oral history suggests how London working women came to use the greater range of cheap consumer goods in ways that not only followed the promptings of popular fashion and femininity but realized a more independent sense of self.[50] Although a blithely manipulative mode, musical comedy may have stimulated such new imaginative gains for women in a more overtly sexualized identity that was no longer merely hostage to the designs of men.

NOTES

1 The quotation is from Jonathan Rose, *The Edwardian Temperament,
  1895–1919* (Athens, Ohio, 1986), p. 165. There is no trace of musical
  comedy in the important work of John Stokes, *In the Nineties* (London,
  1989), and Karl Beckson, *London in the Eighteen Nineties: A Cultural History*
  (New York, 1992).
2 Kathleen Tynan, *The Life of Kenneth Tynan* (New York, 1987), p. 227.
3 The musical was nonetheless a late addition to the agenda in film studies,
  but see Rick Altman, ed., *Genre: The Musical* (Boston, Mass., 1981); Jane
  Feuer, *The Hollywood Musical* (Bloomington, 1982; 2nd edn, 1993); Bruce
  Babington and Peter W. Evans, *Blue Skies and Silver Linings: Aspects of the
  Hollywood Musical* (Manchester, 1985).
4 William Archer, *The Theatrical World of 1894* (London, 1895), p. 245. His
  statistical analysis over four years is reported in *The Theatrical World of
  1897* (London, 1898), pp. 351–72.
5 I have, however, defaulted on a prime priority of the historian by
  treating the period indiscriminately as all of a piece. A fuller account
  would be more specific. There is, for example, the contention that the
  Wilde trial effectively marked the end of the nineties. Did this so register
  in musical comedy, however indirectly? The year 1914 is plainly a social
  watershed, but in the history of the form the first major developmental
  break comes in the mid-1920s with the impact of film and a more
  pronounced Americanization.
6 See George Rowell, *The Victorian Theatre, 1792–1914* (Cambridge, 1978),
  pp. 143–4; Hugh Hunt, Kenneth Richards, and John Russell Taylor,
  The Revels History of Drama, VII, 1880 to the Present Day (London, 1978),
  pp. 65–6; Andrew Lamb, 'Music of the Popular Theatre', in *Music in
  Britain: The Romantic Age, 1800–1914*, ed. Nicholas Temperley (London,
  1981), pp. 97–104; Michael R. Booth, *Theatre in the Victorian Age*
  (Cambridge, 1991), pp. 196–8. For useful popular treatments, see
  Raymond Mander and Joe Mitchenson, *Musical Comedy: A Story in
  Pictures* (London, 1969); Ronald Pearsall, *Edwardian Popular Music*
  (Newton Abbott, 1975). See also Dave Russell, *Popular Music in England,
  1840–1914: A Social History* (Manchester, 1987), pp. 71–2, 193.
7 For a stimulating treatment of the American equivalent with its
  imported English female stars, see Robert C. Allen, *Horrible Prettiness:
  Burlesque and American Culture* (Chapel Hill, 1991). See also Peter G.
  Buckley, 'The Culture of "Leg-Work": The Transformation of Burlesque
  after the Civil War', in James Gilbert *et al.* (eds.) *The Mythmaking Frame of
  Mind: Social Imagination and American Culture* (Belmont, Calif. 1993),
  pp. 113–34, and forthcoming work on the Ziegfeld Girl by Linda
  Mizejewski.
8 *Oxford Companion to the Theatre*, ed. Phyllis Hartnoll (Oxford, 1983). See
  also Walter Macqueen-Pope, *The Gaiety: Theatre of Enchantment* (London,
  1949); Ursula Bloom, *Curtain Call For the Guv'nor: A Biography of George*

Edwardes (London, 1954); Alan Hyman, *The Gaiety Years* (London, 1975).

9 Tracy C. Davis, *Actresses as Working Women: Their Social Identity in Victorian Culture* (London, 1991), pp. 27, 29 and *passim*; James Jupp, *Gaiety Stage Door: Thirty Years Reminiscences of the Theatre* (London, 1923).

10 Arthur Roberts, *Fifty Years of Spoof* (London, 1927), pp. 189–90. Edwardes was represented on stage in the character of Carlton Smythe, impresario, in Sir Arthur Pinero's play about the musical comedy world, *The 'Mind the Paint' Girl*, 1912.

11 'A Chat with George Edwardes', *Era*, 12 September 1894; Ada Reeve, *Take It for a Fact: A Record of My Seventy-five Years on the Stage* (London, 1954), pp. 77–84.

12 Doremy Vernon, *Tiller's Girls* (London, 1988); 'Tiller Training Schools,' *Era*, 22 August 1903.

13 Musical comedy play scripts can be consulted at the British Library, Lord Chamberlain's Play Collection. The Lord Chamberlain's office was responsible for licensing and censorship.

14 The caption reports on a bill before the New York Legislature to suppress the nuisance of 'Stage Door Callers', noting that at big theatres 'every chorus girl, every stage hand and, indeed, all principals must register their arrival and departure, as employees in shops and factories are required to do', *Sketch*, 13 January 1909.

15 *Sketch*, 28 November 1894. Archer noted 'the close reproduction of the external phases of everyday life' in musical comedy. By 'external', Archer may have been emphasizing the public setting of much musical comedy action, which contrasted with the more private, domesticated realism of contemporary mainstream drama.

16 Compare the drudgery of shop life as exposed by Cicely Hamilton, the feminist activist, in her *Diana of Dobson's*, 1908, reprinted in *New Woman Plays*, ed. Linda Fitzsimmons and Viv Gardner (London, 1991).

17 Theatrical agents prowled the West End stores for new recruits to the chorus line, Jupp, *Gaiety Stage Door*, p. 51. For the enhanced visibility of young women service workers and an expanded public zone of licit sexual exploit, see Peter Bailey, 'Parasexuality and Glamour: the Victorian Barmaid as Cultural Prototype', *Gender and History*, 2 (Summer, 1990), pp. 148–72. The tensions between pleasure and danger implicit in this theme are developed in Judith Walkowitz, *City of Dreadful Delight: Narratives of Sexual Danger in Late-Victorian London* (Chicago, 1992), pp. 43–52.

18 On this theme and the promotion of haute couture in particular, see Joel Kaplan and Sheila Stowell, *Theatre and Fashion: Oscar Wilde to the Suffragettes* (Cambridge, 1994). For other innovative scholarship, see Erika Rappaport, 'The West End and Women's Pleasure: Gender and Commercial Culture in London, 1860–1914', Ph.D. dissertation, Rutgers, 1993, ch. 6, 'Acts of Consumption: Musical Comedy and the Desire of

Exchange'. I am grateful to the author for the opportunity to read this chapter ahead of publication.

19 Madeleine Bingham, *Earls and Girls: Dramas in High Society* (London, 1980).

20 *Saturday Review*, 30 October 1909.

21 *Sketch*, 22 April 1896.

22 *Stage*, 20 November 1902. For the new resonance of the seaside girl as male fetish and consumer icon, see Thomas Richards, *The Commodity Culture of Victorian England: Advertising and Spectacle* (London, 1991), ch. 5.

23 I owe this point to Joel Kaplan.

24 For further definition, and its deployment elsewhere, see Bailey, 'Parasexuality and Glamour'. See also, for a similar concept, 'spectation', Laurence Senelick, 'Private Parts in Public Places', in William R. Taylor, ed., *Inventing Times Square: Commerce and Culture at the Crossroads of the World* (New York, 1991), pp. 329–53.

25 E. M. Forster, *Howard's End* (London, 1910; Harmondsworth, 1989), p. 151.

26 Davis, *Actresses as Working Women*, pp. 78–86.

27 Edwardes of the Gaiety was also Edwardes of the Empire music hall, who was at the same time defending himself against charges that he encouraged high-class prostitution in the Empire's promenade. As part of his counter-attack, women with loose unbonneted hair were being ostentatiously denied entrance to the Empire as likely prostitutes, *Evening News*, 13 October 1894. (The Empire scandal is returned to, yet again, in Beckson, *London in the 1890s*, pp. 118–28, with no acknowledgement of Edwardes's other role.) These associations were made plainer when the 'artless Flo' of the song loses her virginity to, or rather proves the seducer of 'a friend of Mrs. Chant', the leading reform critic of Edwardes. See also *The Theatrical World of 1894*, pp. 316–20, and, for Hicks, *Theatre in the Victorian Age*, p. 129. Victor Emeljanow informs me that Hicks was notorious in the business as a sexual predator.

28 *The Theatrical World of 1894*, pp. 59–61. For knowingness on the halls as discourse and social formation, see Bailey, 'Conspiracies of Meaning: Music Hall Song and the Knowingness of Popular Culture', *Past and Present*, 144 (1994), pp. 138–70. There are significant continuities here between the early stage form and the later film musical, which combines a modernist reflexivity with a cultural conservatism; see Feuer, 'The Self-Reflective Musical and the Myth of Entertainment', in *Genre: The Musical*, pp. 159–74.

29 Davis, *Actresses as Working Women*, pp. 137–46.

30 Holbrook Jackson, *The Eighteen Nineties* (London, 1913; New York, 1966), p. 31.

31 Country youths had their own refrain: 'Lottie Collins has no drawers / Will you kindly lend her yours.' See Flora Thompson, *Lark Rise to Candleford* (London, 1973), p. 502.

32 *Era*, 8 October 1892.

33 Jose Collins, *The Maid of the Mountains: Her Story* (London, 1932), pp. 16–17.

34 See Bailey, '*Ally Sloper's Half-Holiday*: Comic Art in the 1880s', *History Workshop*, 16 (Autumn, 1983), pp. 4–31.

35 See Joel Kaplan, 'Edwardian Pinero', *Nineteenth Century Theatre*, 17 (1989), pp. 20–41.

36 The nineties was the take-off point in the commercial production and sale of rubber contraceptives: see Angus McLaren, *Birth Control in Nineteenth Century England* (London, 1978), ch. 12.

37 'Edwardian Pinero', p. 44. Edwardes's shiftiness is apparent in his evidence to the Select Committee on Stage Plays (Censorship), *Parliamentary Papers*, 1909 (303), VIII, pp. 240–8.

38 On Hardy's 'sensuous suavity', see M. H. Spielmann, 'Posters and Poster-Designing in England', *Scribner's Magazine* (July 1895), pp. 42–3. I am grateful to Bridget Elliott for this and other material on Hardy.

39 Robert Roberts, *The Classic Slum* (London, 1973), p. 168. See also Fred Willis, *101 Jubilee Road* (London, 1948), and C. Stella Davies, *North Country Bred* (London, 1963), pp. 48–9.

40 Archer, 'The Case for National Theatres', *Monthly Review* (July 1902), pp. 140–55.

41 *Victorian Theatre*, p. 144. Edwardes was anxious to foster the same impression before the 1909 Select Committee when he spoke proprietorially and protectively of the 'great middle classes of the theatre', receiving some incidental confirmation from a committee member who recalled going to see *The Shop Girl* in 1896 as an Eton schoolboy.

42 William Archer, *The Theatrical World of 1896* (London, 1897), pp. 298–301.

43 *Gaiety Stage Door*, p. 21; D. N. Pigache, *Cafe Royal Days* (London, 1934), pp. 41–2.

44 *Gaiety Stage Door*, pp. 70–1; 'Chat with Ada Reeve', *Sketch*, 8 August 1894. See also Margaret Penn, *Manchester Fourteen Miles* (London, 1982), p. 213.

45 Significant here is the great appeal of the music (unfortunately a missing dimension in this account). But see Russell, *Popular Music*, pp. 72, 192, on the popularity of musical comedy selections with the brass bands of the industrial districts and their mostly lower-class audiences. Presumably the gramophone also gave the music increased currency among the middle class.

46 As an Oxford undergraduate he had been infatuated with the 15-year-old music hall star, Cissie Loftus; see David Cecil, *Max: A Biography* (London, 1964), pp. 80–8.

47 *The Theatrical World of 1896*, pp. 299–300. For a searching analysis of the meaning of musical comedy's consumerism for women and the question of female spectatorship, see Rappaport, 'The West End and Women's Pleasure'.

48 Meta Zimmeck, 'Jobs for the Girls: The Expansion of Clerical Work for Women', in *Unequal Opportunity: Women's Work and Employment in England,*

1800–1918, ed. Angela John (Oxford, 1986), pp. 165, 170. I owe this reference and other suggestions on this point to Arlene Young.

49 Kathy Peiss, *Cheap Amusements: Working Women and Leisure in Turn of the Century New York* (Philadelphia, 1986), pp. 107–14, 126. Allen, *Horrible Prettiness*, pp. 201–4, dates the popular characterization of the working-class chorus girl as 'gold digger' – a strong motif in the later American musical – from this period. Though it has little to say on musical comedy, Taylor, ed., *Inventing Times Square* is richly suggestive on the turn of the century promotion of New York's equivalent of the West End, and the construction of new styles of pleasure, sexuality, and consumerism that exploited the higher visibility of women and an intensive nexus of theatres, night clubs, and restaurants.

50 Sally Alexander, 'Becoming a Woman in London in the 1920s and 1930s', *Metropolis London: Histories and Representations since 1800*, ed. David Feldman and Gareth Stedman Jones (London, 1989), pp. 245–71.

CHAPTER 3

Varieties of life: the making of the Edwardian music hall

Dave Russell

The history of Edwardian music hall, or variety theatre as contemporaries increasingly termed it, is well known but little explored. Key processes and events – syndication, the 1907 strike, the Royal Command – are acknowledged in even the most cursory examination of the halls, but close consideration is unusual. Moreover, what has been written is often hostile; this was, apparently, an age of 'decline' when a supposedly manufactured, syndicate-dominated product destroyed its somehow more authentic Victorian ancestor. However, it is equally possible to depict the Edwardian phase as a formative moment in the history of popular entertainment when changed business practice, patterns of audience demand and response, technological development and the growing influence of American popular culture combined to transmute music hall from a form dominated by a long-established tradition of comic song into a hybrid which, for all its subsequent difficulties, held within it the seeds of many of the most successful elements of later twentieth-century popular culture. This essay, after demonstrating how contemporary reaction to changes in the music hall industry has coloured much later writing, attempts to demonstrate why Edwardian variety should be seen as a significant entertainment form in its own right, before moving on to consider aspects of its wider cultural role and meaning.

From its inception music hall's organization and product were constantly reshaped by endless negotiation between entrepreneurial innovation and audience expectation. Edwardian variety was the culmination of a particularly marked phase of this 'remaking' process, beginning in the 1880s and accelerating rapidly from the late 1890s. It was not the result of a coherent, planned strategy; individual managers and owners utilized numerous approaches. Nevertheless, broad patterns of causation and outcome were clear. A generation of

relatively young provincial music hall owners and managers foresaw
rich possibilities emanating from their reading of considerations of
both demand – rising living standards, improvements in suburban
transport, shifting religious sensibilities, increased demand for public
leisure by women – and supply. It must be allowed that some
elements of variety's 'refining' mission did stem from deeply held
individual moral positions. Sir Edward Moss and Sir Oswald Stoll in
particular have so often been represented as philanthropists who
accidentally strayed into the entertainment business that scepticism
perhaps takes over too readily.[1] Ultimately, however, their innovations
represented adjustment to an altered market situation. In a period
when local governing elites increasingly either shared or were
influenced by the opinions of well-organized temperance and social
purity lobbies, the music hall, with its close association with the drink
trade, was increasingly vulnerable, both to direct attack and a more
general atrophying of profitability and potential future expansion.
Smaller halls were particularly susceptible to closure via the apparently
neutral mechanism of increasingly stringent safety regulations, while
newly erected halls were increasingly denied a drink licence; crucially,
the London County Council made this a formal policy in 1897.[2]
Faced with the loss of a vital source of profitability (drink receipts
comprised perhaps 15–20 per cent of total takings in the 1890s), it was
not surprising that the assumption of respectability marked the way
ahead. Entertainment had to be the major source of profit, drawing
on consumers from constituencies previously hostile to the music hall.
Women's attendance was sought with particular vigour, not simply
because they represented a less than fully exploited audience sector,
but because the cachet that their attendance conferred might prove a
stimulus to previously recalcitrant males.

The result was the series of changes in architectural, artistic, and
business practice, already relatively well documented by music hall
historians. Music halls with neo-classical exteriors and an array of
exotic interiors increasingly came to resemble legitimate theatres.
Strenuous attempts were made to reconstruct audiences by excluding
poorer elements and imposing restraints on behaviour. The Bradford
Empire, for example, combined a high minimum admission of
sixpence with the stern admonition 'children in arms not admitted', a
revealing commentary on their notion of the ideal woman consumer.[3]
On stage, the individual comic singer's hegemony finally ended and
the variety theatre became more and more the preserve of novelty
acts, sketch artists, bioscope exhibitors, magicians and others.

To meet the expense of instituting such changes, 'syndicates' or 'tours' emerged, designed to drive down labour costs by asking artists to exchange the possibility of uncertain but highly paid engagements at individual independent halls, for the guarantee of slightly less well-paid but regular work in a related set of halls. By 1914, some sixteen syndicates controlled about 140 halls.[4] Further efforts to increase profitability resulted in attempts at raising performers' productivity through the large-scale utilization from about 1900 of both the twice-nightly system and the matinée.

Not surprisingly such pace and extent of change led to controversy, and the word 'variety' attracted a considerable ideological detritus which needs removing before serious discussion can begin. The term began life innocently enough in the 1880s, in acknowledgement of the increasing number of conjurors, strongmen, and similar performers in the halls. By the early 1900s, however, variety became the subject of often intense disputation, forming part of the wider episode later termed the 'mass culture' debate. For critics, the pursuit of a mass family audience by increasingly powerful syndicates was leading to the victory of a soulless variety (the term now describing the whole industry) over an older, more authentic music hall tradition where songs had been 'the mouthpiece, the oracles of the people', where audiences had gone 'not as spectators but as performers'. The new leisure entrepreneurs had 'improved' the music hall only 'as a Gothic Cathedral would be by the hacking off of gargoyles ... interesting as is the variety theatre and its myriad developments, the music hall is much more interesting and a thousand times more vital'. These are the words of W. R. Titterton, whose 1912 publication *From Theatre to Music Hall* drew, with a blend of wit and crude prejudice, a picture of an amiably gullible public led astray by profit-orientated entertainment entrepreneurs. In passages that resonate with post-Arnoldian cultural pessimism and pre-empt much of the criticism levelled at the mass media after 1920, Titterton saw variety destroying a vulgar but healthy proletarian Englishness (he did not use this phrase) and replacing it with a culture that ranged from the mildly irritating to the morally corrupt (the new imported dances were 'rank poison') and the radically threatening. 'When the nigger-minstrel can wash his face off after office hours he is harmless; but the true negro singer is often a dangerous fellow to be let loose in a hall – we dare not be familiar with him.'[5]

Variety, of course, had its supporters, and unsurprisingly many of them were to be found in the trade press. Celebrating Stoll's staging of

an albeit truncated *Parsifal* at the Coliseum, the *Era* dismissed
Tittertonesque criticism as misplaced nostalgia. 'We occasionally
come across in the daily newspaper a plea for the ancient music hall,
with its torpor of melancholy, its dingy surroundings, its chairman,
even its music. Such eccentric writers seem to ignore the existence of
conditions in the old days that paralysed the better impulses of the
artiste and degraded his art.'[6] Significantly, these partisan conflicts
have permeated even the best histories until the late 1980s. One
school, undoubtedly the predominant one in both popular and
academic literature, maintains the critical line: syndicate chiefs such
as Stoll 'devitalized' the music hall, which was 'given its final kiss of
death with the achievement of a Royal Command Performance in
1912', an oft-rehearsed sentiment.[7] Alternatively, a minority view
sees Stoll and his contemporaries as 'farseeing ... progressive music
hall promoters' transforming a cultural product with a disreputable
image into 'an inexpensive family entertainment that became
immensely popular after 1900'.[8] Consideration of 'variety', it seems,
has always led to the taking of sides. While not denying that both
positions contain extremely valuable insights, close identification
with the contemporary representations of engaged disputants is not
especially helpful to the historian. In particular, the fact that
Edwardian audiences found the comic singer rivalled by sketches,
revues, performing dogs, opera singers, origami artists and clay
modellers signifies not that it was necessarily bad, devitalized, impure
or inauthentic, but merely different. Little is gained when approaching
a cultural form by presuming it to be merely the degenerate end of a
once heroic phase of popular entertainment. Notions of 'decline',
with its implication of music hall as a fixed category, too easily
disguise key processes of development and change that took place in
the Edwardian period.

Negative assessments of variety underestimate its success in
constructing new constituencies of support and its fostering of new
entertainment styles and practices, while overestimating the extent of
its 'respectabilization'. However contemporaries and subsequent
writers viewed variety, it was undoubtedly extremely popular. The
number of variety theatres grew over the late Victorian and
Edwardian periods, with growth perhaps particularly rapid in the
periods from 1896 to 1901 and 1910 to 1913, although more research
is needed here. Expansion was especially marked in London, where
the number of halls listed by the *Era Almanack* rose from 40 in 1900 to

66 in 1914, with increased suburban provision especially noteworthy, and in provincial towns with populations of between roughly 30,000 and 70,000. It is difficult to measure the exact scale of the industry, but by 1914 there were perhaps some 250 English venues that contemporaries would have termed 'variety theatres', with another 80 to 100 in the rest of Britain.[9] A further source of performance was 'cine-variety', simply variety shows between films, available in hundreds of cinemas between about 1908 and 1914, suggesting that accommodation as well as competition was possible between the two entertainments at this time.

National attendance statistics do not exist, but variety clearly attracted very large numbers. In 1912, for example, the London County Council licensing district contained fifty-one full-blown variety theatres with a total seating capacity of 76,370, many, probably the majority, operating twice nightly and giving at least one matinée a week, for fifty to fifty-two weeks of the year.[10] Obviously, they did not always run at full capacity, but even a moderate estimate would suggest annual admissions in the LCC area alone of some 25 million and perhaps considerably more. The provincial situation was equally propitious, with managers assuming that about one-third of the local population could be deemed potential customers.[11] Although as Jeremy Crump's study of Leicester demonstrates, the legitimate theatre could maintain a dominant position *vis-à-vis* the music hall in some provincial settings, it was probably the cultural form that suffered most from this rising tide. This was especially the case in suburban London, where, according to one informed source, seventeen out of an initial thirty-six theatres had closed since 1900, with a number actually becoming variety theatres.[12] Frequent poor share performance and deep concern over the growth of the cinema industry do admittedly suggest over-capacity in the industry: the pace of expansion almost suggests an air of desperation at times. Nevertheless, in terms of numbers of buildings and audience size, variety reached its apotheosis in the period from 1910 to 1914, accessible to all of urban Britain and its immediate hinterland.

Edwardian managements were also broadly successful in widening support for the music hall industry. They certainly worked hard to court a 'respectable' image via a number of promotional *coups*. The best known is undoubtedly the Royal Command Performance of July 1912 at the Palace Theatre of Variety. As already noted, this event symbolizes for many the death of the old tradition and the victory of the new, a moment of apparent triumph that actually heralded precipitate decline. Certainly, the evening featured the uncertain *nouveau riche* on its best behaviour. No Marie Lloyd, as everybody knows, omitted probably more because of her private life than her stage persona; the comedians, in the words of the otherwise gushing *Era*, remorselessly 'guillotined' in favour of the speciality acts, especially the dancing troupes; and strong hints of censorship. In fact, the importance of this event has probably been exaggerated or misunderstood. It undoubtedly brought considerable publicity, but in artistic terms it merely dotted the 'i's and crossed the 't's of a process already well advanced. Indeed, 1912 is probably more interesting when viewed as a small but significant element in the construction of a 'democratic' or 'popular' monarchy, than as a key issue in the history of variety. While historians have focussed mainly on royalty's use of ceremony and ritual as a mechanism for maintaining the illusion of power, the Edwardian and Georgian periods also saw a calculated attempt to promote a less remote image for the monarchy, thus helping to create the skilful blend of distance and cordiality, ceremony and informality, that served it so well for much of the twentieth century. It is surely no coincidence that George V's first visit to soccer's FA cup final came only two years after his Command appearance 'in plain evening dress, with a white flower in his button-hole'. The royal family were arguably exploiting the variety theatre as much as variety was exploiting them.[13]

Perhaps the most significant publicity victories were those constantly being won in the provinces. Civic openings of new theatres in the presence of the mayor, senior politicians, and sometimes even local churchmen were an increasingly common feature after 1900. The large platform party that celebrated the opening of the Bradford Alhambra in March 1914 included the widow of one of the leading members of the local licensing committee that had attempted to obliterate the town's public house music halls in 1902.[14] Such modest individual acts were symbolic of much bigger successes. Hidden behind them was a web of business strategy whereby owners courted local elites, encouraged local investment by stressing the improved tone of the industry and erected theatres as part of larger office and shop developments. The very existence of these platform parties, coupled with the overall expansion of the variety industry noted earlier, does suggest that managements were successful in broadening their audience. Admittedly, it is not always clear exactly which groups were being attracted and in what numbers. Evidence for increased attendance by women is largely anecdotal, but managements targeted them so forcefully and claimed their growing presence so often that their enhanced patronage can probably be assumed. The growth of the twice-nightly system implies significant levels of attendance by groups that in the words of one observer 'have not to be up at four or five o'clock in the morning', which for one syndicate head meant a broad group encompassing both 'the shop assistant and the businessman'.[15] The growth of matinée performances again suggests the increased attendance of a slightly more leisured class. According to one informed London source whereas theatre matinée audiences were 'nearly all ladies, that does not apply to music halls', and there is some evidence that matinées – and indeed music hall attendance in general – formed part of a new slightly 'fast' middle-class male culture centred also on the golf club and motoring. Certainly, quite novel attempts were made to attract a business-class element, Billy Boardman arguing that his decision to provide 'a row of telephone booths so that clients could transact their affairs' made the Newcastle Pavilion 'a house of rendezvous for businessmen'.[16]

Edwardian audiences saw much that was new to the music hall stage. Obviously, there were strong elements of continuity. Speciality acts such as strongmen, tumblers, and jugglers were already very well represented by the 1880s, while the comic singer did not suddenly disappear in 1900. Much of Marie Lloyd's and Vesta Victoria's careers, for example, fell in the Edwardian period, and many of the best-known music hall songs were written after 1900; that much-quoted study of the 'Victorian moonlight flit', 'Don't Dilly Dally on the Way' (or 'The Cock Linnet Song') actually dates from 1919.[17] Success in blending established and new was indeed one of the major achievements of managements in this period. In 1913, Marjorie Dawson, 'The Crinoline Girl', was reviving Victorian numbers which 'suited the older members of the audience'.[18]

Novelty was in the ascendant, however. One striking feature from the early 1900s was the growth of cinematographic entertainment. The exact economic and institutional relationship between early film and variety must await detailed examination, but clearly 'moving pictures' were provided with one of their first secure homes by the variety theatre, gaining ground rapidly from 1900 to about 1910, from which point their share of the performance fell as exhibitors moved into the mushrooming specialist cinema industry. In a sense, variety did, of course, unwittingly connive at its own decline by giving house room to this new technology. Early cinema was a far more genuine threat to the variety industry than any of the other developments considered here. Nevertheless, as already noted in conjunction with the rise of cine-variety, variety and film could co-exist more readily than is sometimes appreciated. More research is required as to when cinema actually usurped the variety theatre's audience to any significant degree, but pre-1914 cinema, in many provincial areas at least, quite possibly drew on a constituency that previously had not enjoyed enough disposable income to allow for regular attendance at variety performances. The real threat from cinema lay in the future.

Alongside new technology, new song and stage styles also emerged. In terms of popular song, the advent of ragtime was especially important. Syncopated song and dance styles were popular from the very late 1890s, with cakewalk competitions for audience members common practice. However, it was not until 1912 that ragtime, heavily advertised by its main British publisher, Feldman and Company, truly swept the country. Three West End music hall revues of that year, *Everybody's Doing It*, *Kill That Fly* (with scenery by Heath Robinson) and, above all, *Hello Ragtime*, featuring the songs 'Hitchy-Koo' and 'Waiting for the Robert E Lee', were crucial conduits through which ragtime passed into the mainstream of British culture. By 1913, at least 130 American ragtime groups were touring Britain along with countless indigenous imitators.[19] Some commentators have implied an essentially middle-class following for ragtime, but it penetrated deep into contemporary popular culture, the free hall paper the *Magnet* noting the popularity of the new craze even in smaller halls, such as the Black Swan, Leeds, where 'the musical director has been stricken by ragtime fever, and the patrons appear to be willing victims of the infection'.[20] As even this moderate example of the contemporary habit of depicting it as a disease suggests, ragtime was often highly controversial, the fear that its Afro-American roots might contaminate British culture sparking off one of the earliest episodes in the history of the anti-Americanism that has been such a strong feature of twentieth-century popular cultural discourse. Once again, variety seemed to threaten 'Englishness'. Some of this hostile spirit has leeched into the music hall's historical literature, especially its popular variant, ragtime becoming the enemy of old-time music hall. Undoubtedly, its popularity (with established music hall singers in some cases) and its importance in laying the foundations for the acceptance of jazz from about 1919 challenged older styles of British popular song and helped marginalize them within a wider American–international musical context. The ragtime boom of 1912 *was* a highly significant moment. However, within the history of music hall/variety, it is more helpful to see that moment as evidence of variety's capacity to define and meet audience demand for new entertainment styles, and not some form of corruption.

The growth of the sketch was less sudden, and probably less controversial, but again of considerable importance. Sketches first appeared about 1880 and were well established within a decade, but became more popular in the early 1900s, a key element of the attempt to achieve respectability, with many of the larger theatres offering two a night, ranging from 15 to 40 minutes in duration. Ironically, much sketch production was of dubious legality, especially in the Lord Chamberlain's London licensing district in which theatrical performance outside the legitimate theatre was banned under the 1843 theatre legislation. (Most provincial and London suburban halls had 'dual' music hall and theatre licences.) After two decades of alternate compromise and bitter conflict between theatrical and music hall managers, the Lord Chamberlain eventually resolved the situation in January, 1912 by granting theatrical licences to central London halls provided that any sketch was accompanied by at least six variety turns on the programme.[21] Interestingly, the 1912 settlement effectively placed the sketch under the official censorship that it had previously avoided, because most syndicate chiefs, anxious to demonstrate their fitness to receive the Lord Chamberlain's recognition, immediately insisted that all sketches should now be submitted for vetting. Early research suggests that this new arrangement had minimal impact, the overworked Lord Chamberlain's Office largely trusting to variety's self-censorship.[22] More important, the removal of the threat of potentially damaging legal action by theatre managers gave managements confidence to produce dramatic pieces on a far greater scale than before. It can be no coincidence that 1912 saw the real flowering of revue on the English variety stage, as well as an increased borrowing from the repertory and, indeed, the personnel, of the legitimate theatre.

Perhaps the most significant of the various Edwardian sketch genres was the comic, typified by Charles Austin's *Parker PC* series, Harry Tate's trilogy *Motoring*, *Gardening* and *Fishing*, Fred Karno's

Mumming Birds, Fred Kitchen's 'Potts' and 'Perkins' series, and Harry Weldon's *Stiffy the Goalkeeper*. Although actually outnumbered by dramatic sketches such as George Gray's literal celebration of muscular Christianity, *The Fighting Parson*, so successful as to be the victim of four separate illegal sketch prosecutions by London theatre managers in 1904, they are of considerable importance within the history of popular culture.[23] Taking them together is perhaps misleading, since individual performers and writers had distinctive characteristics, but they drew heavily on a common stock of devices including physical and verbal slapsticks, cross-talk, puns, malapropisms and catchphrases. As Lois Rutherford has pointed out in a seminal article, the comic sketch was rooted in a centuries-old theatrical tradition dating back at least to the Renaissance.[24] However, there is a sense that between about 1890 (and especially after 1900) and 1914, it emerged as a distinct genre, a cultural product that had a deep influence on British comedy and indeed, due to the later activities of many of these performers and writers in cinema, broadcasting, and the record industry, in a far wider sphere for decades to come. There are clear resonances of Tate, Austin, Weldon *et al.* in British comedy right through to the Goon Show in the 1950s and beyond, while the visual humour fed directly into the movies through the work of individuals such as ex-Karno actors Charlie Chaplin and Stan Laurel.

At its most sophisticated the sketch blended into 'revue'. A loosely constructed satire on contemporary events, with its initial roots in eighteenth-century French theatre, revue had only a patchy presence in nineteenth-century Britain before re-emerging in the 1890s in a number of London theatres and theatres of variety. However, it was from 1912 that it became a central part of variety entertainment throughout Britain. Revues from this date were generally collections of song and dance routines held together by plots that barely hinted at a unifying theme. The satirical element was strong, but it tended to be directed at theatrical trends far more than at contemporary social and political issues, with the exception of that favoured target, women's rights. *Everybody's Doing It*, by George Grossmith and C. H. Bovill, the opening of which at the Empire, Leicester Square in February 1912 was a major catalyst for the expansion of revue, demonstrates well the genre's great flexibility and capacity to act as a catch-all, containing a ragtime version of *Carmen*, a highland fling, the American two-step dancing of the show's greatest stars, Fred Farren and Ida Crispi, and a patriotic tableau. Revue's pace, lightness of touch and search for novelty – all pointed up in titles such as *Step This*

Way, What a Game, and *Keep Smiling* – demonstrate management's use
of it as a method for brightening variety's image, particularly with
younger audiences. Many contemporaries were as critical of the
revue as they were of all other changes in the period. Certainly, revue
pushed singers into areas of repertoire that were not distinctly 'of' the
music hall, as with George Robey and 'If You Were the Only Girl in
the World', his 1916 hit song with Violet Lorraine from *The Bing Boys
are Here*.[25] However, the popularity of such material is undeniable, the
variety stage once again directing and reflecting shifts in musical
taste. On a wider front, the development of revue, as with a number of
the developments noted above, marks a crucial step in the process by
which, between 1890 and 1930, 'music hall' increasingly shaded into
and drew upon adjacent entertainment types – the musical, musical
comedy, cinema, certain styles of broadcasting – to create a new and
flexible environment for both performers and audiences.

For all the emphasis on novelty, respectability, and improvement,
however, the Edwardian variety theatre was never entirely 'tamed'.
The more officious managements certainly made strenuous efforts to
assert authority. In 1913, a man was ejected from Moss's Swansea
Empire for hissing; a subsequent legal judgment found in his favour
and he was awarded £50 costs. A letter to the *Era* in the same year
claimed that two women in an unnamed hall had been upbraided for
laughing too loudly at a Fred Karno sketch. Similarly, some
managements redoubled the long-running attempt to restrain audiences
from joining in choruses, the insouciant Vesta Victoria satirizing the
procedure in her 1911 song 'Don't Sing the Chorus', in which the
manager threatens the sack if she encourages the vocal efforts of the
gallery and 'upsets my stalls and my boxes'.[26] (There is some evidence
that chorus-singing was deemed far more acceptable during the First
World War, out of respect to soldiers in the audience.) Restrictions
were also often placed on encores and curtain calls, a device partly
explained by the requirements of the twice-nightly system, which
required prompt closure of the first house.

On occasions, audience–management relationships resembled a
kind of guerrilla warfare. Henry Raymond, manager of the New
Cross Empire on its opening in 1899, outlawed whistling and
requested that men keep jackets on. The audience was unimpressed,
and 'even the police engaged at the outset declined to put out men
who indulged in unparliamentary language', claimed Raymond,
who believed that the conversion to his side of a Deptford slaughterman
who had served a prison sentence for threatening him with a knife,

eventually helped tame the gallery. 'Six years hard work', he concluded triumphantly, 'has educated the people to like a high-class variety entertainment and to behave themselves.'[27]

Audiences, however, were never quite the passive dupes that some contemporaries claimed. The very fact that managements worked so hard to create an aura of refinement suggests a continued liveliness, especially at the smaller halls. In extreme cases, when audiences felt cheated or offended, strong displays of disapproval could result, well demonstrated in August 1913 when pressure from the Variety Artists Federation prevented the controversial black American heavyweight boxing champion Jack Johnson from fulfilling engagements at two London halls, the VAF passing a resolution condemning 'engagements based on unsavoury notoriety rather than abilities as legitimate performers'. At the Euston, pro-Johnson factions, found mainly in 'the lower paid seats', listened attentively to the majority of performers, but demonstrated so effectively against those artists who had supported the VAF position that they were unable to begin, let alone complete, their acts. Others, mostly in the stalls and boxes, in turn jeered and hissed those who were disturbing the performance. Similarly, in the same year, a number of Jewish spectators at the Leeds Hippodrome demonstrated against a comedian they felt had insulted them.[28] Performers too could resist, subtly, as with Vesta Victoria above, or more aggressively, Stoll admitting that his house censorship rules could lead 'to friction, and sometimes open defiance'.[29]

Perhaps the significant limit to the push towards respectability was the fact that, as the Jack Johnson case suggests, many managements, while preaching refinement, were anxious to court a certain notoriety. Only a year after hosting the Royal Command Performance, supposedly the defining moment of respectability, the Palace Theatre of Varieties was threatened with the withdrawal of its newly acquired stage play licence unless changes were made to the sketch, *A la Carte*, starring the French dancer Gaby Deslys. Controversy surrounded two scenes, one featuring a lightly-attired Deslys dancing along a stairway into the audience, the other, the 'vision scene', concerning a jealous lover imagining the 'loving endearments between his object of desire and another'. Palace manager Alfred Butt initially refused to make any alterations, arguing that Deslys represented the high artistic qualities that audiences now demanded. The discourse of respectability adopted by the variety industry was clearly a conveniently flexible one, adept at appropriating helpful concepts at moments of crisis. Butt eventually beat a diplomatic retreat when the issue fuelled a national press debate including calls from a resurgent reform lobby for a national inspector of music halls.[30] Such campaigns – and they continued well into the inter-war period until cinema became the main object of criticism – were irritating but not fatal. Indeed, perhaps they were positively helpful. They reminded managements of their vulnerability and thus maintained largely bourgeois-defined social norms which could not be transgressed, but they also provided much useful publicity. A hint of controversy and salaciousness was necessary for the success of even the restrained fare that the Edwardian variety industry served. The 'new' audience accepted it, perhaps even demanded it in the case of some of its male habituees, especially as if with Deslys and others, it was (lightly) dressed in the convenient cloak of 'art'.

The final section of this essay considers the wider meanings of Edwardian variety performance. Apart from the 'standard' interpretative problems posed by cultural analysis – complexity of audience structures, typicality of product or venue considered, mediation of sources, and so forth – Edwardian variety offers a particular challenge because 'variety' was such an apt description. All human life, or at least large chunks of it, really was represented there, thereby producing a theatre characterized by a richness of dramatic opposition, parody, and counterpoint, and generating a plethora of possible meanings not always easily discernible eighty years on. The very late Victorian and Edwardian periods, for example, witnessed (in the words of one provincial paper) a 'strong man craze', at first sight viewable as a 'reflection', if that word is still acceptable in academic discourse, of contemporary preoccupation with the fitness of the imperial race and 'national efficiency'. This might then be added to arguments suggesting that music hall provided a conduit for imperialist ideology. However, strongmen often used 'normal' assistants or audience volunteers to provide comic counterpoint. Did members of the audience grasp the national efficiency agenda while watching, for example, Eugene Sandow (who could apparently hold 684 lbs in weights plus four men and ten women on a board stretched from knee to shoulder while he leant backwards on his arms), or were such notions deflected by attention to the assistant who struggled with the lightest weights? Yet again, the strongmen may have had very different meanings for women in the audience, providing opportunity for displays of pleasure in the male form – Sandow kept a box supposedly containing 'all sorts of jewellery – rings, brooches, bracelets ... thrown on the stage to him by ladies attending the performance' – or the opportunity to poke fun at their less then Herculean partners.[31]

Definitive readings of individual performers and performances are, then, ultimately neither possible nor desirable: the polysemic nature of all cultural products has to be acknowledged. However, such acknowledgement should not preclude the hunt for certain broad patterns transcending the disparate and disputed meanings of individual acts. The broad conclusion offered here is that Edwardian variety provided a site in which certain social, political, and moral issues and conflicts could be aired and worked through, but which ultimately tended to be resolved in the interests of dominant social groups. There is only limited space to explore these issues here and therefore only three disparate but informative themes have been selected: depiction of 'illicit pleasures', the meaning of local, regional and 'Celtic' identity, and the representation of women. Obviously, a very similar case can be argued in regard to the socio-political functions of the Victorian music hall, but all three areas covered here, either because they focussed on elements of social life previously largely neglected by the halls, or because they gave new inflection to existing ideas, do represent distinctly Edwardian manifestations of, and contribution to, the music hall's larger impact.

Some historians of Victorian music hall, while acknowledging its essential conservatism, have placed emphasis on the potential for a sub-political 'subversiveness' inherent in much of the industry's celebration of pleasures, sensual and cerebral, that challenged dominant modes of 'respectability'.[32] Such challenges to propriety were certainly still present in the period from the late 1890s, as exemplified by the vogue for sketches entangling 'innocents' such as maiden aunts and vicars in the world of gambling.[33] In an age of growing middle-class hostility to popular gambling, demonstrated by the introduction of the 1906 Street Betting Act, consideration of gambling, even in its legal forms, might imply a mild protest. Similar arguments might be made in regard to the 'fleshly' songs of Lloyd, Vesta Victoria, and even the early Harry Lauder, always far more than the Presbyterian moraliser of hostile caricature, as is illustrated in 'Stop Your Tickling Jock' (1905) with its celebration of 'the treacle roly poly' enjoyed by singer and girlfriend while her parents 'went to the kirk'.[34] In general, however, the potentially subversive thrust of such material became ever more muted as variety established improved credentials through its appropriation of a growing section of the lower-middle and middle-class audience and establishment of alliances with certain sections of local civic elites. Celebration of beer, idleness, easy winnings, and the pleasures of the opposite sex carried far less subversive weight in this context than in previous decades. Here possibly is support for Peter Bailey's stimulating suggestion that the 'music hall's particular mode of conceit, parody, and innuendo constituted a second language *for all classes*, whose penetrations had a powerful integrative force in English society'.[35] This is complex and as yet largely untilled territory, but it was undeniably the Edwardian period, when music hall's place was so much more broadly and securely rooted, that offered the best possibility for the full blossoming of such a lingua franca, and particularly the element of innuendo. Shared comic codes perhaps did define an 'Englishness' that transcended class, that increasingly unified rather than divided.

Historians have paid only limited attention to the second issue, the question of local and regional identity, but the music hall and variety stage should prove an important focus for their much needed attentions. Despite the vigour of local and regional cultures right through to 1914 and beyond, late Victorian and Edwardian Britain witnessed shifts in the internal balance of power whereby Britain increasingly became identified with England (and often southern England at that), and the social, cultural, and economic dominance of London and the home counties took on new dimensions.[36] The Edwardian variety stage, to a far greater extent than before, constructed notions of provincial (and Celtic) 'otherness' which were to have powerful resonances in popular culture for the rest of the twentieth century. In terms of provincial representation, the most common archetype was the 'northerner', with the 'north' defined very narrowly as essentially the manufacturing districts of Lancashire and Yorkshire. This limited focus derived partly from the strength of the existing stereotype of what actually constituted the north of England, partly from the fact that these areas enjoyed perhaps the strongest regional dialect entertainment culture from which definable local personae could be created (although by this reasoning, the north-east should have featured more widely). For much of the Victorian period, most northern singers had disguised or played down their distinctiveness, Yorkshire comedian J. W. Rowley, for example, performing many of his numbers in coster cockney. From about 1900, however, perhaps benefiting from the success of stage cockneys like Albert Chevalier and Gus Elen in establishing an enthusiasm for 'local' colour in the previous decade, a number of northern performers began to experience success in London, including George Formby senior, Maggie Walsh, Morny Cash and Whit Cunliffe from Lancashire, and Charles Whittle and Jack Pleasants from the West Riding.[37] Probably only Formby was dependent on northern-oriented material, and all used a modified language unencumbered with dialect, but their 'northern-ness' was apparent. Much material revolved around two stock characters, the provincial innocent abroad, the northern 'loon' typified by Formby's 'John Willie' and Knowles's 'Billy Muggins' characters, and the wistful émigré conjuring up memories of his or her partner at home, in songs such as 'The Girl in the Clogs and Shawl' and 'My Girl's a Yorkshire Girl'. In both instances, though, here were sentimental, näive provincials in sharp, sophisticated London.

Similarly limited visions were offered in representations of the Irish and Scottish. A key factor here was that many stage Irishmen and Scotsmen were exactly that. The leading Edwardian music hall Irishman, Talbot O'Farrell, was actually a Yorkshireman, Will Parrott, who had begun his career as 'scotch' comedian Jock McIver.[38] Many such artists were then effectively stereotyping an existing stage culture rather than anything else. The Edwardian music hall Irishman (representations of Irishwomen were less frequent), tailored to suit towns with large Irish populations, was almost indistinguishable from his Victorian forebear. He was a skilful talker, drinker, and fighter, the latter virtue often demonstrated by loyal service to the British Army. There is some evidence that Irish characters and issues were less frequently featured after the end of the Boer War, with a corresponding rise of interest in Scottish matters. Scottish performers and celebration of the valour of Highland regiments had long been an element of music hall entertainment, but commentators noted a late Edwardian craze for Scottish sketches and songs, resulting in a number of English comedians hastily changing national identity.[39] Two not necessarily mutually exclusive explanations might be offered here. It is possible that with the re-emergence of Irish issues on to the political stage from 1910, audiences and managements found comic Irishness a little less comfortable, and transferred their taste for stage Hibernianism to the Scottish. That this change was so easy points up the second explanation: the flood of 'genuine' Scottish comedians such as Neil Kenyon and Sandy McNab and numerous 'imitators' was made possible by the phenomenal success of Harry Lauder.[40]

Music hall commentators have not always been kind to Lauder, his sometimes abrasive public persona, manufactured Scottishness and chauvinistic political utterances hardly appealing to late twentieth-century intellectual sensibilities. However, he was undoubtedly one of the most popular and highly paid performers of the Edwardian age, much of his success attributable not to any intrinsic appeal of the stage Scotsman, but to his considerable talents as singer, writer, and comic actor. His stage 'Scot' was nevertheless a skilful creation, tailored to meet English audiences. While Scottish comedians with broad dialects like W. F. Frame achieved only limited success, Lauder used English with a Scottish accent, and then built a succession of characters appropriate to existing English visions of Scotland. Despite his lowland accent and lowland shepherd's stick, his was an essentially rural Highland and Island Scotland, symbolized by kilts, riotous wedding parties, whisky, and 'bonnie, bonnie lasses'. On (and off) stage, he ruthlessly exploited the notion of the canny Scot. While not actually inventing the stage Scotsman, he gave much of the shape and substance to the character that was to become a major element of twentieth-century popular entertainment, and one that some later twentieth-century Scots find far less appealing and positive than did his usually enthusiastic contemporaries.

All this is not to deny that local pride could not be expressed and reinforced, even within as 'national' a form as the music hall. 'Home' audiences might see these various representations in a different way from their southern and metropolitan counterparts. In their local setting, performers such as Lauder and Formby tended to return to more authentic dialects and embellished local styles, and their material was probably read far more positively. Formby's characters, for example, were never quite the 'jays' that they appeared, 'The Man from Lancashire' in the eponymous song of 1904, for example, successfully besting some London cardsharpers who like everybody else 'think aw'm biggest mug in the town'. Similarly, some northern love songs articulated the supposed opposition between northern virtue and simplicity and southern falseness and showiness, so common in northern views of the south, and of London in particular. 'My Girl's a Yorkshire Girl' exclaimed

Though she's a factory lass, and wears no fancy clothes,
I've a sort of Yorkshire relish, for my little Yorkshire rose.[41]

The gentle tone of much of the humour outlined above, coupled with the provision made by the halls for limited displays of local patriotism, demonstrate that the näive northerner, the fighting Irishman and the drunken and/or canny Scot did not form such negative and disabling images of 'otherness' as those constructed around, for example, the subject races of the British Empire. Nevertheless, in the early twentieth-century context, non-English and English regional cultures were given an extra coat of 'quaintness' that served to reinforce the supposed superiority of metropolitan and national cultures in the century ahead.

Music hall's depiction of women was clearly complex. From the late Victorian period, and perhaps even earlier, it could be seen as the location for a set of potent challenges to domestic ideology: here was a public space, where male inadequacy could be guyed, where large earnings could be accumulated by women performers. Alternatively, it is equally possible to emphasize that managerial blandishments to potential women customers were rooted in the highly traditional notion of women as agents of moral improvement – angel of the hearth becomes angel of the halls – and that the potentially subversive power of some women performers' acts was counterbalanced by the popular association of actresses with prostitution, and various notions of the male as possessor. Final interpretations tend to depend to some extent upon individual political predilection, but the evidence offered here, mostly related to women as performers, would suggest that for the most part the Edwardian music hall represented women's roles in highly traditional ways and that, in extreme moments, it demonstrated 'the common music hall trait' of 'violent hostility to women' which J. S. Bratton found to be a feature of its Victorian predecessor.[42]

Useful light is shed by consideration of the later Edwardian vogue for the highly flexible category contemporaries termed 'classical dance'. While ballet had long appeared on the music hall stage, variety entrepreneurs seized the opportunity to enhance their industry's image by trading on its increasingly elevated artistic status and add to the number of (often solo) dancers on Edwardian programmes. The process culminated with the contracting of Russian star ballerinas Kyaksht, Karsavina, and Pavlova to London variety theatres between

1908 and 1910.[43] As the Gaby Deslys incident suggested earlier, variety's real achievement here was to capitalize on the subsequent positive publicity in such a way as to facilitate a partial fusion of dance of almost any type with ballet/art, and thus legitimize a certain sexual *frisson*. Maud Allan's eight-month engagement at the Palace in 1908 was seen by many contemporaries as ushering in a renewed interest in dance on the variety stage. The use of a property head of St John the Baptist in her 'The Vision of Salome' caused controversy in London, while concern over her supposedly scanty clothing led to bans in at least two provincial venues.[44] The subsequent publicity guaranteed good houses wherever she went and managements speedily booked a number of other, mainly European acts, many of which were, in the word of one unsympathetic commentator, more 'acrobatic' than Allan. Unsurprisingly, purity campaigners attacked many of these performances, 'conceived in passion and [which] have no other object than to stir passions', and some managements were forced to respond. In 1912, for example, French dancer Jeannette Denarber lost a £37 per week contract at the Empire, Leicester Square, following allegations that she had stripped to the waist in front of stagehands during a quick change routine behind a screen or 'shadowgraph', and that her dresser had pointed out her silhouette on the screen to the audience at a crucial moment in her disrobing. *The Era* celebrated 'the care which our variety entrepreneurs exercise to see that nothing indecent shall be included in their entertainments'. Yet, by July 1913 Denarber was performing almost the identical act at the Brixton Empress with great success. As so often, managerial opportunism and male audience prurience secured a place for the sexual display of women on stage. Here, surely, is a key example of what Peter Bailey has termed 'parasexuality ... a sexuality that is deployed but contained, carefully channelled rather than fully discharged ... the less august branches of capitalism converting sexuality from anathema to resource, from resource to commodity, in the development of a modern sexualised consumerism'.[45] As Bailey demonstrates, parasexuality predates the Edwardian age. However, its manifestation on such a large stage as the Edwardian variety theatre gave this particular male construction of glamour a potentially powerful place in contemporary gender politics.

A second element of 'hostility' was provided by the often extraordinarily vituperative attitude shown to the suffragette movement, and indeed the whole suffrage cause, in the immediate pre-war years. Variety stage opposition to women's political rights ranged from mild but effective lampooning – one sketch included a 'Mrs Spankfirst' – to head-on attack. A common vehicle for this was the 'world-turned-upside-down' fantasy in which audiences were asked to peer into a comic (but threatening) future in which women had gained the vote and placed men in a totally subservient position. A number of songs dealt with this notion, including Whit Cunliffe's 'Do You Believe in Women's Rights?' (1910), in which a suffragette at last learns the error of her ways:

> At last the woman came to man, and murmured on his breast,
> The Women's Rights you gave to me with the marriage rites are best,
> And she who'd smacked a policeman's face, and magistrate defied,
> Then whispered, 'As the rib of man, my place is by your side'.
> And even pretty Christabel, the ardent suffragette,
> Found out the true Women's Rights – and pushed a bassinette.

Significantly, many women performers seemed just as comfortable with such material, Marie Kendall warning that the man who married 'a suffering suffragette'

> Soon will be wearing skirts
> And the women wearing the trousers,

while Mrs Langtry (Lady de Bathe) starred in the 1912 sketch *Helping the Cause*, which satirized the role of the monied suffragette supporter.[46]

As always, audience response was probably varied, with much of this entertainment working at a number of levels. *Helping the Cause*, for example, could be seen as a satire on the ignorance of the aristocracy – the central character Lady Vanderville assumes her prison gaoler to be her servant – or, relatedly, as a comedy of misinterpretation. Threatened with the padded cell Lady Vanderville replies, 'Oh, yes, by all means the padded cell. It sounds so comfortable.' Again, certain of these pieces, especially the fantasies of woman's future power, may have opened up potent utopian visions, fulfilling very much the enabling function that some recent theorists have suggested for much romantic fiction. Nevertheless, pushed too far, such speculation becomes a form of wish fulfilment all of its own. The lasting impression is of an entertainment industry as unsympathetic as ever to challenging this, and indeed any other element of the political and social status quo.

The emphasis here on the conservative role of the variety stage is not intended to imply a unified audience response or a unified industry attempt at overt political control. Rather, the political and social tone of the music hall stage grew from managements' need to attract the broadest-based audience by drawing on themes that had the maximum purchase within contemporary society, and by avoiding controversy, or by deflating and deflecting it in ways that suited contemporary opinion. The culture of the Edwardian variety stage articulates broad contemporary social and political currents as much, and probably rather more, than it does the personal statements of entertainment entrepreneurs. There is also no intention to deny that variety could challenge certain powerful contemporary trends. Hunters in search of 'oppositional' elements might glimpse one in variety's relentless pursuit of novelty, modernity (both often expressed in the absorption of non-English performers and cultural forms), and the urban. In an epoch when commentators from so many political backgrounds drew inspiration from the rural and the ancient, the variety theatre represented a site where the denizens of the modern city could fight back. Music hall had always focussed on the urban, the current and the new, but this tendency increased from about 1900 with the use of new technology such as the cinematograph and new musical forms such as ragtime. To term this 'oppositional', in the Williamsite sense of challenging dominant culture, might be an overstatement, but the variety theatre should at least remind historians of Edwardian England that the present as well as the past was well represented in popular cultural discourse.

The 'story' has been taken here to 1914. Almost no serious research has been undertaken into the variety industry beyond that point and the existing literature is thus full of very loose generalizations concerning the 'death' of variety. In as much as any generalization is possible, it would seem that the variety *theatre*, as institution, had clearly reached the limits of its expansion by 1914 and was to come under increasing pressure from the cinema during the second decade of the twentieth century, pressure that became intense by the early 1920s as the dance hall and broadcasting added their weight. The 1920s increasingly saw variety theatres converted into cinemas, the abandonment of variety in favour of musical comedy, and a number of syndicate bankruptcies. However, it is noteworthy that the later 1930s saw the re-appearance of variety at a number of previously converted venues. It was not until the 1950s that the variety theatre really became an endangered species; its problems were shared to a considerable degree by the cinema and dance hall, all three victims of the rise of television and huge changes in patterns of youth culture. Variety as an entertainment style, especially a *comic* style, most certainly survived 1914, with some of its greatest names, Gracie Fields, Sid Field, Max Miller, Billy Bennet, the Crazy Gang, still to come. At the same time it diffused into other entertainment forms, radio, cinema, and television, and has powerful resonances to this day.[47] As always, it seems, Edwardian variety can be depicted as much a fertile point of departure as the end of a once virile music hall culture.

NOTES

I am grateful to the editors for helpful observations on an earlier and much flabbier draft, and to Chris Berry, both for taking on the typing of this following a word-processing disaster, and for making a number of helpful comments on the text.

1 For useful biographical material on Moss and Stoll see G. J. Mellor, *Northern Music Hall* (Newcastle, 1970). For Stoll in particular, *Dictionary of Business Biography*, ed. D. J. Jeremy and C. Shaw (London, 1986), pp. 355–61.
2 *Report from the Joint Select Committee of the House of Lords and the House of Commons on the Stage Plays* (Censorship), Parliamentary Papers VIII (1909), [5757]. On the general issue of music hall and excise licences, C. Waters, 'Manchester Morality and London Capital: the Battle Over the Palace of Varieties', in *Music Hall: The Business of Pleasure*, ed. Peter Bailey (Milton Keynes, 1986), pp. 141–61, and C. Waters, 'Progressives, Puritans and the Cultural Politics of the Council, 1889–1914', in *Politics and the People of London, London County Council 1889–1914*, ed. Andrew Saint (London, 1989), pp. 49–70. Tea lounges were preferred to bars in new halls in Cheltenham and Preston. See *Performer*, 15 May 1913.
3 *Bradford Daily Argus*, 31 December 1899, 28 February 1900.
4 Figure based on analysis of 1914 trade press.
5 W. R. Titterton, *From Theatre to Music Hall* (London, 1912), pp. 124, 121, 115–16, 213.
6 *Era*, 16 July 1913. A line much closer to that argued by Titterton can be seen, however, in the *Magnet*, the Leeds-based trade paper which spoke largely for the non-syndicate, so-called 'free halls'. This journal deserves far more attention than it usually receives.
7 G. Stedman Jones, 'Working-class Culture and Working-class Politics in London, 1870–1900: Notes on the Remaking of a Working Class', in *Languages of Class* (Cambridge, 1983), p. 233.

8 *Dictionary of Business Biography*, p. 356.

9 There were also several hundred public house music halls or concert rooms still holding on to their small stages, chairmen, and waiters. Crucial to the social life of small industrial towns and villages, and training grounds for the variety industry, they were nevertheless clearly seen as a separate formation. Many carried on into the 1920s and beyond, and the whole phenomenon is worthy of historical study.

10 LCC, *London Statistics*, vol. xxiii, 1912–13, pp. 265–6.

11 *Era*, 13 January 1913.

12 J. Crump, 'Provincial Music Hall: Promoters and Public in Leicester, 1863–1929', *Music Hall: The Business of Pleasure*, p. 69; evidence of J. B. Mulholland, *Joint Select Committee Report* (1909), [4081].

13 *Era Special Supplement*, 3 July 1912. J. Gore, *King George V: A Personal Memoir* (London, 1941), pp. 270–3, 337, is useful for this theme. On ceremony, D. Cannadine, 'The Context, Performance and Meaning of Ritual: The British Monarchy and the "Invention of Tradition", c. 1820–1977', in *The Invention of Tradition*, ed. E. Hobsbawm and T. Ranger (Cambridge, 1983), pp. 101–64.

14 *Northern Music Hall*, p. 183; *Bradford Daily Argus*, 31 January 1899, 18 March 1914. For the attack on Bradford pub halls, *Magnet*, 25 January and 1 February 1902.

15 *Report From the Select Committee on Theatres and Places of Public Entertainment* (1892), [3737]; evidence of Henry Tozer, *Joint Select Committee Report* (1909), [4939].

16 W. H. 'Billy' Boardman, *Vaudeville Days* (London, 1935), p. 48.

17 Richard Anthony Baker, *Marie Lloyd, Queen of the Music Halls* (London, 1990), p. 137.

18 *Magnet*, 8 March 1913.

19 R. Middleton, 'Music of the Lower Classes', in *Athlone History of Music in Great Britain*, ed. N. Temperley, vol. v (London, 1981), pp. 88–9.

20 *Magnet*, 12 April 1913.

21 *Era*, 13 January 1912.

22 For evidence of censorship, see comments on scripts of *Heard in Camera*, Lord Chamberlain (British Library Manuscripts Room), 1912/3, which contains anti-Russian material, and the *double entendre*-laden *Winning the Wager*, Lord Chamberlain 1912/12.

23 For *Fighting Parson, Joint Select Committee Report* (1909), Appendix D.

24 L. Rutherford, '"Harmless Nonsense": the Comic Sketch and the Development of Music-Hall Entertainment', *Music Hall: Performance and Style*, ed. J. S. Bratton (Milton Keynes, 1986), pp. 131–51; *Era*, 17 February 1912.

25 George Robey, *Looking Back on Life* (London, 1933), pp. 166–7.

26 *Magnet*, 26 July 1913; *Era*, 8 February 1913; 'Don't Sing the Chorus', British Library, Music Room, H. 3990 K. 34. All song references from this point refer to the British Library collection.

27 *Era*, 29 July 1905.
28 Johnson's 'sins' included having had a white wife who committed suicide, bail-jumping, and breaking contracts. R. Roberts, *Papa Jack and the Era of White Hope* (London, 1983), *Era*, 27 August 1913, and *Magnet*, 30 August 1913, give interestingly different accounts of events. For the Leeds incident, see *Performer*, 15 May 1913, and *Yorkshire Post*, 6 May 1913.
29 *Joint Select Committee Report* (1909), [5019].
30 For Deslys's life, J. Gardiner, *Gaby Deslys, A Fatal Attraction* (London, 1986). For *A la Carte*, *Era*, 3 September, 23 October, 30 October and 19 November 1913.
31 *Bradford Daily Telegraph*, 2 February 1904; Lady de Freece, *Recollections of Vesta Tilley* (London, 1934), pp. 54–5.
32 A. Howkins, *History of Workshop Journal*, 9 (1980), pp. 202–3. He consciously avoids the word subversiveness; '"Harmless Nonsense"', p. 144.
33 For example, *The Lady and the Parson*, Lord Chamberlain 1912/3; *The Big Race*, *Era*, 28 February 1912.
34 In *Francis and Day's Album of Harry Lauder's Popular Songs* n.d., F. 1840.
35 Peter Bailey, 'Making Sense of Music Hall', in *Music Hall: The Business of Pleasure*, p. xviii.
36 For a helpful introduction, J. Harris, *Private Lives, Public Spirit. A Social History of Britain* (Oxford, 1993), pp. 17–23.
37 G. Mozart, *Limelight* (London, 1938), p. 44: G. S. Jones, 'The "Cockney" and the Nation', in *Metropolis London, Histories and Representations Since 1800*, ed. David Feldman and Gareth Stedman Jones (London, 1989), pp. 294–300.
38 *Northern Music Hall*, p. 91.
39 *Era*, 8 February 1912; *Limelight*, p. 257.
40 His autobiography *Roamin' in the Gloamin'* (London, 1928), while self-congratulatory, is nevertheless full of useful information.
41 'The Man from Lancashire', H. 3986 tt. 51, 'My Girl's a Yorkshire Girl (Eh! By gum she's a Champion)' (1908), H. 3986. j. 37. On north–south representations, P. Joyce, *Visions of the People, Industrial England and the Question of Class, 1840–1914* (Cambridge, 1991), pp. 290–328, is a stimulating starting-point. For metropolis against provinces, see D. Smith, *North and South. Britain's Economic, Social and Political Divide* (London, 1989) and D. Read, *The English Provinces* (London, 1964).
42 J. S. Bratton, 'Jenny Hill: Sex and Sexism in Victorian Music Hall', in *Music Hall, Performance and Style*, p. 106.
43 On this and the popularity of Russian ballet in Edwardian Britain, see N. Macdonald, *Diaghilev Observed* (London, 1975), pp. 17–25.
44 *Northern Music Hall*, p. 203; R. Busby, *British Music Hall. An Illustrated Who's Who from 1850 to the Present Day* (London, 1976), pp. 15–16. For a memorable parody see 'Salome' (1908), H 3988 U. 44.
45 *Daily Chronicle*, 20 November 1913; *Era*, 3 January, 2 July 1913; Peter Bailey, 'Parasexuality and Glamour; the Victorian Barmaid as Cultural

Prototype', *Gender and History*, 2,2 (1990), pp. 147, 167.

46 'Do You Believe in Women's Rights?' (1910), H 3991 zz. 39; 'Never Oh! Never Get Married' (1908), H 3986 tt 52. For sketches dealing with future fantasies see, for example, *The Heid o' the House*, *Bradford Daily Telegraph*, 3 February 1914, *In the Future, ibid.* 24 February 1914, *And Very Nice Too*, *Magnet*, 22 November 1913, *The First of April*, Lord Chamberlain 1912/12. For *Helping the Cause*, Lord Chamberlain 1912/5.

47 All forms of Listener Research in the inter-war period demonstrated that the albeit very loosely defined category of 'variety' was consistently the most popular among radio audiences. M. Pegg, *Broadcasting and Society, 1918–1939* (Oxford, 1983), pp. 138–9.

CHAPTER 4

Beating the bounds: gender play and role reversal in the Edwardian music hall

J. S. Bratton

One of the things the first and last decades of the twentieth century share is a fascination with sexual ambiguity and with cross-dressing as an element of performance. Just as images from Madonna videos and the stage and private lives of Boy George have permeated our consciousness, so the Edwardians toyed with pictures of people in costumes of the opposite gender, or of no determined gender at all. Pin-up postcards are ephemeral, but dozens survive that show female impersonators, often in army shows or pierrot troupes, and many more of women dressed in the clothes of men or boys. They are very various: some seem to attempt to create a perfect illusion of masculinity; others wear dancing shoes, or corsets under their military uniforms. A few select elements of masculine dress and couple them with feminine frills, tights and spangles. Some are slender, boyish, charming; others heavy-set and challenging (see plates 3 and 4).

The circulation of such images was very wide. Many surviving cards have been mailed, and bear correspondence between mothers and daughters, or heterosexual courting couples; those preserved from the hazards of posting are often signed, suggesting the customary largesse bestowed on fans. The coincidence of interest tempts us to attribute modern motives to the cross-dressed music hall performers and their followers of eighty years ago. It is I think unavoidable that our first question should be how far, in a popular consciousness not yet permeated by Freudianism, this interest was specifically homosexual, or consciously sexual at all? And then, who were these women? What did they think they were doing when they offered themselves in these disguises?

These are almost impossible questions to answer. Almost nothing seems to be discoverable about their personal or even their professional lives, beyond the leading rank of male impersonators – Vesta Tilley, Hetty King, Ella Shields. One of the few of the mass of pin-ups about

3 Miss Billie Butt. Postcard, author's collection.

4 Miss Pauline Travis. Postcard, author's collection.

whom something is discoverable is Bessie Wentworth; and she proves to be an interesting case. A fatherless City clerk whose mother let theatrical digs, she became a singer of operatic boy roles and a principal boy in pantomime before she developed a highly successful solo act as a coon dancer and singer. According to the press, she was planning to marry, buy a pub and settle down when she died of typhoid in 1901. Her act combined racial and gender impersonation, of sorts: she did not black up, but relied on costume and lyrics to evoke the stereotype of the African-American male plantation slave. Her costume was a loose, open-necked shirt, striped pantaloons and a huge-brimmed, boyish straw hat; the childlike air of the visual image was contradicted by the sexually charged lyrics of her song, 'Looking for a Coon Like Me', which concerns the problems of being so attractive to girls. It ends

> Some sit an' sob until dey're hoarse,
> Some try to get a big divorce;
> You know de reason why, ob course?
> Dere Looking for a Coon like me!
> I'se got in lots o' rows froo gals
> I'se had to skip an' all my pals
> Am Looking for a Coon like me!
> Outside a yeller feller stands,
> Sixteen big niggers he commands,
> Dey'se all got razors in dere hands,
> Looking for a Coon like me![1]

Such material provides a rich field of parodic, distorted, suggestive and transgressive signification; but it does not directly explain the pictures of Bessie Wentworth that were in circulation in the years after her premature death. Labelled 'the late Miss Bessie Wentworth', they show her sitting in various masculine poses on a studio chair (they seem to be all from one photo session) wearing full naval uniform, with a cigarette, an assertive turn of the head, and a prominently displayed little-finger ring (see plate 5.) One can only deduce that the coded pictures relate not to her act, nor to the exemplary life-story assiduously publicized both before and after her death, but to some other persona, in which she was followed, and her image eagerly collected, by her fans. There have been modern instances of such appropriation.

Reading these pictures as if we had discovered an Edwardian k.d.lang will not get us very far in understanding the full range of

5 The late Miss Bessie Wentworth. Postcard, author's collection.

music hall male impersonation; but, equally clearly, the unprece-
dentedly widespread popularity of such images and acts must have
some bearing upon early twentieth-century concerns. To borrow the
terms of the subtitle of Marjorie Garber's *Vested Interests*,[2] my
hypothesis is that there seems to be a correlation to be traced between
an outburst of cross-dressing and a specific cultural anxiety. In
addition, these acts offer material for the analysis of the question
posed by Judith Butler in *Gender Trouble*: 'is drag the imitation of
gender, or does it dramatize the signifying gestures through which
gender itself is established?'.[3]

That there was a level of cultural anxiety surrounding these
performances, if not actually causing and fuelling them, I think can
be demonstrated. In the spring of 1910 the star male impersonator
Hetty King (see plate 6) toured North American cities for the second
time, and returning to London trumpeted her success with a full-page
advertisement in the *Era* of 12 March, quoting her transatlantic
notices. The terms of their praise for her are interesting. In Buffalo
and in Chicago there seems no problem about proclaiming her act as
simply an excellent performance: 'as a regular Beau Brummel sort of
male impersonator she is extremely good' says the *Buffalo Courier*,
calling her then a 'dainty and clever young woman' who 'wears
masculine clothes very effectively as well as very naturally, and her
peculiarly "London Johnny" style and swing prove quite captivating'.
Buffalo, or at least the reporter, has seen this sort of thing before,
knows where it comes from, and can voice the up-to-date estimation
of its interest as a slightly exotic curiosity. The dissonance of his terms,
the 'daintiness' of a young woman wearing masculine clothes
'naturally', is apparently sufficiently accounted for by his placing of
the impersonation as British. *The Chicago Inter-Ocean* does not even
trouble to distance King as a British performer: 'the graceful,
charming, and keenly-humorous impersonator' who 'is dressed
elegantly' 'is to-day the greatest and most fascinating woman in
American vaudeville'. America has taken the male impersonator to
itself. In Montreal King was more of a novelty, and the critic of the
Gazette admitted that the audiences, though enthusiastic, were not
sufficiently knowing in the ways of the London halls to sing along with
the choruses as the performer expected. The writer in the *Herald* was
eager to demonstrate that he knew what was what, however, and
enthused about King as 'a very versatile and dainty little lady' who
'can wear male attire of an effeminate cut' (which he attributes to a

6 Hetty King – 'All the nice girls love a sailor.' Postcard, author's collection.

New York tailor) 'very gracefully' and also 'she can dance a bit, and be saucy' and smoke 'any old thing from a fat cigar to a briar pipe'. He seems to find all this great fun, an amusing novelty in which he is thoroughly well up; effeminacy and the aping of the masculine are all part of the game, enjoyably generating, in Sarah Maitland's phrase, an unfocussed sexual curiosity.[4] By contrast the *Toronto Press*, in a laconic sort of notice, holds King at arm's length across the Atlantic, stressing twice in its opening lines that she is an 'English music-hall artist' and then characterizing her in possibly two-edged statements: 'She wears men's clothes in a style that does credit to her smart London tailor. Miss King sings after the London Music-hall manner; she dances exceedingly well; she changes her walk as completely as she does her costume; and her material is new.' The reserve in this voice, however, seems to me to be to do with a resistance to – a snobbery about? – music hall style and European fashions, rather than any notion of an anxiety about praising a woman for imitating a man. The Canadian critics are responding to music hall modernity, of which King is a striking example, rather than to the specific possibilities and problems of this act. Male impersonation is judged in Toronto on the grounds of realism – King is good at dressing and walking like a man from London; it is a quaint idea, in its way. At least her music hall songs are not too hackneyed, and she dances well.

The American critics so far cited were ahead of this. They perceived themselves as up-to-date in their casual acceptance of male imperson-ation, their knowing ability to read its (sexual) attractiveness to men. When the act is exposed to the New York press, however, the language of its reception exhibits a new unease, a specific need to make sure that the sexuality of the display stays within the realm of titillation addressed to men, by a woman. Sam Mckee in the *Morning Telegraph* greets King as an old acquaintance, and places her very firmly – 'It has been nearly two years since this attractive and talented little Englishwoman has visited America.' A visitor; a little woman; offered for sexualized appreciation – 'attractive'. Then he feels constrained to issue an unequivocal general statement of his position on gender play: 'Male impersonators are not always entirely normal any more than female impersonators are invariably pleasant to contemplate' before tying himself in knots of equivocation and prurience in attempting to place the attractiveness of King and her performance. 'It can unhesitatingly be said' that she 'never become masculine, but is at all times charmingly feminine'; she 'knows how to wear male attire' of advanced styles,

'But no one ever loses sight of the fact that she is not a boy, and everyone is delighted that it should be so. And yet she is boyish, too. Boys are never as nice as Hetty King' and so if this boy of hers really appeared he would eclipse the competition. In her next song she 'is such a pretty naval officer' that 'the boldest buccaneer who ever sailed the sea in his long, low rakish craft would gladly strike his colours' at her approach; and then her jauntiness as a soldier makes it clear why girls love soldiers. This paroxysm of sexualized self-consciousness is not a universal response, but it was not peculiar to the unfortunate Sam. The writer in the *New York Press* was happy to indulge himself in eulogies of her as 'the quintessence of perfection, the pinnacle of delightful femininity essaying the masculine'; but Arthur Angyalfi in the *News* felt it necessary to underline that her act, 'the incarnation of the ideal, the beginning and end of perfection' in male impersonation, captivating and delighting men and women alike, is so because 'she neither loses her womanly attractiveness, nor goes over the line which divides the masculine woman from the mere impersonator'. Lillian Faderman's recent work on the emergence of lesbianism as a category[5] offers a convenient way to understand the response of New York, where the emergence of a female homosexual subculture dates, in her estimation, from the 1890s; these reviews suggest that by 1910 there was an awareness of such women as a distinct and recognizable type to be accounted for in terms of a prurient and pejorative moral discourse, an awareness which changes the reception of the male impersonator irreversibly.

On her return to England as a major star, King put these various responses to her work into circulation in Britain; she would appear to have been confident – rightly so – that they would be read as simple praise and admiration. Their overtones are not influential, perhaps not audible at all, in the British reception of her act. That was determined by its positioning within a very highly developed theatrical mode of representation, whose relation to its audiences was determined by its own set of cultural negotiations. When the terms in which male impersonators presented themselves and were perceived in Britain are explored in the discourses of the press and publicity machine emanating from London, what is revealed, I think, is a primarily political reading of the gender games they play.

I have suggested elsewhere[6] that the best theoretic for this reading might be the concepts of carnival, as best able to deal with the variety and multiplicity of the image-making and gender play of the music hall, and relate that to its political meanings. The inversions of carnival are not, of themselves, to be construed as automatically serving any one politic. Carnival, *pace* Bakhtin, is not inherently subversive when it inverts the categories and hierarchies of the dominant culture; nor is it, as claimed by his Marxist-revisionist commentators,[7] simply a tool of the hegemony calculated to incorporate and diffuse dissent without disturbing the given nature of hierarchy itself. There is, sometimes, treason even in an allowed fool. Historical specificity is essential to understanding. In scrutinizing a particular moment of carnivalesque practice, what matters are the cultural needs and anxieties which this imagery suggests, and what it says about them to the various imaginable audiences on the particular occasions of its enactment. Hence the interest of the range of reviewers' reactions to Hetty King – reflecting different states of awareness about gender concerns and specifically sexual practice and object preference, but capable of being used, by the performer or her agent, to speak different messages to various audiences.

In the Edwardian period King was only one of the leaders in a very crowded field of endeavour and such 'beau brummel' male impersonators were by no means the only women on the halls who were invading or reproducing the acts previously the province of men, or making their comedy out of burlesques of the masculine. Their particular type of act was located in a widespread matrix of gender play that took an active part in challenging boundaries between the sexes. Its negotiations were far more complex than any equation that might suggest itself between the middle-class women demanding the vote and music hall stars donning male clothes. The urgency of the cultural negotiation which the array of cross-gender acts represents is highlighted by the fact that it took place against a background of music hall development which was very hostile to such transgressive activity: increasing self-censorship demanded by the large syndicate halls actively discouraged any act from stepping over the bounds of good taste and respectable family entertainment. Yet reviewers can be seen to be dealing, again and again, with the need to describe the success of acts which, having been permitted because they are not necessarily transgressive in any obvious sexual way, generate an unease about their 'vulgarity' or their oddity, or simply their novel presentation of women in men's positions, or vice versa. These are the marks of carnival: the low, the heterogeneous, the grotesque, the parodic.

The most obviously carnivalesque use made of Edwardian gender impersonation was to police social roles, and enforce, by derision, the unacceptability of their transgression. Many female impersonators eased new anxieties by pressing home the proper behaviour of women and its limits – and also, in fact, the proper behaviour of men, which was now also called into question. The halls were notoriously misogynist. Sketches deriding 'women on top', like the Maples offering in 1906, which had the woman teaching her erring husband the evils of drink 'by the physical force method' when he returned home in the early hours,[8] were very common in the Edwardian period. In individual acts, carnivalesque cross-dressing by men was a very common means of attacking female dominance and independence, and punishing the old, the ugly, and the useless female. Ernest Heathcote singing a song called 'Wallflowers'; Arthur Roberts representing Mrs Twaddles, a boarding-house proprietor, and a 'gushing maiden' called Lucinda; Charles Lillburn singing that 'We ought to grow up to twenty-one, then start all over again'; Steve M'Carthy impersonating 'a female of robust appearance who wonders what a man would do with three wives like her'; Harry Allen mocking 'a dilapidated female who has evidently a sense of what is strictly proper, and is not above the vanities of skirt-dancing'; Charles Dillon cutting a comic figure 'as a lady dancer with impossible legs and of a generally grotesque appearance'; Albert and Edmonds in a sketch about 'an eccentric female' and her servant; Henry Ford commenting bitterly on a husband who wants butter instead of lard and yearns to smoke a pipe; Walter King also remarking on henpecked husbands; Bruce Green, the 'talkative Dame comedian'; Fred Moule's company in a sketch which includes a cross-dressed housemaid, a boxing match and a struggle between a suffragette and several policemen as well as her husband; John E. Conan singing a dame song; and even Tom Jones the Welsh comedian 'as Clara Ap-Morgan who chatters away on all topics in a thoroughly Welsh fashion', are all cross-dressed performers in an antique and normative mould. They are marking the boundaries, punishing transgression, attacking and mocking disliked female traits and unattractive female self-assertion.

If there is a development in this to be observed in the Edwardian period, I think it is in those performances by cross-dressed men that begin to acknowledge and perhaps attack not only the transgressive woman, but, sometimes simultaneously, the characteristics of femininity that have hitherto been valued and imposed, and to question, however obliquely, the constructs of female innocence and the domestic ideology. In Harry Randall's song 'Our Happy Little Home' the dame figure, elderly, wiry, red-nosed, ludicrous, is not the only focus of scorn. The very notion of the happy home, the central pillar of the patriarchy's positioning of the woman, seems to me to come under the questioning and sceptical 'vulgar' gaze of carnival. Such acts were testing the limits. There is quite commonly a rumble of uneasiness from the reviewers of such things as Frank Danby's sketch 'Cupid's Arms' in which an elderly and much-married barmaid is wooed and won by a shabby showman. The image of the woman projected was uncomfortably sexualized: even a man representing a barmaid causes anxiety when he makes her too knowing, too eager, and able, as in this little story, not only to fend off the man when she does not want him, but subsequently to decide independently that she will have him after all, since he is handsome and she imagines he might be rich. 'He works very briskly and dances well' concludes the reviewer, 'but we could wish that some of his patter was missing.'[9] Then there is the odd little act by Cyrus Dare, who impersonated young children. The *Era* reviewer of 19 March 1909, who saw Dare at the Metropolitan, offers without further comment the information 'he is quite successful . . . but he emphasises their precocity rather than their innocence. Especially is this the case in his concluding business, in which an imitation is given of a little girl nursing her dolly.' Such acts were often reprimanded in the press, while their shocking suggestions were perhaps guiltily welcomed and admitted.

Other performers, however, were working very hard to shore up traditional values. The site of the biggest and most revered traditional carnival in Edwardian London was the Drury Lane pantomime. Its roots were deep and very self-consciously valued by the middle-class playgoing audience; it was constructed as the first and best theatrical experience of childhood, the ritual of passage into the imaginary world of Christmas, where an expected text met with magical and comically topical embodiment, enjoyed by adults all the more when it was reflected in the eyes of children. Between 1888 and 1903 the starring combination of Herbert Campbell and Dan Leno, as dame, appeared there sixteen times. Leno's female impersonations were a part of his music hall act, too; but each year in the pantomime his gender clowning was given a topical edge, and the women he represented exposed at length the latest twists in the deeply founded misogyny of the culture. In *Blue Beard*, 1901–2, he played one of Blue

Beard's (Herbert Campbell's) wives, Sister Anne (see plate 7). Not, this time, the elderly widow or the nagging wife, but the ugly, elderly spinster, laughable in her sexual inexperience and need. The *Era* reviewer of 28 December 1901 waxed expansive:

Much was expected of Mr Dan Leno . . . whose Sister Anne is certainly one of the funniest things ever seen in pantomime . . . [she] . . . is bought by Blue Beard as an 'odd lot' when purchasing his wives of the mercenary Mustapha; and all through the piece she forces her undesired endearments upon her husband, the burlesque of sentimentality being irresistible. No one who sees Mr Leno, in a 'check' gown of the most 'modern' cut, reclining in sinuous attitudes by the side of Bluebeard while they discuss the intricacies of Bradshaw can help being amused; and as for 'Dan's' coon song with chorus, it simply sends the house into screams of delighted laughter. Mr Leno is a good dancer, and has all the tricks of the trade at his fingers – or rather his toes'-ends; and his caricature of the corybantic efforts of the up-to-date 'coon' singer is supremely ludicrous and most cleverly reminiscent of the original . . . he will, I believe, work up the burlesque of the Play scene from *Hamlet* into something even more fully diverting than it is at present. As it is, the spectacle of Sister Anne wrapping herself up in a bear-skin rug, and waiting for the cry of 'Lights!' to come from her conscience-stricken spouse, is sufficiently funny to create laughter long and loud.

Leno is never content with one joke; his old maid is the vehicle for a series of evocations and comments. The burlesque tradition that Victorian pantomime inherited allows him to draw on the semiology of other performance texts. The more obvious reference is the scene from *Hamlet*, laden as it is with the Oedipal threat of sexuality to the patriarchy. Spoof Shakespeare was common currency; Leno complicates it by choosing the already self-reflexive 'Play scene'. It is striking that when he applies the same technique to a non-canonical text, he chooses the coon song and dance, as practised by Bessie Wentworth. He thus becomes a man playing a woman playing a man, and his impersonation is an ugly version of a Shakespearean gender-game.

If men like Leno were moved to deride male impersonators, these women were perhaps felt to be trespassing into the masculine territories of the halls. The policing of the boundary of the male impersonator's activities has already been suggested in the reception of Hetty King. The terms in which she could be approved are duplicated in reviews of many women with similar acts. Vesta Tilley is approved for her realism, as King is, and for her similar version of male appearance – she is not like a man, but like a *boy*; her

7 Dan Leno as 'Sister Anne' in *Blue Beard*, Drury Lane Pantomime 1901–2. (*Tatler*, 26 February 1902)

presentation of herself in male clothes is smart, immaculate, precise –
feminized, or at least liminal. The key terms, applied to her act and to
others like it,[10] are words like 'dapper' and 'dainty'. Rita Reasden in
her trade card is 'The dainty gifted male impersonator'. 'The Ideal
male impersonator' calls herself Marie Winsome. 'Maud Vera is a
dainty comedienne who makes a truly swaggering major'; Louie
Tracy, year after year, advertises herself as 'The Dapper Dandy Boy',
Ella Shields is 'the dandy militaire'. The emphasis is on order, rather
than disorder; restraint, rather than excess: little, pretty people,
wearing attractive *clothes*. The costumes themselves perform, and are
reviewed, and their wearers are often praised for their knowledge of
how to wear them, to show them off – as were beautifully gowned
women with other acts. There was a type of act that consisted of quick
changes between various signifying sets of clothes, which included
cross-gender dresses. In March 1910, Marie Jones was touring the
halls with *Wanted, the Co-respondent*, a playlet in which she represented
men – an office boy of 15, a pensioner of 70, a young and blushing
curate – and females from a 'sturdy and defiant suffragette to the
coaxing woman of the world'.[11] Each change was made in less than 5
seconds. In the same month May Beatie and Edward Lauri had a
sketch called *In Her Boudoir* which was 'a protean melange' of
cross-dressing.[12]

There was an awareness that dress was a signifying procedure
connected with the ordering of the social world. On a bill at the
Ealing Hippodrome that same March 1910 Ella Shields sang three
songs in which she appeared alternately in male and female characters,
and Monte Walker sang a song about women dressing in petticoats or
pants.[13] The idea was not new. Ten years earlier, in 1900, the musical
comedy *Girls will be Girls* premiered at the Royalty, Llanelly, and took
as its initial situation the notion that the girls in question asserted
their girlishness by dressing up as boys, in khaki uniforms; its best song
was called 'The Two Genders'. As Mary Wollstonecraft had pointed
out a century before, consciousness of clothes is associated on the one
hand with women and on the other with soldiers. The explosion of
uniform on to the music-hall stage in these years leading up to 1914
can, of course, be read as an aspect of the militarization of the nation.
There is a wonderful example of the male impersonator whose
political message is enthusiastically chauvinist and militaristic in
Sable Fern, appearing in March 1910. In khaki breeches, puttees
and tunic she impersonated a Scoutmaster, surrounded by what she

claimed were a genuine troop of Boy Scouts, exhibiting their patriotism in a 'thrilling camp scene' and singing songs about teaching the rising generation to be prepared. The display culminated in a song called 'Only a Boy', in which great men from Lord Nelson to Lord Kitchener were extolled as their (no doubt uniformed) images were projected on a screen.[14] Here the message is absolutely unequivocal in its appeal to sentimental militarism. But it was not the only sort of use that was made of these sign systems.

Equally, military uniform and its offshoots into show business were made to signify in much broader ways that have to do with defining by dress what a man or a woman is or may be. The girls in khaki, the dandy militaire, and the swaggering major are part of a constellation of playful, and serious, use of uniforms in this way. Women in men's jobs could assert their fitness by donning the proper uniform, like the 'Lady Orchestras' who played at the Women's Exhibition at Earl's Court in 1900; the reviewers could not be prevented from writing archly about the possibility of a 'susceptible player neglecting the bow to smile at a beau',[15] but they were constrained to acknowledge that the women in the uniforms of Swedish Hussars or American sailors played their unladylike instruments with the proper discipline and style. Smartness on the stage was most simply claimed by donning a uniform, whether to sing or dance hornpipes. Reviewers found realistically correct uniforms and parodically or provocatively modified ones equally appealing: 'in "Our Brigade" the Sisters Guest successfully appear as a couple of very smart military men, obviously possessing many "killing" ways; and if their uniform would not exactly meet the approbation of the War Office it must be extremely cool, and certainly looks most becoming.'[16] John Hayman and Co., whose telegraphic address was 'Realistic, London', were compendiously and indiscriminately 'Naval, military, livery, and Theatrical Costumiers'.

Again, the mythical significances were quite consciously present in the minds of contemporary audiences: there is an interesting sketch, *A Man of Spirit* by Frank Price, reviewed by the *Era* at the Stratford Empire on 14 August 1909, that makes the links between uniform, gender, power and domination in patriarchal sexual relationships. 'A middle-aged, steady-going householder has a young and very attractive wife, who is completely gone on the military, and untiringly extols their manly qualities' and also secretly joins the 'Mounted Nurses' Brigade' and puts on the uniform. But he remembers he has a uniform 'and the smart nurse is confronted with a spick-and-span colonel of horse. With change of clothes the meek individual becomes a veritable man of spirit, asserts his authority in no measured terms, and finally orders his wife, now thoroughly subdued, to take off her uniform. The two parts are played with power and finesse' by Daley Cooper and Mabel Lait.

The sexual fascination with dominant women, as well as their vilification and repression, is at the heart of music hall misogyny and it is obviously powerfully involved here. The boyish male impersonator, and the flaunting of girls – and boys – in pretty uniforms is the acceptably titillating face of this obsession in the Edwardian period. When the women represented are older, larger, more womanly in shape and more powerful, a stronger unease and a greater need to punish and repress was beginning to be felt. The 'impressive physique' of the Victorian principal boy was going out of fashion, though it did still occur – Harriet Vernon was praised in *The Era* of 15 September 1900, for having 'enriched her wardrobe with a superb field marshal's uniform, which admirably sets off her fine proportions'. But increasingly the fine figures of women, like Elaine Ravensburg, the principal boy in the Drury Lane pantomimes in Leno's time, were succeeded by slender androgynes like Vesta Tilley who rejected the padded tights and shapes with which their predecessors had enhanced their charms; in some cases they were even replaced, as Ravensburg was, by men. Reviewers began to suggest, unhistorically, that women were invading and taking over acts that had been the preserve of men. They distanced themselves from the popular response to acrobats like the 'sturdy elder lady' amongst the Zaros, who 'has a "frame" of mighty power' 'evidently exciting intense admiration' at the Bedford in 1900.[17] The jocular *Encore* editorial of 23 February 1905, asked 'If lady juggling turns are not growing much in evidence? If the conjuring business will next be exploited by the all-pervading female? If the dainty little hands of the fair ones are not all against them in this line of business?' Women doing disorderly, physical, or burlesque acts on the halls tried to defuse such comments by incongruously claiming dainty femininity for themselves, advertising as 'Alethea the most graceful lady artist, contortionist and gymnast' or 'the beautiful Miss Vulcana, and Miss Gwennie Atlas, the society athletes'. Few had the chutzpah to assert, like Nellie Coleman, that they were proud of being 'the only lady wearing baggy trousers, bald wigs, whiskers and flap shoes'.[18]

There was perhaps some truth in the assertion that women no longer had the decency to keep out of the most masculine performances, and a growing fear that their derided aggression – the curl-papered wife with the rolling pin – was beginning to take new forms that presented it as acceptable behaviour and linked it with success rather than failure. For example, there was the interesting phenomenon of the wrestling craze of 1902, in which more than one troupe of female wrestlers took part, appearing in well-orchestrated and publicized rivalry at several London halls. They represented themselves as national champions of Belgium, Spain, Italy, Switzerland, India, England and Scotland, and the French Mlle. Appolina, who claimed to be champion of the world. They staged several matches at each appearance, and issued challenges to 'any lady under ten stone' and even to male lightweights. On 31 May *The Entr'acte* reported a Miss Bradford upholding 'the honour of Old England' by defeating Miss Fournier of France, who was then allowed a victory over Miss Macgregor. The spectacle of women fighting was becoming a part of the vocabulary of the halls. There was a fashion in pantomime at Christmas 1905–6 for women to take the dame parts of the quarrelsome ugly sisters in *Cinderella*, making them whimsical portraits of 'different types of old maids' with knockabout physical humour: Nellie Coleman's clowning was not unique. A more solemn and sentimental approval of violent activity by a woman – dressed as a boy – appeared in a sketch staged by John Jackson's troupe at the Foresters, Mile End, in May 1901, in which Gladys White played a boy lodging with a drunken couple and in love with their blind daughter. First he belaboured the old couple with a poker and a shovel when they robbed him and came home drunk on his money. Then he rescued the old woman from a fire, she all the while shrieking for a drink, and fell dead himself, leaving the father to repent his wickedness and take his helpless daughter to his arms.

The necessary question is, what are the politics of these particular carnival dramas and displays? The girl playing a boy is sacrificed to the restoration of patriarchal relations; Cinderella's sisters do not become sisters of any other kind when women represent them. The wrestlers are locked in an indissoluble set of ambiguities: they are pornographically presented, in revealing costumes that for extra excitement are also the signs of chauvinism, national costume that is a 'representation' of the soon-to-be-warring nations of Europe and their empires. But it could be argued that they are also breaking out of the denial to women of bodily expression, physical strength, and assertive behaviour, and are in that respect to be regarded as oppositional and challenging. They are not the ugly and laughable representatives of 'women on top' that the dame impersonators presented.

The obvious political significance that one might try to assign to these conflicting signs is contained in David Cheshire's suggestion that it is all to do with suffrage agitation.[19] The suffragette had indeed become one more of the stereotypes of dominating women at whom the *charivari* was directed: men sang songs lamenting the lot of the suffragette's husband, or more suggestively rejoicing in the prospect of sharing a prison cell with one. Quick-change artists could represent one in 5 seconds, as 'sturdy and defiant', and a sketch could climax in the representation of one, played by a man, fighting with a gang of policemen. In December 1908, suffrage agitation began to impinge upon the theatres in a more insistent and personal way than before, with the formation of the Actresses' Franchise League. The AFL rapidly went through the convulsion of choice between constitutional and direct-action methods, and declared itself on the side of direct action; the summer of 1909 saw the escalation of confrontation between the government and the Women's Social and Political Union into daring stunts and imprisonments, and the first hunger strikes. The *Era* leader-writers began to take an interest. They performed comic miracles of fence-sitting and equivocation, and display with wonderful clarity the double-thinking and condescension to which they were natural heirs. An editorial of 16 January 1909 responded to the formation of the League by an argument that runs roughly thus: actresses possess equality with men in their profession already, meeting men on equal terms in the combat of life and leaving it after a drawn battle. Women are as big a draw to the box-office as men; in rehearsals they are sworn at impartially with their male comrades, they have similarly insalubrious dressing-rooms and uncomfortable lodgings. So the leaders of the profession who assembled for this meeting are generously asking for the vote to support their less fortunate sisters. But of course women are not less fortunate. Discrimination in employment, which forbids them to be engaged in dangerous trades, and in marriage, which offers them a life of idleness and maintenance after divorce, is all on their side. They are not really weaker than men – one cannot overlook the 'hockey players, swimmers, acrobats, Dahomey Amazons, charwomen, wrestlers and political lecturers' who all disprove it. So why should they want the inconvenience of a vote, requiring them to listen to canvassers, turn out on a wet night to attend in an elementary school-room to register a choice, and give up provincial engagements to be at home to do so? By 21 August more experience had not brought enlightenment. The leader-writer, beginning this time with a pseudo-objective history of the changes in women's lot due to the removal of the burden of multiple childbearing, leaving women unoccupied and bored, rehearses the same claim that actresses have already 'attained the condition of independence which is desired for all women'. He then frames them as 'exceptional', not sharing the 'ordinary interests' of the rest of the nation, and asks what use the actress as a class could therefore possibly find for the vote. She might vote for a minimum wage – that is 'hardly within the scope of practical politics'; she would be likely to vote for peace at any price – that is clearly against the national interest; and, most dangerous of all, 'the most powerful influence on her exercise of the franchise would probably be an *esprit de corps* with all independent working women'.

A significant element surfaces amidst this defensive posturing that is directly relevant to the question of gender representation: the denunciation, in both articles, of the rhetoric of gallantry and chivalry. In pointing out, apparently with real conviction and approbation, that actresses are not patronized in the way most women are, both articles employ the same terms. 'The conventional attitude of the male, with its insulting "gallantry", its petting, superficial politeness, is exchanged [in the theatre] for a blunt *camaraderie* and merciless frankness which to an enlightened and independent woman must be much more congenial than all the bowings and scrapings of the court of LOUIS QUATORZE' (January). Then in August, 'All the sham chivalries, the contemptuous formalities which distinguish the intercourse between the sexes in ordinary life, and are detested by all intelligent and spirited females are abandoned when stage business has to be done.' The connection between the manners of romance and the construction of gender so as to maintain the oppression of women is very clearly made here. In the halls, there was a corresponding appropriation and subversion of chivalric tropes and romantic imagery. They were used to construct, quite specifically, a proper behaviour for expressing masculinity: taking the rhetoric and hypocrisies of gallantry that were discredited by their appropriation to the oppression of women in modern society, they constructed a male gender, as women might like to see it enacted.

Women began to play the part of the romantic and chivalrous hero in a series of miniature costume dramas. Plate 8 shows Vesta Tilley in the court dress of Louis Quatorze – or what the music hall and musical comedy stage might think would pass for it: tight white breeches, satin coat, the so-becoming ruffles and the big feathered hat, straight out of a Gainsborough Studio melodrama. This was a sideline Tilley did not repeat, but there were specialist women performers who framed their acts in this style, and narratives that depended on its attractions and paradoxes. For example, in April 1910, at a point where the exhibition of films was a staple part of most music hall bills – the Bioscope was featured that month at the Shepherd's Bush Empire, Balham Hippodrome, the Foresters and Walthamstow Palace, for example – Messrs Markt and Co. released *Taming a Husband*. This costume romp is summarized in the Film Gossip column of the *Era* of 2 April. The heroine Lady Margaret, thinking her husband is neglecting her,

confides her fears to her best friend Lady Clarissa, inviting her to visit and advise her. [Lady Clarissa] dresses herself in male attire and assumes the role of a lover. Clarissa as a young gallant makes quite an impression upon the male companions of the husband, and finds her position at times rather embarrassing, especially when invited to join them in drinking and smoking. She blatantly flirts with Lady Margaret, and several times they are surprised together by the husband. He finally catches the young unknown upon his knees before his wife. This is too much, and a challenge is the outcome . . . the seconds for Clarissa try to dissuade their 'man' from meeting his adversary . . . the other man . . . being such a big fellow. This has no effect, and the seconds leave despairing for their friend, as it seems suicidal. They return again with another plea, and find their 'man' in the arms of the wife. This enrages them, and having witnessed his perfidy, they refuse to act, reasoning that the field of honour is too good; he should be slain on the spot.

They tell the husband, who goes

into a frenzy of fury. Into the house they go sword in hand, bent on instantly despatching the vile wretch. Lady Clarissa sees them coming and locks the door, which she realises will prove but a slight obstruction to the raging husband, so she, frightened, dons her conventional habiliments, and when the door yields to their battering, in rushes the husband to learn the truth of the situation and appreciate the guilt of his own negligence.

8 Miss Vesta Tilley. Postcard, author's collection.

Lady Clarissa, in attempting to shake up the assumptions and attitudes about gender roles of her friend's husband, does nothing more masculine than wooing Lady Margaret and smoking and drinking with the lads; she is not allowed to prove herself his equal in actual combat. Live performers were less reticent; there was a vogue in the Edwardian period for swordswomen, and they commonly framed their acts in a dramatic scenario that made clear the association between swordplay and codes of behaviour between the sexes. Esmé Beranger, described as 'the best lady Romeo of the younger generation', studied under Egerton Castle of the Foil Club for her role in *At the Point of the Sword*, given its first public performance at the Palace in September 1901. She played Geoffrey, a 'young Elizabethan gallant' whose sister has been seduced by the dissolute master of fence Savario. 'The artful Geoffrey pretends that he is going to fight a duel, and requests Savario to put him up to all the tricks of swordplay. The unsuspecting seducer confidingly lets Geoffrey into every secret of his "art of fence", and then the avenging brother declares himself, and, with the assistance of the information supplied by the culprit, has no difficulty in "polishing him off", afterwards laying roses on the dead body, and bursting into a passion of tears. Miss Beranger looked very attractive in her boy's dress, fenced beautifully, and acted admirably . . .'[20] By any strict code of chivalry, of course, her deception would be reprehensible; by the logic of realist performance, her roses and tears are hardly appropriate to a young man on killing his hated opponent, the disgracer of his family; but as a dramatization of conflict and anxiety over gender roles, sexuality and social values, this preposterous scenario seems to me to fulfil exactly Butler's description of drag as 'dramatising the signifying gestures by which gender identity is established'.

The idea that sexuality, in the sense of sexual object choice, is part of this scenario of doubt and ambiguity is difficult for the modern observer to escape, especially in the film *Taming a Husband*. It would be very easy to make out a coded second text within the story, in which Margaret and Clarissa are indeed lovers, and the switch to women's clothes that disarms criticism is a Ulyssean trick, the hero(ine) escaping to fight another day by turning the opponent's power against himself and laughing up her immaculate sleeve. Lillian Faderman has pointed out the emergence of the romantic code of chivalric behaviour in the masculine impersonations of the butch in 1950s and 1960s lesbian subcultures.[21] Lesbian women might plausibly be expected to appropriate images of masculinity in this way at a much earlier date. But it is really impossible, until some so far inconceivable revelation comes to light, to determine how far a lesbian subculture, and the covert lesbian identity that it made available to some New York women in the 1900s, might have existed in Edwardian England. My argument about the varied political uses of carnival tropes by these performers does not depend on any such assumption or revelation. The music hall games with gender roles and their imagery, the fascination with clothes, the sharpening oppositions between the representation of disorderly women on the one hand, and disarming androgynes on the other, are nevertheless significant. They contributed a space for testing and contesting gender imagery to the cultural upheaval that surrounded the women's suffrage agitation, and the hostilities and anxieties that upheaval generated.

NOTES

1 Written by John P. Harrington, composed by George Le Brunn; quoted from *Music Hall Memories* (London, n.d.), vol. 1, pp. 207–9.
2 Marjorie Garber, *Vested Interests: Cross-dressing and Cultural Anxiety* (New York and London), 1992.
3 Judith Butler, *Gender Trouble: Feminism and the Subversion of Identity* (New York and London), 1990, p. vii.
4 Sarah Maitland, *Vesta Tilley* (London, 1986), p. 90.
5 Lillian Faderman, *Odd Girls and Twilight Lovers* (New York, 1992).
6 'Irrational Dress', in *The New Woman and Her Sisters*, ed. Viv Gardner and Susan Rutherford (Hemel Hempstead, 1992), pp. 77–91.
7 For a summary of these views and arguments, see Peter Stallybrass and Allon White, *The Politics and Poetics of Transgression* (London, 1986), pp. 1–26.
8 This and all the acts mentioned in the following paragraph are drawn from the review pages of *The Era* over the period discussed.
9 *Era*, 19 March 1910, reviewing the bill at the Oxford on 12 March.
10 Acts and bill matter quoted here are all from *The Era* trade card advertisements between 1900 and 1914.
11 *Era*, 19 March 1910.
12 *Era*, 26 March 1910.
13 *Era*, 2 April 1910.
14 Ibid., reviewing the Rotherhithe Hippodrome premiere of the sketch on 28 March.
15 *Era*, 22 September 1900.
16 *Era*, 25 August 1900.
17 *Era*, 6 January 1900.

18 Bill matter from *Era* cards during 1906.
19 David Cheshire, 'Male Impersonators', *The Saturday Book*, 29 (1969), pp. 245–52.
20 *Era*, 4 September 1901.
21 *Odd Girls and Twilight Lovers*, p. 170.

CHAPTER 5

Edwardian management and the structures of industrial capitalism

Tracy C. Davis

Too often, theatre historians elect flamboyant actresses to be the *sine qua non* of feminist resistance and achievement, considering no other possibilities. On economic and managerial grounds, however, many more names emerge for nomination from the Edwardian period, particularly when social and industrial forces interacting with commerce and gender are emphasized. Theatrical manageresses afford the *only* example of women who were in large numbers up-front business executives in pre-First World War British history, so their career paths and position in the financial community are extremely significant. This chapter sets out two parallel enquiries: one concerns the prominence of women in theatrical management, and the other concerns several aspects of the 'financial environment' (formal and informal capitalist structures) that governed the organization of theatre up to the outbreak of war in 1914 and which had implications for women's access to managerial positions. The terms of the enquiry are influenced by feminist economic historians who show how male privilege is inscribed in the foundations of economic theory, the data sets more or less accepted in standard texts, and the preoccupations of their non-feminist peers.[1] Among these non-feminist peers, much of the British scholarship is in the realm of labour and social history, fields saturated in materialist consciousness, contrasting with the orientation in America towards business history, which, even when examining gender, is more likely to celebrate capital accumulation than to question class. Despite the irreconcilability of these traditions with each other and (increasingly) with feminism, elements of each can be isolated and, through techniques akin to gene splicing, a hybrid can flourish.

A few women achieved notoriety and distinction as managers of entertainments in England and Scotland during the nineteenth century, and at least a hundred more worked in this capacity without being celebrated for it. Proportionately, however, women were not as equally represented in production – that is, the management, ownership, or administration of theatrical ventures – as in performance. Lack of theatrical business experience was not the determining factor, for countless women are known to have gained such experience in family ventures, as their ability to take over in crises and during probate cases demonstrates. Getting money was the obstacle (in most cases, insurmountable) that kept women from starting and controlling business ventures. Anyone with financial savvy and star billing could save money; the difficulty was in raising the additional amounts demanded in this increasingly capital-intensive industry. Allegedly, when the management of Covent Garden threatened to reduce the acting payroll in 1830, Eliza Vestris

at once threw up her engagement, and on the very same day drove down in her carriage to a little old-fashioned shop in the Strand, next door to the Adelphi Theatre, and sought an interview with the honest tradesman who occupied it, whose name was Scott. In addition to the business in the Strand, Scott happened to be proprietor of the Olympic Theatre, which then stood empty. Madame soon let him know the object of her visit, and without more ado they came to terms. She went across the street to Coutts', her bankers, returned to Scott with money to pay as much of the rent in advance as he required, and there and then became lessee of the Olympic.[2]

For less recognizable performers, in banking markets less disposed to extending credit, and for virtually all women, the barriers to acquiring sufficient start-up capital could be prohibitive. Anyone without a personal fortune entering into business required guarantors for the notes of credit by which commerce was conducted, and few women had the social resources of Eliza Vestris. In Carroll Smith-Rosenberg's and Toby Dietz's terms, the power of money floats over those who are its source: discourse 'masculinizes' wealth and speculation while 'feminizing' fiscal irresponsibility. In mercantile writing, femininity was synonymous with dangerous passion and 'ruin' which, for businessmen, resulted in 'unmanning' and financial collapse. This discourse's conflation of sexual realms with commercial behaviour must have been particularly defeating for actresses.[3]

Scholarship in business history suggests that banks applied entirely different criteria to male and female loan applicants who sought to go into business for themselves. Until the Married Women's Property Acts of 1870 and 1874 (England) or 1877 (Scotland), such practices were legal: ancient laws of coverture meant that married women could not enter into contracts, such as loans, on their own behalf. Unmarried women and widows were treated the same way without sanction of law, as if bankers conflated a legal category of adult women (wives) with another category of their own invention (potential wives) and regarded them alike. Successive Married Women's Property legislation culminating in the Act of 1882 (England) should have removed any lingering sex-based prejudicial practices, yet men continued to dominate in theatrical business.

Another aspect of the financial environment also combines the authority of formal institutions with the habits of informal prejudice. It is a factor that antedates the Victorian period and is still with us: namely, the insidious practices of 'gentlemanly capitalism' which circulated wealth among members of Pall Mall clubs, political parties, and fraternal organizations. It is an important but little-documented instrument of conservatism that helped maintain the theatrical managerial cohort's masculine face (and still does, at the Garrick Club). As Alice Kessler-Harris points out:

'Race/class/gender and ethnicity' may appear to be a figure of speech (an overused trope), but our understanding of their interwoven relationship continues to grow with time. Historians who operate in this mode are encouraged to ask how, for example, ideas about masculinity among managers might influence their sense of community and loyalty, their views of family, their economic behavior and social expectations, helping to structure a sexually segmented labor force, and to influence the shape of the female labor market.[4]

The practices of 'gentlemanly capitalism' allowed men to raise money or rally guarantors from acquaintances in a wide occupational and social spectrum. Male actors and managers were invited to join a great variety of clubs in the late nineteenth century; the clubs' socializing hours conveniently complemented actors' working hours, and among fellow members prejudicial judgements along occupational lines were relaxed. Freemasons were particularly accommodating to actors' schedules. Such organizations put lenders and borrowers in touch while perpetuating gentlemanly capitalism and its pattern of gender exclusiveness.

The playing field was truly uneven. The Albemarle, Nineteenth Century, and Russell Clubs, which admitted women prior to 1880, did not admit actresses. The Pioneer and New Century Clubs, which welcomed actresses after the turn of the century, did not admit

millionaires. To take one example, between 1890 and 1914, 8 per cent
of the Reform Club's members were in banking or had bank
directorships.[5] So, while Henry Irving and Bram Stoker, Reform
Club members, could mix with prominent Liberal bankers, including
several Rothschilds and Goldschmids, few prospective manageresses
had comparably legitimate access to this populuation and the
guarantors such bankers would respect. It is such company that
Stoker alludes to in the following passage from his *Reminiscences of
Henry Irving*:

Bankers are of necessity stern folk and unless one can give *quid pro quo* in some
shape they are pretty obdurate as to advances [loans]. Therefore it was that
now and again, despite the enormous sums that he [Irving] earned, he had
occasionally to get an advance. Fortunately, there were friends who were
proud and happy to aid him ... Henry Irving had constant and loving
friends who held any power in their hands at his disposal, and were alike glad
and proud to help him in the splendid work he was doing.[6]

For women, domestic socializing in the form of dinner parties or
daytime 'at homes' was a poor alternative. If working actresses were
not excluded by occupational stigmas, their socializing could be
circumscribed by virtue of being hired as entertainers rather than
attending as guests *per se*, and in any case attendance was not
facilitated by the hours of rehearsal and performance; mixing at such
events was not without sex segregation. Any actress meriting invitation
to such an event was not the type to retire with the gentlemen for
brandy, cigars, and financial chatter.

   Despite this, by the mid-Victorian years it was not entirely
uncommon for women to partake in theatrical business: during the
1850s and 1860s at least three dozen women managed theatres in
Britain and approximately as many more made attempts at
management in each successive decade up to 1910. In contrast, it is
remarkable how few women were *lessees*: that is, the individual
responsible for ground rent and the theatre building itself, in whose
name the licence was written and who was ultimately responsible for
the theatre's conduct. Most women were simply managers, renting
someone else's property for a fixed price and duration without any
responsibility for the premises. This accounts for Mrs Patrick
Campbell, Cissie Grahame, Emily Soldene, Mrs Brown Potter and
countless others.

   The word 'manager', therefore, tends to be ubiquitously and

thereby incorrectly used. Correctly ascribing it is an important step in revealing prescriptions of gendered career paths and another structure governing capital circulation. Even John Hollingshead, after twelve years as lessee of the Gaiety Theatre, describes distinct functions performed by manager and lessee, yet gives them the same name:

There is no brick-and-mortar investment more profitable in London than that of building theatres, and there is no occupation more easy and agreeable than theatrical management [does he mean lesseeship or management *per se*?]. The happy landlord [by which he definitely means the owner] of a London theatre builds in odd holes and corners – in back-yards and blind alleys, in slums and dust-holes; and when his temple of the drama is nearly complete, he obtains a narrow entrance and a frontage in a public thoroughfare sufficient to carry a flaming gas 'device', and immediately lets his property at fifteen per cent rental [to managers, who may or may not hold the lease], reserving various privileges, and taking the fullest security. His choice of tenants is ample and varied. At one end of his list are a host of penniless showmen; at the other are half a dozen belted earls with what are called 'theatrical proclivities'. Undeceived by the Micawberism of one class, or the dazzling brilliancy of the other, he demands and obtains those material guarantees which make business a pleasure and earth a paradise.[7]

Hollingshead does not allow for the differences between owning and leasing (they are not synonymous) but he does make clear the benefits of proprietorship over mere management. Among men, the functions were often or usually coincident: the Gattis, George Sanger, John Toole, Charles Wyndham, Augustin Daly, George Edwardes, Augustus Harris, John Hare, Arthur Bouchier, Ben Conquest, Herbert Beerbohm Tree, Henry Irving (until 1899), William Kendal, Morris Abrahams, Isaac Cohen, J. L. Graydon, the Henglers, Frederick Harrison, Arthur Collins, Frank Curzon, George Alexander, Richard D'Oyly Carte, and Edward Terry all managed, leased, and to some extent owned the London theatres in which they became famous and/or wealthy. They were the most prominent theatrical men of their day, and their business histories constitute the narrative norm posing as a 'universal standard'. Among women of the period – somewhere between the Micawbers and the earls – one can only list Emma Cons, Sara Lane, and Kate Santley with London lesseeships of significant duration. Studying women in counterpoint to the male 'universal standards' helps to reveal some interesting features of the commercial organization of entertainment. Apparently, women were not 'differently abled' but blatantly, unequivocally disadvantaged.

There is an important distinction between 'manager' and 'lessee' analogous to a shopkeeper owning the premises from which business is carried out as against a mere stallkeeper renting a space in the open marketplace. A theatre's manager might be the sole artistic director in complete control of the wares she hawked, but she owned nothing. This distinction has not typically been a subject of concern to theatre historians, but it is a topic of considerable consequence in the history of women and should become a central point of enquiry in our discipline.

To avoid confusion and to underline the coincidence of hermeneutic categories with gender, some refinements to our theatrical vocabulary would be useful. The lexicon of 'impresario' and 'entrepreneur', which have contemporaneous theatrical as well as business connotations, are well suited. While 'manager' has the specific connotation of one who conducts a theatre or other place of amusement, its additional denotations may or may not suggest one who takes financial and operational responsibility for the working of a mercantile or industrial business. 'Manager' is not, in other words, synonymous with one who has either a personal financial stake in the operation or creative input into its design. 'Impresario' is a more precise term describing managers who rented spaces for productions of their own devising. In business terms, *impresari* organized companies, negotiated contracts, and oversaw operations. In addition, the theatrical connotation from the Italian tradition has *impresari* catalyzing public entertainments by bringing together artists and backers.[8] *Impresari* did not necessarily own anything, and were accountable to others for their success or failure, yet they enjoyed some discretionary autonomy not strictly allowed to 'managers'. Nevertheless, 'impresario' suggests a short-term venture: in the Italian operatic tradition the arrangements lasted for a single season or festival.

The term 'entrepreneur' connotes the additional responsibilities of 'lessees' and in some cases 'lessee/proprietors'. In theatre, as in industry, entrepreneurs ventured or undertook the risks of production, brought together capital and labour in what was intended as a permanent installation, and were motivated by the incentive of personal profit. They engineered the general plan, supervised minor details on a day-to-day basis, judged how to balance desired results with the level of expenditure, and were responsible for trying new techniques and ideas. The entrepreneur initiated companies, represented the chief cause of growth and decline in companies, and was rightly credited with innovations. In the neo-classical economic model (predominant in the Edwardian period), entrepreneurs determined the distribution of gross take according to individuals' marginal productivities, and for their pains retained the residual profits, factoring in interest on their capital, a wage for management, a premium for risk-bearing, and a 'rent' on their ability (the latter was often the largest chunk of the salary).[9] Whereas entrepreneurs were often the first to be paid, *impresari* were the last.

This terminology helps to delineate a limitation binding the careers of women. The custom of family succession in proprietorship that was so typical of the eighteenth-century theatre broke down in the nineteenth century, though it remained viable in certain instances (particularly in the provinces and metropolitan areas beyond the West End of London). In the late nineteenth century a few women were hereditary lessee/entrepreneurs of such enterprises: Ellen Poole, Marie Saker, Sara Lane, Mrs James Baylis, and Mrs Nye Chart. Significantly, they all inherited responsibility and property from their husbands, not fathers, suggesting that they had performed business-related functions all along in partnership but without credit. Their theatres were long-term ventures, in most cases with paid-off purchase prices. The capital needed to start up a new venture rose significantly in the high Victorian and Edwardian periods and thus the financial demands of buying out an existing theatre, constructing a new building, or starting up a company from scratch and establishing a repertoire or even a single show (the functions of an entrepreneur) presented significant obstacles, and virtually no women overcame the prejudices of bankers to raise sufficient venture capital. However, being managers (and in some cases *impresari*) was within the financial reach of many women: this meant renting rather than leasing real estate; hiring rather than making costumes, properties, and sets (a practice possible after 1873 thanks to the boom in independent theatrical outfitters); and paying copyright per performance rather than outright buying of untried scripts on speculation.

When inheritance is not an issue, lessee/entrepreneurs and manager/*impresari* present patterns clearly demarcating gendered career paths. The mobility patterns from performer to manager/impresario and thence to lessee/proprietor/entrepreneur are as bounded by gender as in British textile manufacturing, agriculture, and domestic service. The adolescent winders at Courtauld's silk and rayon weaving factory, for example, were tracked to become weavers and then warpers or twisters if they were female, or spindle-cleaners and machinery attendants if they were male. The women's paths never led to more than 10 shillings a week; the male track, in contrast, led additionally to mechanical or overseeing functions that paid up to 32 shillings a week.[10] This pattern pervades industry and is similarly reflected in the theatre.

Despite the muddle of theatrical nomenclature perpetuated in primary documents and almost invariably ignored in secondary histories, the distinctions between managers and lessees are indirectly conveyed; managers who were not also entrepreneurs were likely to come and go in a given theatre and season, while lessee-entrepreneurs stayed for as long as they were solvent and often stamped their artistic and business practices on a particular venue. Women were far more likely to be in the first category than the second. Again, the implications for the narrative norm of male prowess at producing and artistically innovating are momentous. Emma Cons is the proverbial exception challenging the rule: her energies launched the temperance Old Vic in 1880. She held the lease, sat on the Board of Directors, and steered the repertoire (though she hired men actually to manage the stage for the first fourteen years). Combining her aspirations for social reform, working-class adult education in the conjoint Morley College, the instigation of a public limited liability company (1880–4), relationships with wealthy philanthropic donor/investors, and the good will of the Charity Commissioners, Cons was able to raise £17,500 in a period of four months to buy the theatre's freehold while also securing an annual guaranteed endowment. She was a true entrepreneur, retaining the lease and remaining on the Board of Directors after Lilian Baylis took on the day-to-day responsibilities. Cons would probably count among the Edwardians' strong individual identities some see as the only possible hope for today's West End,[11] joined in later years by Lena Ashwell and Annie Horniman, but at the turn of the century she was still unique.

Many of the most famous actress-businesswomen on the late Victorian and Edwardian stage were *impresari*. They are distinguishable from the hordes of fly-by-night London manageresses in that they persistently and successfully toured on the strength of relatively brief but celebrated London self-promotions. The evidence strongly suggests that touring was a consolation for the gender obstacles involved in entrepreneurship, as it is in the category of touring *impresari* that the turn-of-the-century ventures of Millicent Bandmann-Palmer, Geneviève Ward, Ethel Irving, Lydia Thompson, and Matilda Caroline Wood should be classified.

The proverbial jewel-box stuffed with bills landed in few women's laps: perhaps none besides that of Lena Ashwell, who purchased the Kingsway lease by such means in 1907.[12] Almost invariably, women's access to management came through the artistic reputation *and* money accrued from their own acting.[13] Emma Cons – housing reformer and founder of clinics, day care centres, and libraries[14] – was exceptional among female entrepreneurs in that she ventured into the Old Vic without theatrical experience or her own private wealth. Annie Horniman, an heiress without performance experience who first backed the arts in 1894, was less content to hover silently in the early days of the Abbey (Dublin), and was a full-fledged entrepreneur at the Gaiety (Manchester) from 1908.

Concurrent with these women's careers, a new kind of business organization emerged in the 1890s: the ownership of multiple venues and brokering of whole music-hall programmes concentrated in tight proprietorial firms. Edward Moss and Oswald Stoll, like Bronson Albery in later decades, were not performers. They were businessmen. On a lesser scale, perhaps Cons and Horniman were their peers, Cons having garnered some experience in the string of temperance cafes she founded in the 1870s and Horniman getting her wings as an angel. With this new corporate system, women without independent means had even less chance of gaining a proprietary interest in their exploits; had Cons tried to set up the Old Vic venture fifteen years later she too might have had to settle for being an impresario. All along, there are records of women who held the reins of authority without simultaneously acting on the stage – making a distinct career path as executives – but just as women were becoming more visible in such capacities the scale of operations changed and they were cut out of the most financially significant ventures. The phenomenon developed swiftly. In the early 1890s, the Pavilion emerged as part of the first major London syndicate. Among the fifty-nine London music halls licensed and operational in 1907, however, forty-two or 70 per cent were owned by just four conglomerates (Syndicate Halls, Stoll, Gibbons, and Macnaghton) or the LCC, and women were nowhere to be seen.[15]

The second part of this chapter is more exclusively Edwardian, focussing on new types of theatrical organization that arose around the turn of the century and their currency with business practices in

British commerce generally. The ownership of Victorian business shifted successively from families to partnerships (often of non-relatives), then to limited liability companies, and eventually to publicly traded companies. This is well documented in business history. Dates cannot be fixed on these changes like absolute signposts, nor are the managerial distinctions between categories, particularly between partnerships and limited liability companies, necessarily meaningful. The shift does not inevitably entail what Peter Bailey laments as 'the publican and his checktaker . . . [being] superseded by the managerial bureaucracy and faceless shareholders of modern business'.[16] Most early limited liability companies, beginning with the National Opera Co. Ltd (1855), kept the controlling stock under tight control of partners (the legal owners), later using public stock issues to raise cash with non-voting debentures or bonds. Limited liability companies gave the owners the advantage of limiting their collective and individual responsibility for debt arising from the bankruptcy of the business or any partner. Most firms had a small number of shareholders (the law stipulated a minimum of seven, though often some were bogus) and typically in the theatre the managers owned and the owners managed.[17] This form of organization picked up in popularity after the middle of the century. After the Companies Acts of 1855, 1862, and 1867, public limited liability companies offered the advantage of a wider population from which to garner investors – theoretically, though not, it seems, in fact, a more sexually egalitarian development – but control of the companies still tended to rest in a tight proprietorial group, with debenture and other classes of non-voting stock sold at the London and provincial stock exchanges.[18] Several hundreds of these theatre-related firms have been traced.

Various theatrical firms led the turn-of-the-century trend to transform ownership and management from limited liability partnerships to large publicly owned companies. The shift is classically illustrated by the Lyceum's reorganization in 1899: when transformed into a public company, artistic and financial power was transferred from one manager with proprietary interests solely in that company to several managers with other similar syndicated investments as well as to public stockholders. This particular venture was not successful, though others such as the Empire Palace Ltd (1887) were highly profitable.

The next logical development in organizational form was the merging of two or more separately functioning companies, centralizing managerial responsibilities and thereby reducing costs, increasing the margin of profit, making dividends less liable to fluctuation and thereby increasing the value and demand for shares, dealing with opposition more effectively, and mobilizing large sums to acquire other businesses quickly or start new ones. In British industry generally, Leslie Hannah finds the merger movement most intense in the late 1880s and between 1897 and 1902, particularly in brewing and textiles.[19] He might have added entertainment, had he thought to look beyond the categories in the USA's Office of Management and Budget *Standard Industrial Classification Manual.* The Moss and Thornton Empires, superseded in 1899 by Moss Empires Ltd (an amalgamation of Moss, Thornton, and Stoll theatres) provides an obvious corrective to the record. Originally registered with joint capital of £1,650,000, based on ten separate companies with fourteen music halls, Moss Empires built up to £2,086,000 in 1906 with the addition of the Coliseum in London and other properties. With thirty-five houses in 1906 it was the largest theatre enterprise in the world.[20] A history of cooperation antedates the official merger: Stoll's original expansions in Cardiff, Swansea, and Newport were followed by additional entrepreneurial ventures in five more cities, then a period of cooperation with Moss and Thornton to build up nine more halls in Scotland and the northern Midlands. (This is comparable to the 'agreement of cooperation' between Moss Empires and the Variety Theatres Consolidated 'syndicate' of suburban halls after 1924. The VTC was largely rentier-owned, yet shared administrative offices with Moss Empires.[21]) Moss and Thornton cooperated in the same ways that Cadbury and Fry, two rival chocolate makers, maintained their distinct offices and respective brands while joining forces to control cocoa plantations in West Africa, conduct research and development, and distribute the finished product throughout Britain. Bailey observes that the merger of Moss, Stoll, and Thornton shows 'the Victoria music hall had been successfully assimilated to the cultural apparatus of a capitalist society and its history can be read as an analogue of the capitalist transformation of industrial manufacture'.[22] This comes across as something of an understatement when one notes that if Moss Empires had been ranked by market value of capital in 1905, it would have been approximately the forty-fourth largest industrial enterprise in Great Britain.[23] There is considerably more to note about Moss Empires, capitalist transformation than what it indicates about the industrial takeover of the populist roots of music hall.

Moss Empires, like Cadbury–Fry, was an industrial combine (or to use the more common British term, a holding company). Holding companies could be comprised of dozens of small single-function, sometimes family-run enterprises. These were usually horizontally integrated; that is, all specializing in a single process such as weaving or, in the case of entertainment, forming a circuit of separately owned but cooperating venues to facilitate the movement of whole programmes from place to place. The other type of holding company consisted of just two or three leading family firms engaged in the same industry. This is typified by the affiliation of Howard and Wyndham Theatres Ltd with the Robert Arthur Theatres group, engaging in producing, joint management, and booking from 1909 to 1911.[24] This type of holding company was more likely to integrate vertically. In the case of the metals industries, concerns would combine ownership of coal and ore mines with plants for iron founding, forging, rolling, and sometimes fabricating; in entertainment, vertical integration can imply cooperating to cast, rehearse, manage, book, and tour shows. The diversified holdings of David Allen Theatres Co., a family firm of theatrical printers which went into theatre management in the 1890s and held the freeholds of five theatres by 1915, offer a more complex example. The Allens vertically (or forwardly) integrated their printing and advertising business with the ownership of theatrical real estate.

Alfred Chandler's studies of the roots of managerial capitalism provide useful criteria for modelling such developments at the turn of the century.[25] In early and mid-nineteenth-century Victorian theatres, the capitalist entrepreneur was usually both manager and owner (of the enterprise, though often not the land), actively involved, and on site. Later, the capitalist controlled as a financier rather than as an artist and could be a remote figure from the day-to-day operations. This is the difference between Laura Keene and Phineas Barnum or, in the British context, William Charles Macready and Walter de Freece. With this change, the evolution of the present corporate economy can be traced through theatre; indeed, entertainment may be the first sector of the British economy to evince the organizational characteristics of centralized management and integrated production and distribution, though this possibility has not previously been noted.

Enterprises on the scale of J. & P. Coats Ltd, Boots Pure Drug Co. Ltd, and Moss Empires were unprecedented much before the Edwardian years. They have important implications for systems of control, particularly managerial structures, and the whole financial environment. Chandler, the leading historian and theorist of this phenomenon, writes:

Until the late nineteenth century, owners nearly always managed their enterprises. Those few that hired managers rarely employed as many as four or five, and they retained a close personal relationship with their managers, often making them partners in the firm. Such an enterprise may be termed a *personal* one. As firms grew large and began to carry out more than one function, the number of salaried managers increased, reaching 20 or 30 or even 50. Such employees or, to use the British term, servants of the company rarely held large holdings of its stock. These shares remained in the hands of the entrepreneurs who built the company, or in those of their families. These share-holders continued to have a major say in the selection of managers, in the making of over-all policy, and in long-term planning and allocation of resources. Such manager-manned but owner-controlled enterprises can be termed *entrepreneurial* ones. As firms grew larger and as their activities were extended and diversified, stock ownership tended to become widely scattered. Full-time, salaried career managers who owned little or no stock took over positions in top as well as middle and lower management. They made long-term as well as short-term decisions. Owners became rentiers, more concerned with the dividends than the operation of their company. The owners had neither the time, information, experience nor commitment required to manage. Such manager-dominated enterprises can properly be termed *managerial*.[26]

Chandler found that though the third business metamorphosis was common in America by the end of the First World War, British businesses most often were still 'personal', occasionally what he terms 'entrepreneurial', but virtually never 'managerial'. Of the fifty largest British firms in 1919, he writes:

British Dye-stuffs was just getting under way; while United Alkali, Borax Consolidated and also Associated Portland Cement remained federations of small firms. After completing the mergers that created them, these enterprises did not adopt the strategy of the successful American mergers. They did not rationalise the production facilities of the constituent enterprises, nor centralise their administration, nor build extensive buying and purchasing organizations.[27]

Entertainment was no exception in the Edwardian business world. For Chandler, the crucial criteria for identifying the modern corporation are simultaneous investments in manufacturing, marketing, and management. Management decisions must be publicly driven and enacted by ranks of professional hired managers.

Entertainment went some way toward this, but stopped short of the last criterion. The theatrical corollary to manufacturing is the centralized brokering of talent, such as a London agency putting together whole packages of music hall or theatre programmes for distribution on tour to distant provincial or foreign locations. This was the *modus operandum* of Klaw and Erlanger (also allied with Frohman, Nixon, Hayman, and Zimmerman) operating as the Theatrical Syndicate in America. The corollary to the investment in marketing might be the cachet enjoyed by sponsorship in a chain of similarly ranked venues, such as the Howard and Wyndham chain, the de Freece and Mouillot chain, or the Empire Palaces, with the consumer recognition this implied. This type of trading on a name was precisely what the Shuberts laboured for, in contrast to their rival the Syndicate's avoidance of brand-name trading in the early days of that organization. In Britain, the theatre enjoyed extremely well-developed transportation networks which facilitated fast distribution; this market condition was essential to fast high-volume circulation, an efficiency synonymous with the modern corporation.[28] So far, the Edwardian music hall appears to fit the model modern corporation, more so than theatres which (though packaged out of London) toured on the name of the play or star rather than the collective identity of the manufacturer (whose functions combined agent and entrepreneur). Chandler's third criterion, management, is the least understood, partly because of the perennial muddling of terminology and partly because very little scholarship has been devoted to this area, in preference to understanding the nature and politics of performance itself.

There was a population of hired theatre managers, indicating the existence of a professional managerial class. Albert Gilmer progressed from being assistant manager under John Hollingshead at the Alhambra to manager at the Princess's, general manager at the Oxford Music Hall, then general manager of Stoke Newington Palace.[29] Thomas Courtice was another manager for hire: originally an architect, then in stock with Sarah Thorne and Olga Nethersole, he became resident manager at the Theatre Royal Margate 1896–8, toured as business manager with Ben Greet in 1899, was acting manager for Madge Macintosh at the Comedy the same year, was resident manager at Her Majesty's, Carlisle 1900–2, toured as business manager with F. Mouillot in 1903, was press representative for Sir Henry Irving in 1904, and served Charles Frohman as business manager 1904–5.[30] George Edwards-Minor (aka George Edwards, no final 'e') was secretary to D'Oyly Carte at the Opera Comique and Savoy, acting manager at the Alhambra and Royal English Opera House 1891, Shaftesbury and Prince of Wales's 1892, Lyric 1894; and from 1894 until last report in 1906 was acting manager at Daly's.[31] As a final example, Frank Curzon had a comparable history with Charles Hawtrey, lessee of the Avenue; he was made manager of the Coronet before taking its lease and launching into a successful entrepreneurial career in the West End.[32]

Though these individuals demonstrate the existence of a professional managerial class widely employed in entertainment, Curzon's succession from employed manager to lessee or producing manager (or George Edwardes's or Edward Moss's, for that matter) is not appropriate to Chandler's view of the new form of managerial capitalism. There were not twenty or more managers in a given organization, taking decisions on behalf of rentier stockholders. Instead, for the most part, control of the theatrical holding companies was maintained by managers who owned and owners who managed. Significantly, control was frequently family-based, either titular or with a familial succession of chairs of the board. This is equally true of the Littlers, the Simons, and Heilbron families (which were long involved in the Howard and Wyndham theatres),[33] and the heirs of Mary Moore and Charles Wyndham. While entertainment was perhaps the first British industry to illustrate what Chandler calls an entrepreneurial structure (manager-manned but owner-operated, with wide public stock holdings), it remained in line with other kinds of firms in not shifting to the managerial forms of monstrous corporations such as those in America and Germany.

Supposedly, this financial environment leads to setting shorter-term priorities, since decisions are not driven by non-owning managers whose interests lay in guaranteeing themselves a profitable lifetime job. Supposedly, owner-managers are more interested in immediate profit than long-term corporate stability. Supposedly, when the manager's name is also the company's name, capitalism is driven by a 'visible hand', to use Chandler's famous phrase, one which is likely to be aware of being 'confronted by a condition, not a theory';[34] the 'visible hand' acts on the basis of business experience rather than the kind of knowledge contemporaneously expounded by the graduates of business programmes in America's universities.

These typical themes of business history are complemented by the themes expressed in the first part of this chapter. The number of women attempting impresarial managements remained steady in the late Victorian and Edwardian decades. In the latter period, a few might arguably be classed as lessee-entrepreneurs: Lena Ashwell at the Kingsway, Annie Horniman at the Gaiety in Manchester, and Mary Moore at the New Theatre, though she would more correctly be called an entrepreneur-proprietor. Yet as far as is known, women cannot be named in any of the Edwardian examples of the more complex modern corporations or in the professional managerial class emergent in the 1890s. By the turn of the century, women had considerable experience in many types of theatrical speculation, though not extensive involvement in lessee-entrepreneurship or apprenticeship in non-familial companies. Their absence from limited liability companies' Boards of Directors and the corporatist metamorphosis in business structuring (with the possible exception of Cissie Grahame, wife of William Allen) suggests that the financial, social, political, and prejudicial forces that kept women from raising the capital necessary either to be entrepreneurs or middle managers was indeed a severe business handicap. Just when we might expect women to consolidate collectively and make other, perhaps new, kinds of leaps into the financial environment their activity becomes repetitive. They reappear in the same old kinds of organizational ventures, among which we may include the agitation around women's suffrage.[35] What accounts for it?

Since, as was noted at the outset, the theatre affords the only example of women who were up-front corporate business executives in pre-twentieth-century British history, the forces that limited their career paths need to be studied inseparably from the financial environment as a whole. Extensive study is required of the ownership of publicly and privately held companies, without respect to their repertoire, geographical location, or longevity in the industry; and of managerial structures in British theatre, along with the formal and informal forces that maintained them.

It is not just what we enquire into, but also how we ask that matters. Theatre managers like George Alexander, William Edward Allen, Squire Bancroft, Lilian Baylis, Charles Cochran, Henry Irving, George Sanger, Oswald Stoll, Herbert Beerbohm Tree, and Charles Wyndham all appear in the *Dictionary of British Business*, but it is important to understand their achievements in line with the Cassels and Rothschilds (merchant bankers and international financiers) or Cadburys and Rowntrees in whose company they are memorialized. This commerce (in all the word's senses) can also be understood in terms of the privilege of education, sex, and class status which underscores the relationships between the performer, manager, impresario, and entrepreneur when they seek partners to found, merge, expand, and corporatize companies. With the growing opportunities to raise capital and the complexities of the money market before and after joint stock limited liability was feasible, it is even more important to understand the Victorian and Edwardian theatre as a consequence of entrepreneurs and backers and the community they forged in business, leisure, and politics.[36] And particularly, with the corporatization of business prior to the First World War, it is crucial that we consider entertainment's response to new forms of organization before we pretend to understand the commercial ascendancy of film as a rival genre, the dominance of Hollywood rather than Elstree, and the cinema as a more cost-effective form of production and distribution.[37] The answers may not lie in repertoire or audiences' thirst for novelty after all.

NOTES

1 The work of Nancy Hartsock, Heidi Hartmann, and Nancy Folbre is particularly appropriate. See also Tracy C. Davis, 'Reading for Economic History', *Theatre Journal* (December 1993), pp. 487–504.

2 [Matthew Mackintosh] An Old Stager, *Stage Reminiscences: Being Recollections, Chiefly Personal, of Celebrated Theatrical & Musical Performers during the Last Forty Years* (Glasgow, 1866), pp. 68–9.

3 Carroll Smith-Rosenberg, 'Dis-Covering the Subject of the "Great Constitutional Discussion', 1786–1789', *Journal of American History*, 79.3 (December 1992), pp. 841–73; and Toby Dietz, 'Shipwrecked: Imperiled Masculinity and the Culture of Risk Among Philadelphia's Eighteenth-Century Merchants', Berkshire Conference of Women Historians, 1993.

4 Alice Kessler-Harris, 'Ideologies and Innovation: Gender Dimensions of Business History', *Business and Economic History*, 2nd series, 20 (1991), p. 48.

5 Y. Cassis, 'Bankers in English Society in the Late Nineteenth Century', *Economic History Review*, 2nd series, 38.2 (1985), p. 216.

6 Bram Stoker, *Personal Reminiscences of Henry Irving* (New York and London, 1906), vol. II, p. 315.

7 John Hollingshead, *Plain English* (1880); reprinted in *Victorian Theatre: The Theatre in Its Time*, ed. Russell Jackson (New York, 1989), pp. 271–2.

8 This is too restrictive a description for the Italian opera *impresari* of the late eighteenth and nineteenth centuries. Some of them were personally interested in making a market for their costume stocks and some participated in unlimited or limited liability companies. See John Rosselli, *The Opera Industry in Italy from Cimarosa to Verdi: The Role of the Impresario* (Cambridge, 1984). I wish to state a narrower and more precise definition.

9 Economists, sociologists, and business theorists scarcely agree on the concept of entrepreneurship. This description is based on Alfred Marshall's concept published in his *Principles* in 1890, which held sway at least until 1930. See Humberto Barreto, *The Entrepreneur in Microeconomic Theory: Disappearance and Explanation* (London and New York, 1989), pp. 53–5, and Peter L. Payne, *British Entrepreneurship in the Nineteenth Century*, 2nd edn (London, 1988).

10 Judy Lown, *Women and Industrialization: Gender at Work in Nineteenth-Century England* (Cambridge, 1990), pp. 50–9.

11 For example, Michael Billington, 'Making a Drama out of a Crisis', *Guardian Weekly*, 5 July 1992, p. 26.

12 Lena Ashwell, *Myself a Player* (London: Michael Joseph, 1936), pp. 134–5.

13 Theatrical salaries, like those in other sectors, were not impartially divided by sex. See Tracy C. Davis, *Actresses as Working Women: Their Social Identity In Victorian Culture* (London, 1991), pp. 24–35. It is astonishing to see women's earnings decline so markedly with the entrenchment of industrialization, migration to cities, rise of literacy and schooling, and women's departure from paid labour. The differential between actresses' and actors' pay may not be so large as in the general population, yet the general trend helped reinforce society's view of actresses (a prominent subset of women) as normatively poorer.

14 Sybil Oldfield, *Spinsters of this Parish: The Life and Times of F. M. Mayor and Mary Sheepshanks* (London, 1984), p. 299.

15 *The Stage Year Book*, ed. L. Carson (London, 1908), p. 113.

16 Peter Bailey, 'Custom, Capital and Culture in the Victorian Music Hall', *Popular Culture and Custom in Nineteenth-Century England*, ed. Robert D. Storch (London, 1982), p. 187.

17 A. E. Musson, *The Growth of British Industry* (New York, 1978), p. 248.

18 This results from a series of Companies Acts: 25 & 26 Vict. ch. 89 (1862); 30 & 31 Vict. ch. 131 (1867); and 63 & 64 Vict. ch. 48 (1900). A few dozen theatrical ventures were registered in the 1860s and 1870s, but the records do not show great numbers until after 1886.

19 Leslie Hannah, 'Mergers in British Manufacturing Industry, 1880–1918', *Oxford Economic Papers*, n.s., 26 (March 1974), p. 10.

20 *The Green Room Book of Who's Who on the Stage. An Annual Biographical Record of the Dramatic Musical and Variety World*, ed. Bampton Hunt (London, 1906), p. 249. Edward Moss arose from a family management and developed 'brand name' entertainment extremely early. His father was a music hall entrepreneur, and Edward first assisted with the management of a theatre of varieties in Greenock, establishing the foundations of what would become the first 'Empire Palace' in Edinburgh's Gaiety in 1877.

21 *Theatre Ownership in Britain. A Report Prepared for the Federation of Theatre Unions* (London, 1953), p. 19. The report notes: 'Moss Empires stock was always quite a favourite of the small rentier investor (apart from the London Stock Exchange it is also quoted at Birmingham, Cardiff,

Edinburgh, Glasgow, Liverpool and Newcastle – an unusually wide spread) who no doubt feels that he can always keep an eye on the state of his investment, or part of it, by paying a visit to the local Empire' (p. 14).

22 'Custom, Capital, and Culture in the Victorian Music Hall', p. 202.

23 Peter L. Payne, 'The Emergence of Large-Scale Companies in Great Britain', *Economic History Review*, 2nd series, 20 (December 1967), pp. 539–40; Christine Shaw, 'The Large Manufacturing Employers of 1907', *Business History*, 25 (1983), pp. 42–60; and J. Scott and M. Hughes, *The Anatomy of Scottish Capital: Scottish Companies and Scottish Capital* (London and Montreal, 1986), p. 19.

24 *Theatre Ownership in Britain*, p. 20.

25 *Managerial Hierarchies: Comparative Perspectives on the Rise of the Modern Industrial Enterprise*, ed. Alfred D. Chandler and Herman Daems (Cambridge, Mass. and London, 1980).

26 Alfred Chandler, 'The Development of Modern Management Structure in the US and UK', *Management Strategy and Business Development: An Historical and Comparative Study*, ed. Leslie Hannah (London and Basingstoke, 1976); rpt. in *The Essential Alfred Chandler: Essays Toward a Historical Theory of Big Business*, ed. Thomas K. McCraw (Boston, 1988), p. 361.

27 'The Development of Modern Management Structure in the US and UK', p. 369.

28 See Alfred Chandler, *The Visible Hand: the Managerial Revolution in American Business* (Cambridge, 1977); rpt. in *The Essential Alfred Chandler*, p. 401.

29 *The Green Room Book and Who's Who on the Stage*, ed. Bampton Hunt (London, 1907), p. 151.

30 *The Green Room Book* (London, 1906), p. 86.

31 Ibid., p. 114.

32 Ibid., p. 95.

33 *Theatre Ownership in Britain*, p. 20.

34 David Belasco citing Grover Cleveland in 'The Business of Theatrical Management', *Saturday Evening Post*, 7 June 1919.

35 See Julie Holledge, *Innocent Flowers: Women in the Edwardian Theatre* (London, 1981); and Sheila Stowell, *A Stage of Their Own: Feminist Playwrights of the Suffrage Era* (Manchester, 1992).

36 Some progress toward this has been made. See Peter Bailey, *Music Hall: the Business of Pleasure* (Milton Keynes, 1986).

37 Firms like the London and District Mutoscope Co. boomed *c.* 1898–1900, but their costly equipment was soon obsolete. By 1910, cinematograph firms such as University Varieties Syndicate and Standard Electric Theatres floundered in the midst of excess competition and erratic licensing practices, suggesting that the theatre was a surer investment in this depressed period. Extremely few cinema screening firms survived the First World War. See *Register of Defunct Companies* (London, 1990); *Stock Exchange Loan and Prospectus Index 1824–1901* (Guildhall Library); and annual reports of companies traded on the London Stock Exchange.

CHAPTER 6

The New Drama and the new audience

Dennis Kennedy

Of the many issues connected to the rise of modernism in the arts in Europe at the end of the nineteenth century, one of the most intriguing and least discussed is the position of audience. Instead of working within profitable styles and subjects that ratified habitual attitudes on the part of the public, modernism privileged novelty over custom and unease over solace. Reflecting the anxiety of modern life, modernists regularly transferred the artist's disquietude to the artist's patrons, eventually implying a radically new relationship with the bourgeois audience. They thus turned the Victorian concept of the audience upside down, especially the assumption that art should have a comfortable, one-for-one relationship with the tangible facts of the quotidian world.

Perhaps this is most readily apparent in the realm of painting. The affronts to convention that took place in the latter part of the century – the proto-modernist movements of Impressionism and Post-Impressionism, culminating in the full-blown modernism of Cubism just before the First World War – posed serious challenges to the traditional alliance between artist and viewer. The earlier breakdown of the aristocratic patronage system had forced painters in the nineteenth century to *find* buyers. Since these buyers were chiefly industrialists and merchants with nouveau cash, and did not have an established or in-bred method of verifying the value of art, when they sought to purchase contemporary pictures they often looked for an external stamp of approval. The stamp was provided by the official academies which, through their gallery exhibitions, also provided the place of mediation between the buyer and the seller. Economically speaking, galleries were sites of transaction; theatrically speaking, they were sites of the performance of art. The power of the academies derived from their right of exclusion: painters and paintings not admitted were denied conventional approbation and ready sale.

Thus it is not surprising that the great revolutionary movements in modernist painting date back to the Salon des Refusés in Paris in 1863. That famous occasion exhibited the pictures that had been passed over by the regular Salon jury, including Manet's *Déjeuner sur l'herbe*, firmly marking them with official repudiation. The avant-garde artist was thereafter defined as the rejected artist, forced to seek a small public against the grain.

As Peter Bürger points out in his influential book *Theory of the Avant-Garde*, the major quest of European art in the nineteenth century was for independence from 'life praxis'. Having lost the patronage of the church and of the aristocracy, bourgeois art began to claim the status of an organic entity, idealist in nature, complete in itself and subject only to its own laws. It privileged form over content by insisting on art's autonomy from cultural forces external to its artists, justified by the Romantic demand of freedom. Emphasis on the signified gave way to emphasis on a coherent set of signifiers; meaning receded and art became 'about' itself and the artist who made it. No longer a servant of the aristocracy, the artist in a commodity society became a maker of independent objects. But as Russell Berman notes, 'the autonomous work is, from the start, not only autonomous but also an object to be possessed; the idealist description of art also aims to make art a pure commodity'.[1]

Near the end of the century, however, avant-gardists rejected the bourgeois blueprint – not by finding new patronage in the aristocratic model, but by disavowing the hold on art exercised by the purses of the middle class. The chief technical strategy for accomplishing the avant-garde project was a strong insistence that art is a cultural artifact. Bürger's summary is useful:

> The European avant-garde movements can be defined as an attack on the status of art in bourgeois society. What is negated is not an earlier form of art (a style) but art as an institution that is unassociated with the life praxis of men.

The avant-gardists created art that self-consciously looked like art in order to re-establish art's position within the social order, thus permitting their work to comment on and criticize that order. Avant-garde art denied the succour of Realism in order to call attention to its own artifice, its manufacturedness (what Bürger calls *montierte* or its 'fitted' quality), deliberately attempting to shock the bourgeoisie by contradicting trustworthy expectations. 'The organic work of art seeks to make unrecognizable the fact that it has been made', Bürger writes. 'The opposite holds true for the avant-gardiste work: it proclaims itself an artificial construct, an artifact.'[2] Cubist painting, with its emphasis on 'reality fragments' forged together in montage fashion, is a clear early example. But avant-garde painters, by definition attacking commodity society, still lived in a commodity society and still found their clients among the bourgeoisie.

In the theatre, with its much greater need to attract spectators assembled in groups, the issue of an audience for modernism became even more paradoxical. The reform movements that originated in Europe in the last decades of the nineteenth century flew in the face of the established theatrical system which treated plays as commodities and audiences as consumers of product: what Brecht would later call 'the culinary theatre'. In different ways these movements attempted to find not traditional theatrical success but rather to take their audiences into a new kind of seriousness. Here we join the well-known tale, the foundation of most of the narratives we have constructed about the revolutionary nature of *fin-de-siècle* theatre: Nora slamming a door, Antoine pushing a handcart filled with his mother's furniture, Yeats shocked by the toilet-brush sceptre at the dress rehearsal of *Ubu Roi*, the Freie Bühne and the Independent Theatre Society avoiding the ban on *Ghosts*, the nocturne of tea-drinking by Vladimir and Konstantin as they argued over an art theatre. These are the reigning theatre myths of our century, deeply inscribed in our consciousness and in our official histories. Indeed, much of the subsequent discourse for modernist theatre was shaped as early as 1914 by the rather peevish tone in the writing of Edward Gordon Craig, that ultimate example of the *refusé*, who was confident that the nineteenth-century audience was ignorantly trapped by the fussy overdecoration and inflated acting of the regular theatres.

I suppose he was right. But strangely it has not much been noted how thoroughly convinced these reformers were that audiences were like children who needed to be led. The very term *avant-garde* implies this, with its heavy-handed military metaphor. The avant-garde artists of the end of the nineteenth century expected to lead audiences into a social and aesthetic promised land that would cast off the mendacity and the habits of intellectual compliance long associated with the burgher's life. *La vie de bohème* contained a huge and unacknowledged contradiction: though avant-garde practitioners in Europe disdained middle-class values and tastes and revelled in that disdain, their only hope of success lay with middle-class audiences, whether established or emergent. *Epater le bourgeois* was a self-defeating motto: consumers will not pay to be offended for very long. Thus the idea of an audience for the avant-garde was from the start inherently problematic.

Of course avant-gardists strove to transfigure the notion of the audience as mere purchasers of product. They sought to change the spiritual or interior aspects of 'middle-classness', not necessarily to change the economic and social group that bought their pictures, listened to their music, read their books, or watched their plays. His purpose as a young artist, intoned Joyce's Stephen Dedalus, one of the founding fictional priests of avant-gardism, was 'to forge in the smithy of my soul the uncreated conscience of my race'. Extending the Romantic notion of the artist as saviour, this avant-garde construction was continued through the modernist period and often still affects our cultural notions of what artists should be and how they should think. Wave after wave of reforming movements – Symbolists, Expressionists, Dadaists, Futurists, Surrealists, Absurdists – actively scorned or reviled their audiences or potential audiences. Indeed a powerful notion in the twentieth century has been that artists of high seriousness should not be popular or financially successful. This means, in effect, that the dominant perception about advanced art in the west has accepted the Romanticized avant-garde premise. To put it as simply as possible, avant-garde art equals small audiences and something close to financial failure. If the audiences get too large, or the monetary rewards too great, by definition the work is not on the cutting edge.

Obviously this is a limited view of the serious artist's relationship to the public. Prior to the Romantic movement western culture found no necessary relationship between penury and artistic greatness; the historical shift that brought about the change was thoroughly analysed by Karl Marx. In our own century many serious artists have maintained an ambiguous position regarding success, from Pablo Picasso to Andy Warhol, from Bernard Shaw to Woody Allen. It is therapeutic to recall what Harold Clurman said: 'All artists dream, and when they dream they dream of money.' Yet the Romantic view that artistic success means financial failure reflects what was a profound dilemma for most of the avant-garde theatre reformers around the turn of the century.

The organizations devoted to theatrical renovation began small, often as restricted clubs. Constituting themselves as private societies rather than as commercial ventures, they achieved a number of cultural goals at a stroke: they eluded the censor's power and other licensing restrictions; they ensured a small but determined audience at each event, already committed financially to the season; they enabled the events to be mounted on an irregular basis; they freed themselves from audience repudiation of unconventional plays; and they validated their own advanced status by controlling the admission of the general public. But it was extremely difficult to survive under the harsh financial regimes forced on these troupes, which helped to promulgate the notion that art in the theatre was bound to be a losing proposition. There were 349 seats available for the first performance of André Antoine's Théâtre Libre, and not all of them were filled.[3] Had they been filled, that would still have been quite a small audience for 1887, and not large enough to sustain a company: in 1894, after seven years of intermittent productions, Antoine was bankrupt. When he reappeared on the scene it was in a larger theatre, and eventually in a heavily subsidized one. Otto Brahm dissolved the Freie Bühne less than five years after its founding, when he moved on to the stability of the Deutsches Theater, where financial problems disappeared. The Moscow Art Theatre seemed an exception to the rule of the impoverished free stage, but its first years were secured by private subsidy.

In England, a country without a tradition of subsidy of any type and with a theatrical system attuned to commerce and the long run, circumstances were even more difficult for the alternative societies and their audiences. In the seven years of its life the Independent Theatre Society never had more than 175 members. Its founder, J. T. Grein, wrote that 'the income was barely £400 a year during the whole of its existence',[4] and he remained convinced during the Edwardian years that advanced drama could not be made to flourish on the regular stage in London. The Stage Society, offering more varied plays and with better rehearsed productions, was substantially more successful. It limited membership to 300 in its first year, and performed only on Sunday evenings. In his memoirs of the period Alan Wade recalled that Sunday performances, officially prohibited in Britain, 'caused considerable nervousness to theatre lessees', who agreed in the end to hire out their houses only when assured that there would be no advance publicity or reviews in the press. Even so the police arrived at the Royalty Theatre for the Society's first event, Shaw's *You Never Can Tell* in 1899, to question the legality of even a private performance on a Sunday. (Frederick Whelen kept them 'adroitly involved in a long argument' until the play was over.[5]) The single Sunday performance meant that the Stage Society was able to take advantage of professional actors working in the regular theatres on their one night off. The small membership was meanwhile authenticating itself as the elite vanguard of dramatic art.

In its second season the Society was pressured to raise its number to 500 and to give an additional performance of each production on Monday afternoons. In the interests of the actors who were working for nothing or next to nothing, newspaper critics were now invited; the legal worries over Sunday performance had apparently receded. By 1907 the Society had increased its rolls to about 1,200. The expansion spoke well for the growing interest in the New Drama, but put a severe strain on accommodating the membership for popular events. When Granville Barker's play *Waste* was refused a licence that year, for example, the Society hurriedly mounted two private performances. (There was great trouble securing a venue, as theatre managers were reluctant to offend the Lord Chamberlain, who might retaliate by withholding renewal of their own operating licenses. By a stroke of luck the Imperial Theatre in Westminster became available; since it was about to be torn down, the usual fear was eliminated.) The controversy surrounding the play ensured a heavy demand for tickets, which could only be obtained by a potential spectator becoming a member – indeed, it may have been the *Waste* affair that artificially inflated the Stage Society's membership. The secretary, A. E. Drinkwater, was 'a firm disciplinarian', according to Wade, 'quite imperious to blandishment, and it was reported at the time that Henry James and two duchesses had to be content with seats in the gallery'.[6]

Despite its modest size and modest programming, it was the Stage Society that established the model for the New Drama and the new audience in London. In 1903 Barker wrote to William Archer with a plan to take the Court Theatre for 'a stock season of the uncommercial Drama' – he was thinking of Hauptmann, Sudermann, Ibsen, Maeterlinck, Schnitzler, Shaw, and Brieux. Barker's chief justification was his belief in the potential for an expanded new audience:

I think there is a class of intellectual would-be playgoers who are profoundly bored by the theatre as it is. Matinée productions don't touch these people (who are all workers) and Sunday evening is expensive and incapable of expansion ... I think the Independent Theatre – the New Century – The Stage Society – have prepared the ground, and the time is ripe for starting a theatre upon these lines, upon a regular – however unpretending – basis.[7]

The audience would be greatly expanded, though still small, as the Court had only 614 seats. Barker knew that subsidy was necessary (he suggested a start-up fund of £5,000), and that subscription sales were important. But he also knew that if the advances made by the Sunday societies were to be consolidated, the theatre had to be a public one, accessible to all. Barker even suggested that the highest price should be 5 or 6 shillings, which would have been a great bargain in the Edwardian period, about half the cost of a standard ticket for the stalls, which was 10 shillings and sixpence.

In the event most of these goals were not reached. When the famous Vedrenne–Barker performances began at the Court in 1904, they were on Tuesday, Thursday, and Friday afternoons only. These were days on which the regular theatres did not hold matinées, so that gainfully employed actors could be used in the manner established by the Stage Society. Rehearsals were squeezed in whenever possible, often lasting until the small hours. Only gradually and cautiously did the new management expand into evening performances. A small guarantee fund was established, mostly from Charlotte Shaw, and favourable rental terms for the theatre were provided by its lessee, J. H. Leigh, but no large subsidy was provided. The tickets cost the same as they did at the St James's Theatre or at Drury Lane. The subscription scheme was completely unsuccessful; at the end of the second season, when the venture had achieved significant fame, only twelve subscriptions had been sold.[8]

'The plain fact is', said the *Referee* during the first Vedrenne–Barker season, 'Mr Vedrenne has succeeded in drawing to the theatre a class of playgoer for whom too scant consideration is shown by the theatrical managers; playgoers, I mean, with a purely artistic taste for the theatre.'[9] But who were these people with a purely artistic taste? Shaw boasted they were 'not an audience, but a congregation'.[10] The 'great British public', Mario Borsa wrote in *The English Stage of Today* (112–13), 'artless, coarse-minded, and dull-witted – does not frequent the Court ... The Court audiences are composed of persons of culture and students, with a goodly percentage of society people.' In an interview in 1907, Barker said his audiences were mainly women, male sentimentalists who had not obtained their majority, and older people who had not grown up.[11] Most contemporary comments reinforce this conclusion. It is a new audience, *The Bystander* noted (10 Jan. 1906: 72):

> The Court theatre is now become a cult. The matinée-goers are an audience apart. A decade ago they would have been termed 'Soulful'. But the elect who crowd to the productions at the Court Theatre are bizarre, not so much in appearance and dress as in point of view... Outspokenness brings no blush to their cheek. They are mostly women.

F. C. Burnand, the editor of *Punch* (13 Dec. 1905: 422), went to one of the first matinées of *Major Barbara*, and found that 'the female element in the audience preponderated over the inferior sex by something like twelve to one'. This was not an ordinary matinée audience of women, he thought, for it 'had not a theatre-going, but rather a lecture-going, sermon-loving appearance' (see plate 9).

Matinées were not new to the regular theatres when Barker instituted his reign at the Court. They had grown during the 1870s and 1880s as a result of the popularity of the theatre among the leisured classes and were used for both regular productions and for untried plays. The persistent audience for matinées during the late Victorian period encouraged managers to experiment with more unconventional fare and paved the way for the Ibsen movement of the nineties.[12] But the big thing to say about matinée specators, the thing Barker emphasized in his letter to Archer, is obvious: they were not workers, whether from the working class or the bourgeois class. In fact the female matinée audience seems a marvellous demonstration of Thorstein Veblen's theory of vicarious leisure: wives and daughters of hard-working men of commerce sent out in daylight in flagrantly impractical dress to proclaim the freedom from drudgery for women bought by their masters' successful toil. Unable to afford the leisure of the aristocracy themselves, the male merchant class showed off women as surrogate signifiers of wealth.

And the matinée hat, that ultimate example of needless sartorial provocation, was a leisure-signifier of great cultural resonance. These hats, which 'spread in a vast radius around the head' and were 'piled high with ornamentation of birds, flowers or fruit', were very difficult to set on straight, requiring a mirror, an assistant, and a number of remarkably long hatpins.[13] Removing them, therefore, was an action of major consequence, not to be undertaken merely for the convenience of lesser mortals who happened to be seated behind them in the house

9 The audience at *You Never Can Tell* at the Savoy Theatre. A sketch by Charles
Sykes from *The Bystander*, 2 October 1907. Three matters are notable: that the rigid
dress distinctions in the different parts of the auditorium were in force even for a play
by Shaw; that the artist has attempted to inscribe parallel class distinctions in the
faces and postures of his figures; that serious-looking women dominated the Circle.

10 'Mr. Punch's Patent Matinée Hat, fitted with binocular glasses for the benefit of those sitting behind its wearer.' (A cartoon from *Mr Punch at the Play*, London, n.d.)

(see plate 10). Critics railed against their absurdities to little avail; Shaw started a campaign in the press as early as 1896.[14] As a private club, the Stage Society could ask ladies to remove them with success; even George Alexander got some of his clientele to consider their fellow spectators at the St James's through a combination of discreet good manners and a free cloak room.

As to the Court, reported *The Tatler* (21 Dec. 1904: 432), 'the hat question is very rife there because the stage is unhappily unusually low, and in the back rows of the stalls it is very difficult to see over mountainous hats'. Still it was with considerable surprise that critics noticed, at the very first Vedrenne–Barker matinée in 1904, that the new management had induced all but 'Three Ladies' to remove their hats. 'Cheerfully conforming to the new Edict',[15] these bare-headed spectators were signifying that they wished to belong to a new class of playgoer, separating themselves from Borsa's 'great British public' and from the mindless members of the middle class. Of course manners changed with resistance. A columnist for *The Lady* (8 Dec. 1904: 933) who called herself 'Cuckoo' attended a matinée of *Candida* and objected to the new policy: 'We were aghast at having to tear our hats off our heads as best we could, for at the Court it is a rule to prevent "matinée hats" obscuring the view of those behind, and I must say that most people looked dishevelled and untidy in consequence, for hats do disarrange the hair and flatten the front waves, etc., in a way that no man can understand!'

Convinced that audience manners and attitudes had to be changed, the management urged compliance in other new ways as well. It attempted, for example, to regulate the anarchic habits of applause that survived from the nineteenth century. Some programmes announced that actors would not take curtain calls at the end of each act, but only at the conclusion of the performance. This desire to make audience habits conform to a more serious approach to drama connects Barker to the general modernist desire to control the nature of perception.

It was not only leisured women who attended the Court matinées, especially for the Shaw plays. 'The adoring audience at the Court yesterday afternoon'[16] – that is, for the premiere of *John Bull's Other Island* in October 1904 – included a number of politicians. Prime Minister Balfour sat in the Royal Box with Beatrice and Sidney Webb on 10 November. At a special evening performance in March, King Edward, the heavy embodiment of the unreformed theatregoer, royally sat there – and laughed so hard that he broke his chair. This oft-told story, which ensured the success of the first Vedrenne–Barker season, was actually the wrong signal for the new audience Barker was seeking. In any event, the King never made it to a matinée. By the time *Major Barbara* was in matinées a year later the nature of the audience had been well established and the critics were regularly commenting on its distinctiveness. Balfour, who saw *John Bull* three times, was in the box for the new play with the Webbs and Sir Oliver Lodge, 'heading a brilliant and intellectual audience'.[17] 'There was intelligence – alert and expectant – on both sides of the footlights at the Court yesterday afternoon', said the *Daily Chronicle* about *Major Barbara* (28 Nov. 1905); 'the house was crowded to the doors' with 'a gathering altogether of quite surprising people'. The surprising people were exceedingly responsive:

They leapt at every utterance; they laughed long before the bright lines came; they said 'hear, hear' at each twist of the argument, in low solemn voices, like the 'amens' of a prayer meeting.

There was, indeed, something almost oppressively solid about this spirit of Shaw-worship that was spread abroad. 'Colossal!' 'The greatest mind in Europe!' Such were the hardly apt phrases that were bandied about in the entr'actes.

The Standard (same date) added that the enthusiasm of the audience 'almost succeeded in outlasting the severe long-windedness of the last act'.

Matinées clarify one of the chief issues about the Edwardian audience for the New Drama. After the first precarious months, the Vedrenne–Barker seasons shifted into a different and more prosperous mode, in which new productions were given six matinées and, if successful with the audience, were moved to evening performances. This procedure was much closer to Barker's original intention, as it allowed people gainfully occupied during the days to attend at night. But the plays that succeeded in the evenings were chiefly those by Bernard Shaw, the mainstay of the Court repertoire, and some of the more accessible Realist works. The poetic dramas of Maeterlinck, Yeats, and Masefield, for example, which helped to establish the versatility of the Court experiment and tied it to its European counterparts, never made the transfer. Gilbert Murray's translations of Euripides, which gathered much positive attention in matinée performances, did very poorly when they became evening fare. In its original six matinées in January 1906, *Electra* took in an average of almost £100 per performance, a respectable box office for what was surely a minority taste. Of the first performance, *The Era* (20 Jan. 1906: 17) said 'That theatre of the intellectuals – the Court – was filled on Tuesday afternoon with a highly cultured audience.' Yet when the play ran for two weeks in the evenings in March, the six performances in the first week averaged only £26 each. 'The business so far is suicidal', Barker wrote to Murray; 'it is all the fortune of war, war with the public'. *Hippolytus*, which did very well as the first Vedrenne–Barker matinée in 1904, did even worse than *Electra* when it was tried at night in April of 1906.[18] The audience with a 'purely artistic taste for the theatre' was apparently limited. One night a man was refused admittance by the box-office attendant because he was intoxicated. 'But of *course* I'm drunk', he countered. 'Do you think I should come to the Court Theatre if I was sober?'[19]

'I prefer addressing minorities', Barker wrote; 'one can make them hear better'.[20] The unconventional spectators attracted to the Vedrenne–Barker seasons constituted a self-defined and distinct culture. They matched the elitism of Barker's theatrical reform with a sense of their own superiority. They did not like the transfer of the Court operation in 1907 to the larger and more commercial environment of the Savoy, where they felt ill at ease and assimilated, and made their objections quite plain. The best example relates to printed programmes, which can be revealing documents of theatrical intention. At the socialist Court the programmes, beautifully printed in red and black ink on heavy linen paper, were single-fold pages that contained no advertisements or other distractions. Like the Stage Society programmes, they suggested seriousness of purpose; they contextualized the performances with an uncluttered elegance of design and a complete absence of commercialism. In most of them a large notice was printed in red, announcing there were 'No Fees' at the Court. Edwardian theatres were inconsistent about this issue, some assessing extra charges for programmes and for cloak rooms, others not. At the Savoy, Barker's business manager, J. E. Vedrenne, accepted advertisements and then made the mistake of selling the programmes. Some of the committed audience, a precarious coalition of Shavians, Fabians, feminists, and theatrical pioneers, thoroughly disapproved of this mercantile consequence, and took their revenge. When Barker made his first appearance as Sergius in *Arms and the Man* in December 1907, he was greeted by an organized demonstration from the gallery, 'a loud chorus of shouts of "No Fees!"'[21]

The failure of the Savoy venture, and the failure of Barker's experiment in repertory at the Duke of York's Theatre in 1910, suggested that the new audience, no matter how committed and vocal, was not large enough to support an art theatre that was self-sustaining. Here we notice the big difference between conditions in England and on the continent. Antoine in Paris and Brahm in Berlin, after their few years of apprenticeship in poor theatre, moved on to the security of external subsidy; Barker in London did not. His subsequent attempts with his wife to create a repertory theatre seemed to be getting somewhere, but they were getting somewhere very slowly. The Little Theatre in Adelphi, where Barker and Lillah McCarthy established management in 1911, was a severe house that looked like a lecture hall; it was all stalls except for seven boxes in the back, and seated 278 people. The Kingsway in Great Queen Street, where they operated in 1912, held but 564.[22] The three revolutionary Shakespeare productions at the Savoy, which brought much larger audiences, were made possible by a private subsidy; and the two that were successful paid for themselves through the kind of long runs that violated Barker's repertory principles.

Of these enterprises, the one that is most interesting for our subject occurred at the St James's Theatre in 1913. Here Barker's attempts to create a repertory theatre, and to move beyond the confines of his original Court audience, met their severest test. The St James's, the most fashionable theatre in London, had been the home of Society Drama since *Lady Windermere's Fan* in 1892. Its location in Piccadilly, its repertoire of plays by Pinero, Jones, and Wilde that made Ibsen's issues palatable, and the extreme etiquette of Alexander's management – all these colluded to attract society, the haute bourgeoisie, and the lesser classes who admired their betters. Alexander, who was elected to the London County Council in 1907 as a Conservative, operated his theatre like an expensive club. It 'exuded the same gracious dignity as himself', Macqueen-Pope wrote, and the audience 'felt it as soon as they entered'. Even the box-office manager wore a tall hat when on duty.[23] Complimentary tickets were special cards reminding the bearer that evening dress was imperative for admission.

Evening dress was regularly worn in the stalls and dress circle everywhere, even for Shaw's plays, as is apparent in the illustration reproduced above. Perhaps it is hard for us, with our culture of prodigious informality, to imagine the strict protocol this imposed on the audience in Victorian and Edwardian London. The resolute distinctions between classes, plainly marked by their degrees of dress, separated the audience into discrete areas of the auditorium. J. T. Grein recalled that on his first visit to London, as the critic for a Dutch paper, he did not know the rules and arrived at the Lyceum wearing tweeds to see Henry Irving in *Faust*. Irving's manager, Bram Stoker in the flesh, barred the way, pointing to the notice on the ticket, 'Evening Dress Indispensable', and escorted the shamed foreigner to the family circle, tenth row, where, he said, 'I saw little and heard less.'[24] The wealthy classes, 'shirtfronts and sables', as Macqueen-Pope called them, established a tone for the entire audience similar to that expected in their drawing-rooms.[25]

The St James's was the very opposite of a socialist theatre

attempting to reform the stage. Alexander did not want reform; he wanted continuance. He wanted a stage world that reflected the manners and dress of his leading spectators, one in which they could see themselves righteously manipulating the status quo. The wealthy members of the audience and the actors portraying wealthy figures on stage were engaged in a reciprocal semiosis, in which their dress was the leading signifier. Even the advertisements in the programmes reinforced this mentality. In 1913 they were dominated by elegant clothiers: furs from Revillon Frères of Regent Street, 'French Model Gowns' from the Elite Company of Grosvenor Mansions, Paquin designs, theatre gowns from Liberty's.[26]

Alexander insured that decorum went beyond the walls of the theatre, insisting that his actors who played society people on stage also dress like society people in their private lives. Once early in the century he caught Henry Ainley and Lilian Braithwaite walking together in Bond Street on their day off. Ainley wore a Norfolk jacket and a floppy hat, while his friend had on a tweed outfit. Alexander spoke magisterially, addressing them in the third person: 'I would remind them that this is Bond Street and at the fashionable hour, and that they are members of the St James's theatre company. Membership of that company entails certain sartorial obligations. I need say no more.'[27] Alexander kept up his standards even during the war. In 1917 he sent for Godfrey Tearle over the same issue:

Tearle, I am told that you have been seen walking in Piccadilly in the forenoon incorrectly dressed. You wear a lounge suit and that is not the right attire for a young leading man in my company. The correct dress for a gentleman in the forenoon is a morning coat and top hat. You will have to rectify this error or I shall take it that you wish no longer to be a member of the St James's company.[28]

So the St James's was not the most obvious venue for the leader of the New Drama to premiere *Androcles and the Lion*, a Fabian extravaganza with feminist overtones. Alexander had taken his sartorially correct company on provincial tour in the autumn of 1913, and from September to Christmas Barker rented the theatre for another repertory experiment. The disturbing merger of the old and the new was readily apparent. Shaw's portrait inside the front cover of the programme was placed opposite an advertisement for the International Fur Store, Britain's leading vegetarian staring at an enticement for 'charming new designs made in Russian Sable,

Chinchilla, Natural Musquash, and other fashionable furs'.[29] Feminists took the persecution of Christians in the play as a reference to their own cause and to the government's ridiculous insistence that suffragist prisoners on hunger strike were answerable for force-feeding, not the authorities; when Ben Webster as the Roman Captain said on stage that Christians have only themselves to blame if they suffer, he was interrupted by 'suffragette cheers from the gallery'. Yet the critic reporting the demonstration also noted that spectators from the stalls were overheard using words like 'vulgarity', 'blasphemy', and 'childish' to describe the play.[30] When Shaw's Lion first came through the forest and shook his mane, one young blood in the stalls, probably thinking he had come to an Alexander production, 'screwed his monocle into his eye and muttered "God! What have they got Hall Caine in it for?"'[31] Strangest of all, Barker had placed a sign near the box-office window – that same box office whose manager always wore a top hat – that read, 'We should like our patrons to feel that in no part of the house is evening dress indispensable.'[32]

I do not know if many people took up his suggestion to violate the class code so flagrantly, but I doubt it. The problem of the new audience in England was not just that it was too small to sustain the kind of theatre Barker wanted. Nor was it simply that it lived inside a larger theatrical community that did not want a reformed stage at all. In addition to those external difficulties, Barker had created a further one. Like the European avant-gardists, he thought that his spectators also needed reform. Both Barker and Shaw, despite their socialist agenda – or perhaps because of it – believed that the audience required management; if spectators were to rise to a higher level, they would have to be steered there. Some of them were like children; some of them were drunk. (Since there was no permanent subsidy to underwrite the cost, spectators would have to pay for their improvement themselves: the bourgeoisie was being asked to fund a theatre that wanted to destroy the bourgeois position.) The desire to lead London to a promised land of the stage was eminently Fabian, a permeation theory applied to art. But Barker lacked Shaw's patience to wait for slow change. Or perhaps he grew to see that permeation was an insufficient weapon in the face of the swift and incontestable alterations forced upon English society after 1914 that moved the theatre farther away from the conditions he sought.

In any event, he never got over a rather distant and slightly disdainful attitude to the audience and its unwillingness to be led. In

1917, just as he was deciding to retire from the stage, he wrote: 'I do believe my present loathing for the theatre is loathing for the audience. I have never loved them.'[33] More than any other characteristic, that loathing for the audience tied him to the early modernists, most of whom were convinced that high art could only be valued by a small coterie of the like-minded. The avant-garde suspicion of popular success eventually split twentieth-century art into two parts: the larger part got the audiences but little lasting attention, the smaller part the critical and historical acclaim. It is a split very much still with us, especially in Britain and North America. Not until Bertolt Brecht, writing around 1930,[34] did any major theatre thinker or theatre practitioner seriously consider that it might not be the spectators who needed reformation, but rather the artists and their art.

NOTES

1 Russell A. Berman, *Modern Culture and Critical Theory: Art, Politics, and the Legacy of the Frankfurt School* (Madison, 1989), p. 48.

2 Peter Bürger, *Theory of the Avant-Garde*, trans. Michael Shaw (Minneapolis, 1984), pp. 49, 72.

3 See Jean Chothia, *André Antoine* (Cambridge, 1991), p. 7.

4 J. T. Grein, *Stage Society News*, 25 January 1907.

5 See Allan Wade, *Memories of the London Theatre, 1900–1914*, ed. Alan Andrews (London, 1983), p. 4.

6 The figures for membership come from Wade, and from Mario Borsa, *The English Stage of Today*, trans. Selwyn Brinton (London, 1908), p. 103. The quotation about Drinkwater is from Wade, p. 19.

7 Letter of 21 April 1903, in *Granville Barker and His Correspondents*, ed. Eric Salmon (Detroit, 1986), pp. 41–2.

8 According to Borsa, *English Stage*, p. 113; I have not found corroboration elsewhere.

9 *Referee*, 16 April 1905, p. 2.

10 Archibald Henderson, *Bernard Shaw: Playboy and Prophet* (New York, 1932), p. 444.

11 'Who Will Be the Director of the "New Theatre"?' *The Theatre*, 7 (September 1907), p. 235.

12 George Rowell, *Victorian Theatre, 1792–1914*, 2nd edn (Cambridge, 1978), pp. 103–4, 128.

13 W. Macqueen-Pope, *St James's: Theatre of Distinction* (London, 1958), p. 167.

14 See *Our Theatres in the Nineties* (London, 1931), vol. II, pp. 77–8.

15 *Referee*, 23 October 1904, p. 2. See also *Pall Mall Gazette*, 19 October 1904, p. 11.
16 Unidentified clipping dated 2 November 1904, in the British Theatre Museum, London.
17 *The Stage*, 30 November 1905, p. 17.
18 Based on box office statements from J. E. Vedrenne to Murray, dated 3 February, 19 and 26 March, 2 and 8 April 1906, in the Gilbert Murray Papers in the Bodleian Library, Oxford. See my *Granville Barker and the Dream of Theatre* (Cambridge, 1985), pp. 38–40.
19 Theodore Steir, *With Pavlova Around the World* (London, 1927), p. 277.
20 'Repertory Theatres', *The New Quarterly*, 2 (1909), p. 491.
21 *Pall Mall Gazette*, 31 December 1907, p. 4.
22 The Little Theatre figures are from C. B. Purdom, *Harley Granville Barker* (London, 1955), p. 122; the Kingsway figures from *Who's Who in the Theatre* (London, 1922), p. 1250.
23 *St James's*, p. 167.
24 Grein's comments, written in 1925, are reprinted in Michael Orme, *J. T. Grein* (London, 1936), p. 44.
25 See J. C. Trewin, *The Edwardian Theatre* (Oxford, 1976), p. 28.
26 All these are contained in the programme for *The Turning Point*, which opened on 6 January 1913.
27 *St James's*, p. 168. Macqueen-Pope's work is not always reliable and must be treated with caution, but his gossipy anecdotes are too good to ignore.
28 Related in Anthony Quayle, *A Time to Speak* (London, 1990), p. 313.
29 St James's Theatre programme of 1 September 1913
30 *Manchester Guardian*, 2 September 1913, p. 2.
31 Barry Duncan, *The St James's Theatre: Its Strange and Complete History, 1835–1957* (London, 1964), p. 287.
32 *The Standard*, 3 December 1913, p. 8.
33 Quoted in Michael Holroyd, *Bernard Shaw* (New York, 1989), vol. II, p. 175. The current revival of interest in Barker's own plays, and in his status as a precursor of late twentieth-century theatre, may well be connected to a parallel crisis in the audiences of our own time. I address this issue in a paper called 'The Transformations of Granville Barker', in *Harley Granville Barker: An Edinburgh Retrospective 1992*, ed. Jan McDonald and Leslie Hill (Glasgow, 1993).
34 See, for example, 'The Modern Theatre is the Epic Theatre', written by Brecht and Peter Suhrkamp, in *Brecht on Theatre*, ed. John Willett (New York, 1964), pp. 34–5.

CHAPTER 7

Towards an ideal spectator: theatregoing and the Edwardian critic

Victor Emeljanow

On 8 January 1907 a notice appeared in *The Times*. It stated that:

A. B. Walkley accepted the position of president of the Society of Dramatic Critics formed with 'social and professional purposes, to facilitate the exchange of views on the material and intellectual aspects of the calling of dramatic criticism and generally to promote the interests of the calling'. Vice-President is William Archer, Honorary Secretary, F. Moy Thomas; Committee: Owen Seamen, Hamilton Fyfe, J. T. Grein, G. E. Morrison, A. F. Robbins, Sydney Dark, Anthony Ellis, E. F. Spence, Charles Palmer.

Seven years later the *Stage Year Book* for 1914 recorded that:

During the year 1913 there has been formed a Critics' Circle in connection with the Institute of Journalists... There was a Society of Dramatic Critics formed in 1906... with Mr A. B. Walkley as president. Interest in the society ... waned and the Society of Dramatic Critics is now moribund. The Critics' Circle was formed in April. The Committee consists of Messrs William Archer, G. E. Morrison, J. T. Grein, Richard Northcott and S. R. Littlewood, Honorary Secretary.[1]

Both of these notices referred to events which had taken place in the years immediately previous to their publication. Obviously something had happened in the Edwardian period by 1906 to suggest the need for a Society of Dramatic Critics. Equally, by 1913, whatever had motivated the formation of that Society had not been strong enough to sustain it. Was the formation of the society, therefore, in the first place premature? Had patterns of theatregoing changed significantly between 1906 and 1913? What was the calling of dramatic criticism and its intellectual aspects which formed the basis of the confident terms of association?

In fact, there is little to suggest that patterns of theatregoing changed radically in the period. In his list of long runs on the London stage, John Parker enumerates 254 plays which reached or exceeded a consecutive run of at least 100 nights during the period from 1901 to 1911.[2] Though this may be a somewhat arbitrary criterion for determining popular theatregoing, it does offer an indicator of taste. Of those 254 productions, musicals, including revivals of Gilbert and Sullivan, counted for sixty-one productions and pantomimes for ten, matched only by Shakespeare with ten. Perhaps predictably, the most popular contemporary authors in order were Barrie (six), Hall Caine, Somerset Maugham, Conan Doyle and Hubert Davies (five), Henry Arthur Jones, Alfred Sutro (four), Pinero, Stephen Phillips and H. V. Esmond (three) and then more surprisingly, Shaw, Arnold Bennett, and Maeterlinck. Translations and adaptions mostly from French accounted for fourteen (four of which were the work of Cosmo Gordon Lennox). An additional fourteen plays were written by women.

How does this measure up to records of actual playgoing? In his book, *Edwardian Theatre*, J. C. Trewin refers to the theatregoing experiences of two ordinary patrons, the one provincial, the other a suburban Londoner. He suggests that their patterns of theatregoing may be, *mutatis mutandis*, typical.[3] The provincial theatregoer, for example, followed his favourite actors from Birmingham to Shrewsbury and then to London. In the course of this he found himself attending performances of *The Oresteian Trilogy* as well as *Pelléas and Mélisande* and *Captain Brassbound's Conversion*. The suburban theatregoer, whose record is admittedly confined to the year 1905, Trewin suggests probably caught public transport to the theatre on a night other than the first. Both included Shakespeare, Shaw, Hall Caine, R. C. Carton in their playgoing; both followed the Neilson–Terry combination, George Alexander, and Oscar Asche whenever and wherever they appeared, especially in costumed melodrama; neither of them appeared to have had any interest in Pinero or Jones. The suburban playgoer went to the Court quite by chance and found that he wanted to see more of Shaw divorced from the lure of personality acting. If we compare these records with that of a professional playgoer, H. M. Walbrook, we find that the differences are few.[4] Walbrook had been a provincial critic writing about both the local Brighton as well as London theatres for the *Brighton Guardian*. In 1906 he joined the *Pall Mall Gazette* on which he remained until 1915. He was not a personality in himself nor a writer distinguished by literary idiosyncrasy or self-regarding waywardness, but one who set out to give an overview of the elements which characterized Edwardian theatregoing. His theatregoing encompassed Sutro, Cicely Hamilton, Masefield, the Sicilian actors, and Shakespeare. Looking at the three records one might be struck by the evidence of catholicity of taste, the significance of Shakespeare and the willingness on the part of the theatregoers to integrate Aeschylus, Shaw, or the visits of foreign companies into their regular theatregoing.

To return to the paragraph in *The Times*. Why should it have been thought necessary at this time to form a craft guild to facilitate an exchange of views and to emphasize the intellectual aspects of the calling of dramatic criticism? That dramatic criticism was flourishing at the time is indisputable. (Tracy Davis and Christopher Kent between them have, after all, identified 241 critics in the period 1830 to 1914.[5]) Moreover, the newly formed Society was to be joined by between fifty and sixty critics within the year. Was this an indicator of critical self-assurance? On the other hand, might the formation of a society reflect not assurance but rather insecurity and a suspicion that something needed to be done about the *données* of critical evaluation? Perhaps theatre critics and theatregoers alike might be sharing the same feelings which the politician C. F. Masterman felt on the eve of being swept into power in 1906:

Expectancy and surprise are the notes of the age. Expectancy belongs by nature to a time balanced uneasily between two great periods of change. On the one hand is a past still showing faint survivals of vitality; on the other is the future but hardly coming to birth. The years as they pass still appear as years of preparation, a time of waiting rather than a time of action... But surprise passes into astonishment in confronting the particular and special features of the age. Here is a civilization becoming ever more divorced from Nature ... protesting through its literature a kind of cosmic weariness.[6]

The Society came into being at a particularly significant point. Henry Irving and Clement Scott had died recently, Joseph Knight had long retired and was to die in June 1907, the Liberal government was promising a new dispensation and the Court theatre was coming to the end of its innovative seasons. All these might indeed bring sharply into focus the need to address the problem which Granville Barker was later to articulate: 'There is an art of theatre and there is a theatrical industry, and it is absurd to expect that the interests of the two can be continuously identical; it is difficult, rather, to see why nowadays they should ever coincide.'[7] From this perspective, it could be argued that the Society may have come into existence in order to respond to an urgent need to redefine the language of criticism and to address such issues as the difference between a 'dramatic' critic and a 'theatre' critic and whether indeed the critic was 'engaged in one of the most difficult and necessary tasks that the varied labours of daily journalism can afford' as the 28-year-old critic for the *Morning Leader*, S. R. Littlewood, wrote in 1903?[8] If the critics were responsible in part for the successes of the Court seasons as the 29-year-old Desmond MacCarthy maintained, then it was perhaps indeed high time to define the calling.

Was the Society equipped to answer these questions? If the business and promotion of this new craft guild was entrusted to its executive committee, were they the right people for the job? The composition of the committee was an odd mixture. Its oldest member was F. Moy Thomas who was 78 when he joined the Society. He was also very sick and had given up active reviewing in 1901. For thirty years the critic for the *Graphic* as well as the *Daily News*, he had edited the collected works of Coleridge and became the first editor of *Cassell's Magazine*. On the surface he might have appeared to represent all that a new society would try to avoid: as an intimate friend of John Hollingshead and a collaborator in a number of Gaiety musicals he was hardly a disinterested critic. His credentials, however, were impeccable: he had been a passionate advocate of the rights of dramatic authors in the 1870s and epitomized a gentleman-amateur tradition which stretched back to the theatrical amateur Charles Dickens to whom Thomas had been introduced by Talfourd in 1850, more than half a century before. He was an uncompromising Victorian whose values were those of Clement Scott and whose intimate involvement in theatre practice might have provoked the kinds of suspicions about critics and their venality which had been voiced at the end of the previous century by George Moore.

Temperamentally, Thomas was close to Sidney Dark who was both a literary and dramatic critic. Dark had been an actor and in fact played Pettersen in the Royalty production of *The Wild Duck* in 1894. In 1907 he was the 33-year-old dramatic critic of the *Daily Express*, to which he had transferred from the *Daily Mail* in 1904.

Dark appears to have cultivated assiduously the persona of a theatrical dilettante,[9] who was elected to the committee because he had manifested admiration for its charter and because it would enable him to rub shoulders with famous people, in particular Walkley whom he admired for his dress sense as much as for his mind. There is little to suggest a sense of urgency or dedication in his habits.

He regularly lunched at the Cavour where he met Charles Brookfield and Hawtrey, and at 5.0 p.m. he progressed to the Café Royal to meet Frank Harris and Max Beerbohm and to fraternize with racing reporters, detectives, and spivs before going to the theatre. In the theatre he was an admirer of the actor-manager to whose glamorous persona he responded. Characteristically he was more interested in the fact that R. C. Carton was a tiny man who wore a toupée and high heels than the reasons why he was a successful dramatist. No one could have been more temperamentally opposed to the other members of the committee, especially to either the president or vice-president.

Neither Hamilton Fyfe nor Owen Seamen was on the committee primarily as a dramatic critic. Rather, they were both editors of significant papers: Seamen, who had joined *Punch* in 1897 and had become its editor in 1906, and Fyfe who had been the editor of the *Daily Mirror* since 1903. Seamen, moreover, had had a distinguished academic career at Cambridge and as Professor of Literature at Durham before commencing a full-time career as a writer of parodic verse, as well as being a wit and raconteur. His career inevitably invites a comparison with Max Beerbohm's who, significantly, played no role in the formation of the Society.

Anthony Ellis and Alfred Robbins represented the interests of the provincial *Manchester Daily Despatch* and the *Birmingham Post* respectively, although Ellis was also a freelance writer for the *World* and the *Academy*. Ellis's career as a critic and thus a member of the Society, however, was to be a short one. He would resign in 1909 to pursue his major interests as a theatre manager and dramatic author. Alfred Robbins, on the other hand, was a playwright as well, and, at the time of his election, was vice-president of the Institute of Journalists, an organization founded in 1890 and of which he would become president in 1908. Robbins was an organization man dedicated as much to Freemasonry as to elevating the position of the journalist. When the Society collapsed, it was he who would revitalize it at the end of the Edwardian period and give it a new direction and purpose with the support of his ally George Morrison, whom he persuaded to join the executive committee. Morrison at the time of his election was dramatic critic both of the *Pall Mall Gazette* and the *Morning Post*. Like Robbins and Dark, Morrison had aspirations as a playwright and he was able to resign his position on the *Gazette* on the strength of his success, particularly his version of *Don Quixote* produced by Benson in

1908. Like Robbins, however, he saw himself as a professional journalist first and foremost.

Charles Palmer is a rather shadowy figure. He was dramatic critic of the *Sun* from 1903 to 1906 and a paragraphist for the *Globe* from 1904, whose editor he became after the Edwardian period. He was also the father of John Palmer who was to become drama critic for the *Evening Standard* and who wrote *The Future of the Theatre*.

Thus far we have a committee composed of dedicated journalists who were occasional critics, critics who aspired to be and sometimes were successful playwrights (common enough Victorian phenomena), representatives of provincial newspapers as well as London ones, and at least one ostentatious dilettante. Thus far there exists little to suggest a commonly accepted sense of 'calling', let alone a sense of the intellectual dimension of drama criticism. Nonetheless, there had already been attempts to define the role of the theatregoer and, by extension, the exemplary model of an 'ideal spectator', the critic. This phrase, although in essence Platonic, is in fact derived from the title of a lecture which the Society's president A. B. Walkley delivered to the Royal Institution in February 1903. And it was with this definition that the four remaining members of the committee had struggled and were to struggle in the Edwardian period.

Perhaps the least well known of the four is E. F. Spence, whose initials appeared in the dramatic criticism of the *Westminster Gazette* and the *Sketch*. He had been educated privately and at Charterhouse. Like Archer and Seamen, he had been called to the bar and began writing criticism three years later, at the age of 33. Unlike Walkley, Archer, and Grein, who were more concerned with the role of the critic either in advancing the cause of the 'serious drama', or in acting as dramatic apologists and as the scourges of the Establishment, Spence had no such platform. As a consequence, it left him little to do but act as a chronicler illustrating what he took to be the erosion of Victorian verities. In his criticisms[10] we see the confusion which many members of the new Society must have felt. He was confronted on the one hand by a drama which either romanticized history or vulgarized religion (*The Exile*, *The Scarlet Pimpernel*, *Claudian* and *The Passing of the Third Floor Back* as examples), and on the other by a drama which promoted new ideas and expressed current life and thought, but whose partisan enthusiasm he felt left the audience powerless to draw its own conclusions. In this basket he would have placed the plays of Cicely Hamilton, Elizabeth Robins, and most of the Court seasons.

Spence was equally disturbed by what he took to be the mesmeric effect of the stage on the spectator, an effect which embraced both the stage's moral propaganda and the actor's ability to suggest a role model. In following their idols about the country, playgoers were exposed to moral and historical paradigms which determined their values and blunted their sensibilities. Wilson Barrett playing King Alfred and Claudian, or Martin Harvey playing Napoleon, or Forbes-Robertson in the Jerome play he felt exerted an undue influence.[11] Similarly, the production of *The Lower Depths* in 1903 and the visits of the Grand Guignol and Sicilian Players in 1908 exposed playgoers to experiences which at the very least were gratuitously shocking and unaesthetic.

We can see that Spence found himself caught in the critical dichotomy between form and content, between the material and its theatrical realization by the performers. It of course anticipates the kind of criticism that has been levelled at the producers and consumers of television. He was also worried by the platforms espoused by some of his colleagues on the grounds that they seemed to invest the stage with even more social power than it already had. Where did this place the critic? If playgoers were powerless to resist the Svengalis of the stage, the critic he felt should perform the role of an informed and active intermediary. Spence's answer was an early suggestion that the critic might act as dramaturg. This role would provide not only assistance to playwrights in shaping unsolicited scripts and in monitoring the progress of established dramatists but also provide an intervention between managements and the dramatic vehicles. Thus the critic would, for example, suggest the suitability of the performer to the role and indeed assume some of the functions of an agent. Spence was encouraged by new casting practices employed by the Stage Society and the Barker–Vedrenne management in which actors were being matched to their roles. This new and authoritative role would demand that the critic be versed in theatre history, modern literary movements, music, and the pictorial arts. What Spence was arguing was to give the critic an active part in the artistic process, to provide expertise based on discernment and taste. In 1906, however, there were few who would be prepared to invest the critic with this sort of power.

We now come to the last three critics, who were arguably the most influential in terms of the new drama and its realization. We need not, however, be concerned with this aspect but rather with their differences in temperament and outlook and how these might have affected the agenda of the new Society. Just before our period William Archer had published *Study and Stage*, and Walkley, *Frames of Mind*.[12] The publications gave Max Beerbohm the opportunity to evaluate the qualities of both men and in so doing, identified them with two quite distinct approaches to criticism and theatregoing. Walkley he found idiosyncratically humorous (which appealed to Beerbohm) but tolerant and ostentatiously erudite (which did not); Archer he found academic and 'ideal' but prone to 'spot and to be grateful for, the soul of goodness in things artistically evil'.[13]

A. B. Walkley in fact had been much influenced by Archer's Victorian works, in particular *English Dramatists of To-day*, and had been the drama critic for the *Star* for twelve years (with Shaw as music critic) until he began his association with *The Times* which lasted from 1900 until his death. He was a complex man: flamboyantly dressed and identifiably French rather than English after dark; during the day dressed in the conventionally sombre apparel of an upwardly mobile public servant (he held a position in the General Post Office until his retirement in 1919).

In 1903, however, he published *Dramatic Criticism*, which identified his position on the business of criticism.[14] As a critic Walkley allied himself uncompromisingly with the dramatists at the expense of the performers: 'The play deals with life, actual or fantastic; it presents therefore as a rule an infinitely richer matter for criticism than the success or failure of the actor to realise the author's personage.'[15] Walkley was equally fastidious and detached when he came to discuss audiences. The critic needed to remain aloof from public opinion; he regarded too many critics as either slavish chroniclers of the public opinion of the stalls or equally slavish reflectors of popular taste. As such, the critic was acting as an accomplice whereby the public was able to sympathize with itself, and be rendered impotent and unwilling to confront the new. This Olympian distaste for the theatregoer allowed him to attack both Pinero and Jones for their apparent willingness to compromise. He was surprised when confronted by a play like *Iris* in 1901 which appeared to avoid compromise.

The distance between Walkley and Archer can be measured by the fact that the former distrusted all talk about drama as an educational force or the theatre as a national institution on the grounds that it was a popular art and should be treated as such.[16] He was disingenuously to tell the Joint Select Committee on Stage Plays (Censorship) in 1909 that 'the importance of drama, is apt to be somewhat overrated nowadays and we take these things a little too solemnly'.[17] It is quite clear where Walkley stood. He was prepared to side with dramatists provided that they did not transgress his personal code of beauty and form. He had no time for the opinion of the stalls and even less for actors who intruded their personalities between the words of the dramatists and their appreciation by the ideal spectator by which, of course, he meant himself. In his evaluation of performance, therefore, he valued those actors who were self-effacing. This even affected his appreciation of performers like Réjane who, although she was French and therefore in his estimation admirable, was at the mercy of plays like *Zaza* written merely to show off the talents of one performer. He understandably had very little sympathy with Granville Barker's 'exemplary theatre', which appeared to place the actor in the foreground at the expense of the author.

So where did this place the critic? 'Critics proper ... are consumers of one art, the art of drama, and producers of another art, the art of criticism.'[18] Criticism therefore was itself a mode of self-expression, an independent art form which had as *its* consumers not the theatregoing public but rather the readers – those who never went to the theatre. 'Criticism can give *the reader* (not the playgoer) a very fair idea of *Hamlet* or ... *The Admirable Crichton* ... It can give only an adequate account of... *A Midsummer Night's Dream* ... With *Charley's Aunt* it can do nothing.'[19] In other words, as the dramatic receded and the theatrical elements took over, the language of criticism became increasingly inadequate. Walkley placed the relationship between critic and reader on the same level of personal engagement as between reader and novelist or essayist. He saw himself as the ideal consumer of the dramatic art through his ability to balance sensibility to impression with power of analysis, and his task was to communicate the fruits of this balance to the reader. From the reader he looked to a reaction that 'the knowledge of this man's feelings has illuminated, expanded, warmed and invigorated my own'.[20] It is little wonder that Walkley's criticisms abound in references which would establish his own direct links with a literary pedigree which included Aristotle, Longinus, Dryden, Johnson, and Anatole France. It led Archer to accuse Walkley of letting aesthetic or philosophic theory intrude between himself and the work of art. Beerbohm thought he had read too much and forgotten too little.

The fundamentalist Christian Scot, William Archer, had established his reputation as a critic well within the Victorian period. Indeed, in the Edwardian period he was to devote himself increasingly to editorial work – he was finishing his edition of Ibsen's collected works in 1906 and would edit Congreve and Farquhar between 1906 and 1912. The battle for the acceptance of Ibsen all but won, he now saw his role as that of a warrior in the causes of a national theatre and the abolition of censorship. Thus in this period he was less than an ideal spectator. He was able, however, to identify the major problem facing theatre criticism – 'One of the great difficulties of criticism is to see the play through the actor and the actor through the play'[21] – but was temperamentally little able to do anything about it. His criticism was coloured by his determination to prove the principle of evolution, to measure both playwriting and performance according to 'the strict requirements of the realistic stage' and to demonstrate that progress in the theatre had been inhibited by the actor-manager since the days of Charles Kean.

To these principles which he carried over from the Victorian period he remained true throughout his working life. Thus Archer saw modern English drama beginning with the work of Gilbert, whose function had been to clean the theatre's Augean stables of inherited meretriciousness. This in turn had paved the way for Ibsen, not in his *Ghosts* or *Doll's House* mode, but rather in that of *John Gabriel Borkman* or *The Master Builder*, which provided the material fit for the palace of art which Archer hoped the English theatre would become. And he measured both playwriting and performance by the extent to which they aspired to the perfection of his models. It was the job, moreover, of critics to guide playwrights and performers towards these goals. This made him tolerant of inanity provided it aspired to nothing more and able to overlook inadequacy provided it aspired to better things. It certainly put him at odds with Walkley, Beerbohm and, indeed, Shaw: 'I would rather see columns of fatuous gush about a foolish play, than a brilliant but discouraging and sterilising criticism of a play with any germs of good in it.'[22]

Like many of his fellow critics, however, he had little faith in the taste or discriminative abilities of the theatregoer. With this in mind, he saw actors and playwrights taking the path of least resistance (a version of Walkley's compromise), thus thwarting the evolutionary process to which they should be devoted. The actor-managers, like the clerics of the established churches, preached a conservative lesson which was comfortable and acceptable when in fact Archer required them to be evangelists. Like Spence, he took exception to their position both in the theatre and society, not on paradigmatic grounds, but rather because their position actively militated against access and opportunity for all. The only way out was the establishment of an exemplary national theatre. To this project he devoted himself as a fervent proselytizer during the Edwardian period.

The first draft of Archer's scheme for a national theatre had been circulated in 1904 and had the support of the most conservative theatrical identities of the time – Henry Irving, Squire Bancroft, Barrie, Helen D'Oyly Carte, John Hare, Henry Arthur Jones, and Pinero. Of course, to give it authority it had to be so. More revealing, however, was the repertoire which Archer proposed and which remained unmodified for the 1907 Duckworth edition despite a new preface in which his co-author, Granville Barker, took the repertoire to task. The reason for this was undoubtedly the successful Court seasons which had intervened. It nonetheless was true that in 1904 Barker had accepted Archer's repertoire choices which had been selected on the principle of plays which were national, representative, and popular. Despite his lack of faith in theatregoers, Archer used the yardstick of established attractiveness to an English public to guide the choice of an eclectic repertoire which included his selection of classical as well as modern plays. Moreover, since the theatre needed to be exemplary the plays needed to demonstrate the essential worth of English drama. The prospective national theatre would assist in the provision of a model 'to similar enterprises in provincial cities, in the colonies and in America . . . worthy of the metropolis of the Empire'.[23] As an imperialist therefore Archer was not going to be responsible for exporting unworthy plays or indeed plays which appealed only to a cultured or literary class. The result was a repertoire which was a paradigm of 'serious' Edwardian theatregoing: Shakespeare represented by *Hamlet, Romeo and Juliet, Richard II*, and *As You Like it* but not *Lear, Measure for Measure, Richard III*, or *All's Well*; the nineteenth century to represent the evolution of comedy including Bulwer Lytton, Robertson, Gilbert, and Wilde; Pinero's *Trelawny of the 'Wells'* and *The Benefit of the Doubt*, Haddon Chambers's *The Tyranny of Tears*, R. C. Carton's *Lady Huntworth's Experiment*, and Jones's *The Liars*, with a taste of Sudermann, Maeterlinck, and Yeats. In other words, a repertoire not dissimilar to the actual plays seen in the records of our theatregoers in the period. Significantly, no Ibsen, no Shaw, and no women. It is little wonder that his obituary read in part: 'His determination not to be wilful or capricious, his desire to avoid inconsistency of judgement, led him sometimes into ... mental stiffness.'[24]

On the surface of it Archer had much in common with J. T. Grein, and indeed Grein held Archer to be the only critic of any consequence. He also shared Archer's belief that the only hope for the drama lay in a form of subsidized theatre whose earnestness would affect acting, criticism, and the creation of a drama which would ennoble the public mind. But unlike Archer, Grein seems to have had little sense of humour. His indefatigible organization of other people, his determination to set English theatre within a European context, alienated him from his critical peers and played into the hands of English insularity. Although he remained as critic for the *Sunday Special* (later *Times*) from 1897 to 1918, his election to the Society was a tribute to his work with the Independent Theatre rather than as an influential critic.

Grein worried like a demented terrier at the bones of the English drama, retrieving a morsel here and there and hoping that eventually he would be able, with the assistance of a few English dramatists, to reconstruct a dramatic creature stitched together with European thread. It was this preconception about what English drama *ought* to be saying that allowed him to welcome English plays insofar as they attempted to emulate continental models and English actors insofar as they were willing to attempt the works of European masters. For these reasons he liked, for instance, Esmond's *Grierson's Way* and Forbes-Robertson for tackling *Pelléas and Mélisande* in his production with Martin-Harvey and Mrs Patrick Campbell.

As a critic Grein shared Archer's missionary zeal. He saw himself not so much as a dramaturg but rather as a teacher-critic sitting in judgement, summing up, pointing out where faults lay and able to suggest remedies. In order to do so a critic needed to be a linguist, intellectually rigorous and completely disinterested. While he thus rejected the comradely fraternization which Sydney Dark enjoyed as well as any interest in performance *per se*, it led him into a curious cul-de-sac. Theatres were there to put on plays which demonstrated European models; those that did not were not doing their bit for the reconstruction of English drama. This principle, as well, determined the functions of both the performer and the critic. About the latter, Grein was intensely pessimistic. To him, critics had all been tarred by the brush of Clement Scott, manifesting favouritism towards actors, cringing servility towards managers and merely paying lip service to new developments while they tolerated the bowdlerizations of Dumas, Augier, and Zola. At the same time Grein, like his critical colleagues, differentiated between form and content: content embraced subject-matter and a vaguely defined concept of 'truth' which tended to be equated with the representation of daily life (in this respect he could compare Haddon Chambers's *Tyranny of Tears* favourably with Ibsen), while form was principally identified with performance. Here he ran into trouble. He was prepared to praise actors who fitted the role but was intolerant of actors who incorporated realistic behaviour. His attitude towards Carton's *Lady Huntworth's Experiment* is illuminating. He found Carton's play to be an interesting experiment in role reversal. However, he was unprepared to accept Dot Boucicault's realistic performance as a drunkard on the grounds that, since the primary object of comedy was to afford a diverting study of manners, such behaviour was merely unrefined and an affront to good taste.

Spence and Grein therefore possessed certain attitudes in common. For Spence the essential conservatism of the theatre was denying it a vocabulary of incident and experience which foreign dramatists enjoyed and which itself was challenging their performers, while Grein was more insistent that it was the duty of the English theatre to emulate these models so that it might be drawn into a European artistic community. Both were struggling to evaluate the proper role of theatre in Edwardian society, but in so striving they found it difficult to come to terms with the difference between 'what' was said or done on stage and 'how'. For instance, how could the stage embrace serious subjects while avoiding a display of viciousness or ugliness? How could one reconcile freedom of expression with an ingrained belief on the part of all the critics that the function of the drama was to be ennobling? The disparity tended to be attributed to the performers. It was they, at least in Archer's and Grein's opinion, who refused to see the theatre as a temple of art at which initiates were invited to worship, with the performers functioning as dedicated acolytes of the Drama.

We can see that Walkley was essentially at odds with all his colleagues on the committee. He would have categorized Archer, Grein, and Spence, with their insistence on logical ordering of ideas, classification, and comparison, and the moral basis on which they evaluated plays as being either frivolous or wholesome, as 'dogmatic'. He would have categorized himself as an 'impressionist', interested in feelings, sceptical about general ideas and external authorities, who allowed the reader a place in the stalls to savour a performance during the white heat of an opening night without the inconvenience of actually attending. Here, however, he was not consistent. But this inconsistency did not arise out of a preconception about the role of theatre as much as a preconception about his own role as an ideal spectator. Walkley desperately wanted to be regarded as authoritative and for criticism to be recognized as an independent art form equivalent to the art of the essayist. It is little wonder therefore that his persona and his criticism signalled his dislike of the herd or indeed any manifestation of organized behaviour. It goes a long way to explain his lack of leadership and enthusiasm as president in the development of a coherent policy for the Society in 1906.

Would a coherent policy have been possible given the conflicting attitudes of its committee? The answer is probably no. Too many questions were being posed, often the correct ones, but which the individuals were incapable of answering. Too many of the committee were caught between the old and the new. The composition of the committee reflected a desire to honour the old warriors and at the same time to give the critic authority. In order to do this, however, the individual members needed to demonstrate a talent for self-abnegation which they did not possess. On the contrary, Walkley, for example, was campaigning to have the very persona of the critic recognized, rejecting the anonymity which newspapers like *The Times* preserved and preferred.

Perhaps the Society would have been better served by some of the notable omissions. W. L. Courtney, drama critic for the *Daily Telegraph*, C. E. Montague of the *Manchester Guardian*, Desmond MacCarthy of the *Speaker*, let alone Max Beerbohm of the *Saturday Review*, were not represented. In fact, the reasons for their absences were partly historical. Although Courtney held the position of chief dramatic critic and literary editor of the *Daily Telegraph* from the middle of the 1890s until 1925, he was a philosopher more interested in literature than the theatre. Moreover, his wife was terminally ill in 1906 and he was never far from her bedside during that year. Courtney's friend Montague remained uncompromisingly Mancunian, so much so that his reputation as a critic did not spread until after the First World War. In any case, he would have been an awkward colleague at odds with most of their declared values: 'to have any critical self of one's own, one must keep off the backs of high horses of all kinds, the high horse of culture, the high horse of moralism, the high horses of critical authority and tradition'.[25] MacCarthy was as yet too young to command much attention. Though he had covered the Barker–Vedrenne seasons for the *Speaker*, he would not come into his own as a theatre critic until he joined the *New Statesman* in 1913. He would, however, have been comfortable with Walkley and Archer, to whose sustained efforts on behalf of the new drama he directly attributed the success of the Court seasons. He would have been less at home with Grein, whom he found truculent and overly propagandist.

It is difficult to imagine Max Beerbohm as a member of any committee, so determined was his strategy to be an ostentatious loner. With tongue only partly in cheek, he gave the impression that he did not take himself seriously at a time when critics were determined that they should be so. Thus Archer and Grein could not forgive him his displays of worldweariness at being called back from the realities of his Italian holidays to the artificialities of the West End stage. He took it upon himself perversely to advocate the cause of Henry Arthur Jones at a time when all his colleagues were looking to Pinero, and criticized Shakespeare's playmaking with Shavian vigour. Nor was he an educator, however much he respected Archer and Spence. At the same time, most criticism he saw functioning as merely the mouthpiece of public opinion and 'the public is the villain of every piece that is produced'.

Even had he been willing to serve on the committee, his presence would have been a difficult one. He would have tended to side with the francophile Walkley, and to dismiss Spence's notion of the critic as dramaturg on the grounds of the essential selfishness and myopia of the actor-managers. Perhaps coloured by his own family connection with Tree, he had made a point of denigrating those performers who relied on their personality and fashionable cleverness, let alone those who took themselves seriously. Beerbohm was outraged at the effrontery of Wilson Barrett presuming to give a curtain speech as King Alfred after the last night of *The Christian King* in which he said that 'the colonies – especially South Africa – were knitting themselves by ever closer bonds to the Mother Country'. He was shrewd enough to see that Edwardian acting was itself at the crossroads. Increasingly he saw instances of plays in which performance styles clashed, which made it impossible to hide the artificialities of the plays themselves.[26] Thus, for example, when Charles Hawtrey and Arthur Williams played opposite each other, spectators were confronted by 'mimes' (his favourite word) who were performing essentially in different plays: Hawtrey who relied entirely on maintaining a sly complicity with his audience and Williams who was intent on sublimating his persona in the character.

In the light of all this, it is hardly surprising that the Society of Dramatic Critics with its resounding statement of intent simply failed to get off the ground. Some of this may be attributed to the inaction of Moy Thomas as secretary and Walkley as president. Mostly, however, it was the indigestible mix of personalities and the fact that a sense of calling or the notion of a commonly accepted craft were new concepts on which few could agree. The formation of the Society, however, did focus attention on the need to answer some fundamental questions which had not been addressed in the Victorian period. Of particular importance was the need to evaluate the role of the critic especially in relation to the new drama and the new audience; how a critic should respond to a new acting style which the new drama required; whether the critic should be an insider or an outsider in relation to the theatrical process; and how the traditional impressionist language of criticism might come to terms with the influx of Russian ballet dancers, Sicilian players, and Japanese acting companies in the period.

When in 1914 the *Stage Year Book* announced the formation of the Critics' Circle, significantly it did not include a statement of objectives. There were some changes in personnel. Since 1906, Moy Thomas had died, Beerbohm had retired, Fyfe had concentrated on being a political journalist, Anthony Ellis had become a theatre manager, Dark had become a novelist and William Archer was on extended overseas trips. Alfred Robbins was now president of the Institute of Journalists and it was he, together with Morrison, who proposed that the new organization be officially connected to the Institute. Indeed it became formally the Critics' Circle of the Institute of Journalists. Archer was elected as a presidential figurehead. Its executive committee included Northcott, who was the archivist of Covent Garden and wrote extensively about opera and singers and, as a practising organist and choirmaster, also wrote music criticism for the *Daily Chronicle*. He was, moreover, a fully paid up fellow of the Institute of Journalists and a nominee of the extremely energetic secretary S. R. Littlewood. Littlewood had been an early member of the Institute and was principal drama critic for the *Daily Chronicle*. He would remain as the Circle's secretary until 1922, becoming its president in 1923. In 1920 he would also be the chairman of the Institute.

In 1939 Littlewood wrote one of the first histories of English dramatic criticism.[27] In his chapter entitled 'The Profession of Criticism' he offers an evaluation of critics he admired as pioneers. His perspective, however, is that of a practising journalist and his admiration of Walkley, Shaw, Archer, and Grein is coloured by the extent to which they contributed to elevating the position of the journalistic profession. Surprisingly, perhaps, he gives no credit to Leigh Hunt, Hazlitt, or Lewes. He tries to rehabilitate Clement Scott on the grounds that his lyrical enthusiasm about performers did wonders for the box office. His advice to would-be critics is down to earth: the critic needs to convey what the play is about, whether or not it is worth seeing, the nature of its production and who appeared in it and in what characters. It was this hard-nosed approach to criticism that characterized the new Critics' Circle while the significance of the new organization was, of course, its formal affiliation with journalism. With the possible exceptions of Archer and Grein, its committee all regarded themselves as professional journalists, which gave substance to the ideas of a calling and a craft. It also sounded the deathknell of the amateur critic. From now on the game of criticism would be conducted by professional 'players', relegating the amateur 'gentlemen' to the pavilions.

∟ NOTES

1 *The Stage Year Book* (London, 1914), p. 140. The subsequent history of the Society is unclear, although it was intended to be run on formal lines as the publication of its draft rules demonstrates (*Suggested Rules to be Submitted at a General Meeting, January 4th, 1907* [London]: For the Society). The Critics' Circle continues to the present day and meets regularly. Grein, Spence, Morrison, Seamen and Walkley from the original Society were each to serve consecutively as presidents of the Circle in the period from 1914 to 1922.
2 *Who's Who in the Theatre*, ed. John Parker, 11th edn (London, 1952), p. 1805.
3 J. C. Trewin, *The Edwardian Theatre* (Oxford, 1976), pp. 7–19.
4 H. M. Walbrook, *Nights at the Play* (London, 1911).
5 See their articles in *Victorian Periodicals Review*, Spring–Summer 1980, Winter 1984 and Fall 1986.
6 C. F. G. Masterman, *In Peril of Change: Essays written in Time of Tranquillity* (London, 1905), p. xii.
7 H. Granville Barker in the preface to L. Housman, *Little Plays of St. Francis*

(London, 1922), quoted by A. Nicoll, *English Drama 1900–1930* (Cambridge, 1975), p. 12.

8 Arthur Lawrence, 'Journalism as a Profession', in *Start in Life*, ed. J. E. H. Williams (London, 1903).

9 His appreciation of the Edwardian theatre is documented in his autobiography, *Not Such a Bad Life* (London, 1941).

10 E. F. S., *Our Stage and Its Critics* (London, 1910).

11 In *The Christian King*, Adelphi, 1902, and Osbourne and Strong, *The Exile*, Royalty, 1903.

12 Both by Grant Richards in 1899.

13 From 'William Archer and A. B. Walkley', *Saturday Review*, 18 November 1899, quoted in *Around Theatres* (London, 1953), p. 42.

14 H. Child, 'Arthur Bingham Walkley', *The Post Victorians* (London, 1933). Walkley's three lectures respectively titled 'The Ideal Spectator', 'The Dramatic Critic', and 'Old and New Criticism' were collected under the title *Dramatic Criticism* and published by John Murray in 1903.

15 *Dramatic Criticism* (London, 1903), p. 63.

16 This must have been particularly galling to both Granville Barker and Archer, who had published their *A National Theatre: Scheme and Estimates* privately in 1904 and were to make it a public document in 1907.

17 Question 3594, Minutes of Evidence, *Report of the Joint Select Committee on Stage Plays (Censorship)*, 20 August 1909, p. 199.

18 *Dramatic Criticism*, p. 51.

19 Ibid., p. 62.

20 Ibid., p. 122.

21 William Archer to W. S. Gilbert in *Real Conversations* (London, 1904).

22 William Archer quoted in Charles Archer, *William Archer: Life, Work and Friendships* (New Haven, 1931), p. 406.

23 William Archer and Harley Granville Barker, *A National Theatre: Scheme and Estimates* (London, 1907), p. xvii.

24 Obituary, *The Times*, 29 December 1924, p. 12.

25 *Dramatic Values* (New York, 1925), p. 273.

26 For example, in his review of Arliss's *There and Back*, May 1902.

27 S. R. Littlewood, *Dramatic Criticism* (London, 1939).

CHAPTER 8

Suffrage critics and political action: a feminist agenda

Sheila Stowell

On 20 March 1914 *The Suffragette*, the radical newspaper of the Pankhursts' Women's Social and Political Union, published on its front page a particularly striking political cartoon (see plate 11). The creation of staff artist Herbert Cole, it depicts the interior of a theatre during what is apparently an unsettling performance. On-stage we find a tableau incorporating a bound and downcast representation of Justice. Her scales lie fallen on the floor before her. On the other side of a curtained proscenium are pictured an unruly crowd of fist-shaking working men and baton-wielding police.[1] Interposing herself between Justice and her opponents is an intermediary figure best described as an emblem of clear-thinking, critical-minded Womanhood. Alluding to the stage spectacle behind her, this figure, in flowing gown and laurel wreath, holds a petition of grievances. Her gaze, calm and far-sighted, pushes past the performance's protesting crowd to engage immediately and directly with the newspaper's readers. It is, all in all, an effective piece of iconographic shorthand that nicely encapsulates suffrage attitudes towards the theatre as a place of significant political activity. I have chosen it as a way of calling attention to two different but related ways in which Edwardian feminists used the stage to articulate their cause. Elsewhere I have discussed the phenomena of suffrage drama and street spectacle.[2] Here I would like to look at both the mediating figure of the suffrage theatre critic and the manner in which by 1914 commercial playhouses had themselves become sites for a new kind of suffrage performance.

First, however, we must consider the auspices under which suffrage theatre criticism was written. There were, during the Edwardian era, four major suffrage newspapers, each the official organ of an influential suffrage society. First to appear was *Votes for Women*, the newspaper of the militant Women's Social and Political Union. Under the joint editorship of Emmeline and Frederick Pethick-

11 An Allegory. Cartoon by Herbert Cole. (*Suffragette* 20 March 1914)

Lawrence, it began publication in 1907, ceasing with the granting of limited suffrage in 1918. 'The pioneer of popular journalistic style in the suffrage press ... it introduced newspaper format (though not dimensions), lead cartoons, banner headlines, [and] "actuality" photographs.'[3] When the Pethick-Lawrences left the WSPU in the autumn of 1912 following disputes with Christabel and Emmeline Pankhurst over the escalating use of guerilla tactics – the Pethick-Lawrences were against it – they took *Votes for Women* with them. It remained an independent paper until January 1914 when it became the official organ of the Pethick-Lawrences' newly founded United Suffragists, a more centrist organization composed for the most part of disgruntled ex-WSPU members. The WSPU itself replaced *Votes for Women* with the *Suffragette* which became, in turn, the voice of the movement's most violent and militant wing. Edited by Christabel Pankhurst from exile in Paris (a warrant was out for her arrest in Britain), the paper endured a number of government efforts to censor and suppress it.[4] As David Doughan has observed, it 'had the air of a barely-tolerated paper on the border of legality'.[5] It ceased publication as a suffrage newspaper in August 1914.

The *Vote* was the official organ of the Women's Freedom League, the other major militant (but non-violent) organization that dominated the suffrage campaign during the Edwardian period. Formed in 1907 under the leadership of Charlotte Despard as a democratically organized alternative to the WSPU, the WFL began to publish its own paper in 1909 and continued until 1933. As its title suggests, the paper's original editors (playwright/actor Cicely Hamilton and writer Marion Holmes) considered the right to vote to occupy 'the first place in the interests' of the paper with suffrage topics receiving 'special attention'. The general aim of the *Vote* was to 'fill in the gaps left on the one hand by the so-called "women's papers", and on the other by the daily newspapers', the resulting product designed to appeal 'primarily to the increasing class of educated women who have intellectual, industrial, or public interests'.[6] Despite their relatively high profiles, however, both the WSPU and WFL were later arrivals on to a battle-ground already occupied by the constitutionalist and law-abiding National Union of Women's Suffrage Societies. The largest of the major suffrage organizations, the NUWSS was formed in 1897 under the leadership of Millicent Garrett Fawcett as an amalgam of sixteen pre-existing societies. Its paper, the *Common Cause*, first appeared out of Manchester in 1909, some two years after the first issue of *Votes for Women*. 'Covering a wide range of feminist topics as well as suffrage',[7] it moved its offices to London in 1911 (in the process significantly broadening the range of theatrical events reviewed) where it continued to publish until 1920. Its editors included social activists Helena Swanwick, Clementina Black, and Maude Royden.

Each of the above newspapers allotted space to regular, if intermittent theatre criticism, sometimes written by figures prominent in their respective societies. Emmeline Pethick-Lawrence, for example, and Emily Wilding Davison, the first woman to die for the women's suffrage cause,[8] contributed reviews to *Votes for Women*, as did Christabel Pankhurst for the *Suffragette* and Charlotte Despard for the *Vote*. Yet the most striking feature of such criticism – apart from the fact of its being written mostly by women at a time when, as Victor Emeljanow points out elsewhere in this volume, the Society of Dramatic Critics (1906) and later Critics' Circle (1913) were male clubs – is that in spite of important organizational, tactical, and political differences between the societies themselves, the attitudes expressed in suffrage theatre columns stake out a markedly common ground. Although generally, aside from securing the vote, there was 'no necessary agreement between suffrage societies, either about the strategies through which that goal was best pursued or on the benefits that it would bring'[9] at least as far as theatre criticism was concerned, the choice of plays and productions reviewed and the kinds of comments afforded are strikingly similar. Across a spectrum delineated by the extremist *Suffragette* on the one hand and the gradualist *Common Cause* on the other, the theatre was seen to offer a platform for powerful dissent, a literal stage for the criticism of current orthodoxies, and a highly visible venue for participants to display either conversion to or reaffirmation of the suffrage cause. Like the Lord Chamberlain's office, with which they found themselves in frequent opposition, suffrage theatre critics recognized in the theatre a force that could be manipulated for a variety of ends although, unlike the Examiner of Plays with his apparent desire to maintain the status quo, they sought to secure that power to promote their own brand of political change. Such were the 'burdens', to borrow a term from Kenneth Burke, that suffrage theatre critics carried with them to the playhouse.

Accordingly, each paper endorsed a process of selection that singled out for review 'progressive' rather than 'commercial' stage pieces, most such works interpreted as arguing either directly or indirectly (how indirectly can usually be measured by the level of rhetorical gymnastics required of the reviewer) the suffrage cause. Not surprisingly regular reviews were accorded the overtly partisan productions of the Actresses' Franchise League, the Women Writers' Suffrage League and Edith Craig's Pioneer Players, the last an organization dedicated to 'playing propaganda plays, chiefly those dealing with the Women's Movement'.[10] Also reviewed were stagings of plays by politically committed women dramatists like Cicely Hamilton and Christopher St John, including St John's translation and adapation of *Paphnutius*, a moral comedy by the tenth-century nun Hroswitha of Gandersheim. Hroswitha, herself celebrated in press notices as 'almost of more interest than her play',[11] was heralded as another 'feminist' playwright,[12] one who provided suffrage reviewers with an opportunity for historical repositioning. Standing shoulder to shoulder with Hroswitha, they saw themselves as the future of a feminist past that provided 'the only connecting link between the Latin theatre and the rise of liturgical drama'[13] and answered, like Cicely Hamilton's *Pageant of Great Women*, the tired anti-suffragist argument that women had produced no figures of cultural or historical significance. In fact, St John herself was allowed to urge, in a pre-production puff published in *Votes for Women*, that readers' interest must needs 'be roused by the production of a play written by a woman, translated by a woman, produced by a woman, and adorned with melodies of the best period of plainsong, which we should never have been able to obtain ... but for the industry and talent of a woman!'[14]

In fact, suffrage reviewers generally gave prominence to women's work in the theatre. The Women's Theatre Week of December 1913, for example, organized by Actresses' Franchise League play department secretary, Inez Bensusan, with the hope of creating a permanent co-operative enterprise run by women, received extensive coverage. So too did plays produced by women managers like Gertrude Kingston, Lillah McCarthy, Lena Ashwell, and Annie Horniman, all committed suffrage supporters, the meaning and credibility of the works they staged explained in terms of their producers' political allegiance. Selected productions by more broadly based alternative theatre organizations such as the Play Actors and the Authors' Producing Society were also noticed. In the case of these latter groups, however, it was invariably the subject-matter of a play that determined whether or not it was reviewed. The Play Actors' production of Bjornson's *The Gauntlet* and the Authors' Producing Society's production of Brieux's *Damaged Goods*, for example, both dealing with the sexual double standard and both banned by the Lord Chamberlain's office, were covered in each of the above papers. *Damaged Goods*, concerning the passing from a husband to an ignorant wife of a sexually transmitted disease, was reviewed by the *Common Cause* because it was, in the words of its reviewer, A.S., 'not an entertainment' but 'a sermon and a warning' that provided dramatic justification for feminists' decision to go 'forth to slay this dragon of prudery and hypocrisy which stalks in our midst, devouring the innocents, and proclaiming shamelessly that it must be let alone, as it is too hideous for respectable people to talk about'.[15] The same play was also commented upon by Christabel Pankhurst in the *Suffragette* because it provided her with an obvious opportunity both to elaborate upon her highly sensational campaign for 'Votes for Women and Chastity for Men'[16] and to reiterate a common suffrage feminist theme that while Brieux should be praised for his courage in writing the piece, 'A woman's play ... would have been stronger still.' 'A woman playwright', Pankhurst argues, 'would have condemned without compromise, the medical secrecy according to which a woman is refused the knowledge that she is engaged or is actually married to, a man who is diseased.'[17] The reviewer for the *Vote* took the occasion yet again to attack the office of the Lord Chamberlain, maintaining that the fact that Brieux's play had been banned was 'the strongest argument we have yet had for the relegation of the Censor and his office to a museum of useless antiquities'.[18]

At the same time that they registered their commitment to a radical, determinedly non-commercial theatre that could be seen to argue the virtue of their cause, suffrage critics formed a united front against musical comedy and what Peter Bailey has called its 'rhetoric of the girl', battling here as elsewhere what they understood to be the compulsory sexualization of women in thrall to male viciousness, a servitude linked to an enforced ignorance of the virulent consequences of trade in sex. Feminists were not slow to point out the connivance between government agencies and the purveyors of musical comedy in the continuance of this practice. Indeed, K.D.S. in *Votes for Women* complained that while Brieux's 'fine piece of moral enlightenment must be played in private', musical comedies of 'coarse suggestiveness' are 'permitted everywhere'.[19] *The Suffragette* similarly used a 'private' revival of *Ghosts* by the New Constitutional Society for Women's

Suffrage to observe that while Ibsen's play is 'withheld from the public in this country, the most low-toned musical comedies and offensive revues are not only tolerated but receive official sanction and authority to do what they can to create that same "heedlessness" of which Oswald Alving speaks, and to surround vice with all the glamour of the most sensuous appeal'.[20] Suffrage theatre critics seconded the widespread efforts of suffrage members to embrace a womanliness which, while often marked by an outward adherence to the tenets of fashionable dress, was emptied of sexual connotation.[21] They shared Inez Bensusan's aim, expressed in an interview with the *Common Cause* in regard to her Woman's Theatre Enterprise, to reject the 'sex standard of physical attraction so often set up by a male management', and 'to give woman her proper chance in dramatic art, both as professional artist and as typical specimen of her sex'. Objecting 'to that style of piece . . . which makes cynical capital out of the sexual escapades of frivolous males and their smartness in deceiving the women to whom they are married, or engaged to be married, as to their true character' Bensusan voiced a desire, often reiterated by suffrage critics, for a drama that would not 'divorce itself from a serious consideration of life and human interests' but that would 'set up a high artistic standard, and stick to it'.[22]

To this end, suffrage theatre reviewers also attended performances of work by such 'progressive' playwrights and male suffrage sympathizers as Bernard Shaw, Harley Granville Barker, John Galsworthy, and Laurence Housman. Their reviews, while often favourable, were not however marked by slavish praise. Thus we find the *Common Cause* attacking Galsworthy's *Strife* for its unrepresentative depiction of striking miners' wives, a view it reiterated in a subsequent number: 'it does seem hard that all the women [in the play] should have been of the sort that men of action can only regard as a clog and a hindrance'.[23] The *Common Cause* also faulted Granville Barker's *Voysey Inheritance* for its halting action and insufficient motivation, although it rushed to the defence of the same playwright's *Madras House*. Condemned by the popular press as a 'Polygamy for the People Play'[24] the *Common Cause* embraced the work, insisting that 'all friends of women owe Mr. Barker their most grateful thanks' for exposing 'the conspiracy of society against a woman's self-development and self-expression'.[25] Nor was Bernard Shaw universally praised. *Press Cuttings* for instance, a one-act comedy about male conscription and female enfranchisement among other things, was accused of being rather too subtle 'in so far as it referred to the liberation movement'.[26] On the occasion of the play's revival by Annie Horniman in Manchester in November 1909, the *Common Cause* also questioned its tone given the current political climate: 'This week some of us laughed with a rather wry mouth at Mr Shaw's quips... When one remembers that women are at the present moment being tortured in prison by a Government whose only remedy for disorder is repression, one can scarcely laugh very heartily at "Shoot em down!" or if the laugh is loud, it is bitter too. The rapid rate of reprisals between the Government and the Militants has so increased that the skit is not far enough removed from actuality to allow of its being enjoyed as mere skit.'[27]

Suffrage reviewers were also willing to criticize work – usually but not invariably in terms of its effectiveness as propaganda – by allied associations like the Actresses' Franchise League, the Pioneer Players and the Woman's Theatre Enterprise. E.H.M, reviewing AFL productions of Harold Rubenstein's *Her Wild Oats* and John Kidd's *Restitution*, observed that 'all the plays which have been written with the idea of converting the waverer or the apathetic are not in the least likely to do so, and Mr Rubenstein's *Wild Oats* is no exception'. *Restitution* is dismissed as 'a piece of sickly sentimentality'.[28] *Votes for Women* condemned both Hugh de Selincourt's *Beastie* as a sentimental episode that 'failed signally' to set the audience thinking and the play's production by the Pioneer Players as 'unconvincing'. Edith Lyttelton's *Thumbscrew*, produced on the same bill, was criticized for its 'interminable conversations' and the actors taken to task for failing to do 'much justice' to the work.[29] Nor did the Woman's Theatre Enterprise escape unscathed. Henry Nevinson, one of the few male reviewers writing for the suffrage press, objected to the company's choice of Brieux's *Woman on Her Own* (in a translation by Charlotte Shaw), criticizing the play for its 'sense of hindrance and defeat' and the extent to which it is overly determined by 'the old masculine conception of "woman's sphere"'.[30] It was a view shared by A.D.A. in the *Suffragette*, who also took the occasion to express yet again the long-felt want to see a woman 'write a play showing the real spirit of the Suffragette. It has never been done yet, and I do not believe that a male dramatist will ever do it.'[31]

Overall, suffrage theatre critics understood their job to be the interpretation of plays and productions from a specifically suffrage point of view. As Nevinson comments in his *Votes for Women* review of

Shaw's *Androcles and the Lion*, 'writing for you, I dwell on the suffragette interest, strong throughout'. While he goes on to note that 'there are other sides',[32] in deference to the perceived interests of his readership he does not pursue them. Agnes Evans makes the same point in *Common Cause*. Discussing a reading of Laurence Housman's censored *Pains and Penalties*, she concludes that 'I have touched only on the "Common Cause" aspect of the play: there is much else in it.'[33] Uppermost in every reviewer's mind was a suffrage agenda, broad enough to encompass a great deal more than the granting of female enfranchisement. Included were such issues as women's work opportunities, their economic deprivation and the sexual double standard, the amendment of existing penal, labour, and marital legislation, as well as more narrowly theatrical matters (with cultural resonances of course) like the numbers and kinds of roles for women. Suffrage theatre critics understood their role and that of the theatre to be pedagogical. Like avant-gardists more generally, they knew what the public should be seeing even while old-fashioned 'playwrights keep on showing it what it ought to be tired of seeing'. They demanded to see themselves and the possibility of a new age, and complained that

it is strange to go out of the world, where women are fighting for freedom and showing unparalleled courage when most despised and rejected, into the theatre, where the dramatist appears unaffected by this new Renaissance. Strange, indeed, it is, too, that Cordelia in 'King Lear' at the Haymarket seems more modern, more of the stuff of which Winson Green prisoners are made, than any heroine imagined by Pinero or Maugham.[34]

Of course, a work's very lack of modernity could be a stick with which to beat the suffrage drum, and occasionally a West End play like Arthur Wing Pinero's *Mid-Channel* (St James's) could be pressed into service, not on the basis of any intrinsic merit but because a tale of a woman's wasted life and suicide seemed 'to constitute one of the greatest arguments in favour of woman's suffrage . . . ever seen on the stage'.[35] Shakespeare's plays, by contrast, were hauled into the service of this twentieth-century cause whenever a case could be made for them as the work of what Granville Barker called 'a still living playwright'. In such circumstances suffrage critics had an answer for Stephen Hawking's rhetorical question, 'Why do we remember the past but not the future?' They maintained that certain of Shakespeare's plays did just that – offered them the memory of their future. Or to put it in 'modernist' terms, they accepted Shakespeare's work when they could interpret its pastness as imitating their present.

This did not, however, signal a wholesale rush in the name of the cause to any and all Shakespeare productions. The fact of a work by Shakespeare on stage did not in and of itself guarantee its modernity, its relevance to feminists. There had to be an additional link to the suffrage cause. The circumstances of a production had in some way to demonstrate an acceptable political bias. It should not be surprising to learn then that in suffrage publications that gave prominence to women's work in the theatre, the first Shakespeare play to be reviewed was Annie Horniman's 1910 Gaiety (Manchester) production of *Much Ado About Nothing*. The meaning and credibility of the work were significantly explained for the theatre critic in terms of its producer's political allegiance. Although praising at the outset the 'finish and interplay that a company only acquires by long practice together', the *Common Cause* reviewer, like critics more generally, focussed upon the tragic cast of Mona Limerick's Beatrice. Her interpretation was able to realize, the paper concluded, 'a great thing of a great scene. She was a tragic Beatrice, a mirthless and a somewhat bitter Beatrice, but she caught one by the throat with her sob, "I am sorry for my cousin."'[36] The reviewer identifies here as the high point of the play a scene that embraced, in the face of male betrayal, the sisterly solidarity that was the mainstay of the suffrage movement, a solidarity that extended to Beatrice and what the *Common Cause* recognized as her 'generosity and greatness of heart which scorn the mere protestations of a lover when there is work to do in righting a wrong'.[37] Such comments were meant to be read analogously – what was true of the circumstances of the play was to be seen to be true of the feminist struggle. For the critic of *Much Ado About Nothing* and her readers, Beatrice was a suffragist, engaged as they were in righting wrongs done by men.

The most formidable heroine in Shakespeare's canon, or at least the one who came to personify the qualities of courage and critical intelligence in the face of state-sponsored injustice was, however, not Beatrice but Paulina in *The Winter's Tale*. Indeed, it was largely the opportunity to raise this comprimario role to star status that seems to have prompted much of the attention suffrage critics gave to Granville Barker's 1912 production of the play. Much has been written about this production in the last decade, most of it stressing the theatrical innovations which rendered the performance, in

Dennis Kennedy's words, 'one of the four or five most important Shakespearian productions of this century'.[38] Although not a financial success – evening performances ceased after six weeks – its visual strangeness assured it a place of notoriety among critics who argued vociferously about its innovative minimalism. Yet despite compelling links that might have been drawn between aesthetic and feminist challenges to Victorian orthodoxies, the suffrage press was not particularly interested in what critic A. B. Walkley had termed the production's 'assault upon conventionalism'. The two papers that contain reviews, *Votes for Women* and the *Suffragette*, both representing the most radical wing of the suffrage movement, were more concerned with political issues debated in the play, especially those raised through the figures of Hermione and Paulina. Indeed, the victimization of Hermione at the hands of a tyranical patriarchy together with Paulina's vocal defence developed themes that had already directed suffrage attention to *Much Ado About Nothing*. Here, however, Shakespeare set his action in both a juridical and theatrical framework, not unlike the staged relationship of (female) social critic and (female) victim depicted in the Cole cartoon described at the beginning of this essay.

This is not to say that the production's innovations were passed over in silence. In fact, the *Suffragette* columnist announced at the outset that she went prepared to dislike it because 'that irritating army whose one idea in life is to advance, no matter where, all thought fit to rave about' it.[39] But she accepts the look, as it were, because it confirms Shakespeare's prescient modernity, visually underscoring his representation of a 'new world' 'fraught with meaning to the twentieth century universe as though Shakespeare had written it from an Adelphi flat'.[40] In the opinion of the *Suffragette* the value of the production lay in its revelation that 'the real heroine ... should be a militant Suffragette', feminism's harbinger and heroine located in the character of

the dauntless, potent, unflinching Paulina – the eternal Suffragette whom all the greatest geniuses of all ages have loved to portray. Paulina, penetrating to forbidden chambers and telling tyrants to their faces of the wronged woman and the helpless child; Paulina turning full on the unjust king the flood of her fierce eloquence, while his attendants fawn and cower for fear of his insane wrath ... The real heroine of 'The Winter's Tale' is the woman who makes things happen – the militant Paulina, just as the real heroines of the twentieth century are the women who make things happen – the militant Suffragettes.[41]

A deliberately perverse reading, we might conclude, of a production Kennedy understandably describes as 'notably apolitical',[42] revealing to us 'not a real world but a world of art'.[43] But suffragettes were bent upon political reality *and* the production of a real new world, and they looked for its confirmation in art.

So for the reviewer for *Votes for Women*, likewise, the meaning of *The Winter's Tale* resided in its immediate political relevance, so much so that she admits that 'the rest of the play did not interest me so much'. Her engagement with the piece rested with what she tongue-in-cheek called the 'modern interpolations' of 'the whole character of Paulina ... [which] could have been written in after 1905, by someone who had just come in contact with the militant Suffrage movement' and which would be 'the most interesting portion of the play to militant Suffragists'.[44] She retitles the play 'The Conspiracy Trial of Hermione' and goes on to describe at length those features of the piece that confirmed suffragettes' sense of their own reality. Accordingly, Lillah McCarthy's Hermione awaits her trial 'like any member of the WSPU'. 'While on remand', the reviewer continues, she

is visited in prison by that delightful Suffragette of the play, Paulina ... whose militant spirit has been well rendered by Miss Esme Beringer. Waiting in the ante-room to see the Governor, and filled, as so many of us have been at the gates of Holloway since 1905, with a sense of the irony of such imprisonments, she exclaims: 'Good lady, / No court in Europe is too good for thee, / What does thou then in prison?[45]

The *Votes for Women* columnist draws extended parallels between the circumstances of the play and the real political struggles of suffragettes; Shakespeare's language was understood as an ally's retort to the crimes of a modern Liberal government and its various representatives, Prime Minister, Home Secretary and members of the Cabinet. For her and her readers *The Winter's Tale* is animated by the suffrage struggle, its art and artifice brought to present life via their actual experience.

While the law-abiding theatre enthusiasts of the National Union of Women's Suffrage Societies remained content to voice their political agenda through columns of drama criticism – as well as, of course, through plays by colleagues in the Actresses' Franchise League and Women Writers' Suffrage League – the more militant membership of the WSPU chose to second such commentary with direct public action in which the commercial theatre, a forum with an audience already assembled, was itself appropriated as a platform for extra-legal resistance. Accordingly, entire theatres became the locus for suffrage performances, which, in the eyes of WSPU members, were both alternative forms of theatre criticism and a new kind of critical theatre organized to run in tandem with scheduled events. A blatant example of such radical theatre, propounded by a predominantly middle-class organization that reviled both the present state of the theatre and its audience, was reported in the 29 May 1914 issue of *The Suffragette* under the head-line 'Militant Events of the Week'. Smaller headings reminiscent of Victorian playbills reporting 'Suffragettes at the Royal Matinee', 'Scenes that Will Live in History', and 'A Woman Speaks from the Stage', preceded an account of the 'impressive protest' that unfolded at His Majesty's Theatre before King George V attending a benefit matinée revival of Henry Arthur Jones's vastly popular melodrama, *The Silver King* (see plate 12). 'It must be confessed', the *Evening Standard* observed, 'that the interest of the opening stages of the piece played a very subordinate part to the wilder spectacle in the auditorium. Ladies were perturbed, and men were not in the calm state of mind which a theatrical entertainment demands for full enjoyment.'[46] Indeed, the *Suffragette* elaborated, using the language of theatrical representation to express the reality of their protest, 'the dramatic thrills of the play were as nothing compared to those roused by the living drama enacted before the eyes of that vast audience'. 'The first scene' or 'prelude' – the terms are those of the *Suffragette* – occurred outside the theatre when a protester tried to present the King with a petition. This was followed, hard upon the rising of the curtain, by the sound of a woman's voice, 'clear, strong and vibrating', raised in protest, over the voices of the actors. Then, the account continues,

the storm broke. Plainclothes men flung themselves upon the woman, excited policemen hurried in from the corridors to their assistance, and she was dragged from her seat in the stalls and thrown roughly into the street, where she was arrested. Scarcely had she been removed when another woman arose and addressed His Majesty... The attempt to eject her was frustrated by the fact that she had securely padlocked herself to the stall. A burly ruffian in plainclothes immediately put his hand roughly over her mouth, while another held her down in her seat. Meanwhile a woman had climbed on the stage across the footlights. Probably no more moving and dramatic scene has ever been witnessed on the stage, as, with arms outstretched

– in, I should stress, yet another theatrical realization of Cole's front-page cartoon which had preceded the event by two months –

12 Lèse-Majeste at His Majesty's Theatre: The Mad Militants' Demonstration at Last Week's Royal Matinee. May 1914

she proceeded to address His Majesty in passionate terms of protest. 'Your
Majesty,' she began, 'why do you permit this torture of women fighting for
their rights?' At this point stage hands rushing from the wings seized her and
carried her off... Again and again through the performance, from different
parts of the house, came the cry – 'Release Mrs Pankhurst', and just before
the falling of the curtain on the first act, a shower of leaflets descended upon
the audience from the higher parts of the theatre.[47]

Although more spectacular than others, this was not an isolated or
accidental event. Particularly as the 'Woman's War' intensified into
what the *Evening Standard* characterized as 'general warfare against
the public [against which] the public demand protection',[48] such
disruptive performances became increasingly common. On the
occasion of a staging of Arnold Bennett's *The Great Adventure* at the
Lyceum Theatre, Ipswich, in February 1914, a suffragette dropped a
banner from the gallery protesting against the forcible feeding of
suffrage prisoners. Her action was accompanied by a shower of
leaflets. Again in June 1914, His Majesty's Theatre, Daly's, the New
Theatre, Globe, Duke of York's, Kingsway, Comedy, Queen's, St
James's and the Coliseum, among others, were made the scenes of
suffrage spectacle. 'In several cases', it was reported, 'the play itself
was interrupted for several minutes, and the actors were obliged to
pause until the [protesting] speakers had been ejected, and the tumult
in the audience had shown signs of dying down.'[49] The Comedy
Theatre experienced a similar display on 17 June 1914, when a
special matinée for the clergy was interrupted by a woman who stood
up to remind the 'Gentlemen [that] while you are enjoying yourselves
here, women are being tortured in prison for fighting for their
principles.'[50] The inevitable chaos followed: a shower of leaflets and
the ejection of the interrupter. Nor were individual audience
members in theatre foyers safe from such impromptu performances.
In a letter to the *Suffragette*, Lall Forsyth records how following the
production of a Galsworthy play at the Kingsway Theatre – the
'playground of the Suffrage cause' – she accosted Winston Churchill
and his party in the central hall to demand 'Votes for Women'.
Although he did not speak, according to Forsyth he 'looked as though
he thought there were 500 suffragettes floating round, waiting to
attack him. Then his mother came to his rescue. She caught hold of
me, clenched her teeth, and tried to pinch my arm. I said to her that
evidently Mr Churchill required the protection of women.'[51]

Amidst such flurries of forcible ejections, harangues from the stalls, stages and foyers, and confiscated showers of suffrage literature, we can catch a glimpse of the type of mutually profitable accommodation the suffragettes were attempting to realize – much as they had used their power as consumers to reach a mutually exploitative stand-off with department store merchants.[52] At the Theatre Royal, Preston, one enterprising manager, upon hearing of an impending suffrage disruption, opted to include the event as part of the evening's bill, displaying a calculated capitulation to suffrage theatregoers' campaigns to reform the stage. A section of seats was reserved for the protestors, and an explanation read from the stage informing playgoers of the circumstances of the demonstration. The *Suffragette* observed after the event that 'the announcement was received with all goodwill by the audience, who listened with close interest to the eloquent speech delivered to them from the dress circle'.[53] Here surely is an early manifestation of the zealous efforts of much twentieth-century 'progressive' theatre to break down what it characterized as artificial boundaries between performance and audience. Yet, when as a result of acting up suffragettes succeeded in over-running such barriers, they did not strive to provoke audiences to further acts of disruption. Instead, they praised what others would go on to condemn as bourgeois good manners. Given the chance, suffragettes wanted to be heard in order to convert; to this end they moved beyond reviews of representations of protest to the thing itself, performed. Oscar Wilde, who in the eyes of early feminists betrayed his promise as a playwright of the future, once quipped that 'the object of living was to become a work of art'. Edwardian feminists might have countered that 'the object of criticism was to bring art to life'.

NOTES

1 The juxtaposition, suggesting the collusion of labour and law enforcement, confirms pictorially the WSPU's increasing disenchantment with the Labour Party. Originally (along with her husband, Dr Richard Pankhurst) a supporter of the Liberals, Emmeline Pankhurst, who founded the WSPU in 1903 in Manchester, moved to the Independent Labour Party in 1894 following the Liberals' exclusion of women from the third Reform Act of 1884. The WSPU's break with the Labour Party began after its move to London in 1906 and its decision to embrace militancy. The law-abiding National Union of Women's Suffrage Societies, on the other hand, although a non-party organization, had always had strong ties to the Liberal Party. These ties were broken when Liberals failed in

any significant numbers to support the Conciliation Bill of 1911 which offered limited suffrage for women. At that time the NUWSS executive opted to cast its support behind the Labour Party, establishing an Election Fighting Fund that would raise money to fund Labour candidates standing against Liberal anti-suffragists.

2 See for instance *A Stage of Their Own: Feminist Theatre of the Suffrage Era* (Manchester, 1992; paperback, Michigan, 1994) and with Joel Kaplan, *Theatre and Fashion: Oscar Wilde to the Suffragettes* (Cambridge, 1994).

3 David Doughan and Denise Sanchez, *Feminist Periodicals 1855–1944: An Annotated Critical Bibliography* (Brighton, 1987), p. 25.

4 The government tried to stop publication of the *Suffragette* in the spring of 1913 by issuing writs against its printer, the Victoria House Press, and members of the editorial board for conspiring maliciously to damage property. The manager of the Victoria House Press was released on an undertaking to cease printing the paper; the others charged were subsequently found guilty and received sentences of from 6 to 21 months. The offices of the *Suffragette* were then subject to a number of police raids, forcing the paper to relocate on a number of occasions. By July 1914 efforts were taken to prevent further distribution of the paper by threatening to charge anyone publishing or distributing it.

5 Doughan, *Feminist Periodicals*, p. 34.

6 *Vote*, 8 September 1909.

7 Doughan, *Feminist Periodicals*, p. 28.

8 Protesting at the Derby, Davison was trampled by the King's horse as she tried to grab hold of its reins. She died four days later and her translation into the first suffrage martyr began in earnest.

9 Lisa Tickner, *The Spectacle of Women* (London, 1987), p. 6.

10 *Vote*, 25 February 1911.

11 *Suffragette*, 16 January 1914.

12 St John's characterization of Hroswitha as a feminist – 'It is improbable that the idea that a woman is not a complete human being, and therefore not entitled to complete opportunities for development, but only to those circumscribed ones which man is graciously pleased to accord her, ever occurred to the playwright nun... Unlike some women of letters of a later time, Hroswitha makes no apology for her sex in her preface' – did not go unchallenged (*Votes for Women*, 2 January 1914). In a subsequent letter to the editor, Ursula Roberts argued that Hroswitha did indeed apologize for her sex and that neither she nor the suffrage movement's reputation should 'be enhanced by a misrepresentation of the facts'. St John responded that 'facts are stubborn things but the impress made by them on each individual mind is bound to vary and my mind is ever more sensitive to the spirit than the letter' (16 January 1914). Needless to say the 'spirit' of the suffrage age was up to the task of locating a feminist in Hroswitha.

13 *Suffragette*, 16 January 1914.

14 *Votes for Women*, 2 January 1914.

15 *Common Cause*, 6 March 1914.

16 In *The Great Scourge and How to End It* (London, 1913), Christabel Pank-hurst argued that 75 to 80 per cent of all men were infected with gonorrhea and a substantial number with syphilis, and encouraged women to protect themselves from such diseased manhood: 'there can be no mating between the spiritually developed women of this new day and men who in thought and conduct with regard to sex matters are their inferiors'. Although her figures were questioned, the medical profession of the time – at the behest one could say of a different political agenda – was coming up with similar numbers.

17 *Suffragette*, 20 February 1914.

18 *Vote*, 27 February, 1914.

19 *Votes for Women*, 3 April 1914.

20 *Suffragette*, 8 May 1914.

21 For a further discussion of suffrage supporters' attitudes to and uses of fashion see *Theatre and Fashion*, pp. 152–84.

22 *Common Cause*, 21 November 1913.

23 *Common Cause*, 4 November 1909.

24 See for example *Sketch*, 16 March 1910.

25 *Common Cause*, 7 April 1910.

26 *Common Cause*, 15 July 1909. It should be said that this criticism of Shaw's play did not go unchallenged. A subsequent letter to the editor regretted the 'tone of disappointment underlying' the review and argued that although 'we women would have liked a play in which all the old arguments were polished up afresh, and presented with irresistible humour ... if I mistake not, this play was written for men – for the men who still believe that they are lords of everything in general, and of women in particular. It is these men who will now help to fill our coffers, and will laugh over the play ... Only gradually will it dawn upon them that Shaw is laughing at them, that he has turned the full glare of the light on to the absurdity of the position. The average Britisher hates to be ridiculous, he will do anything rather – even concede women the right to vote' (*Common Cause*, 22 July 1909).

27 *Common Cause*, 30 September 1909.

28 *Vote*, 18 March 1911.

29 *Votes for Women*, 20 December 1912.

30 *Votes for Women*, 12 December 1913.

31 *Suffragette*, 12 December 1913.

32 *Votes for Women*, 5 September 1913.

33 *Common Cause*, 3 November 1910.

34 *Votes for Women*, 8 October 1909.

35 *Vote*, 4 November 1909.

36 *Common Cause*, 27 January 1910.

37 *Common Cause*, 27 January 1910.

38 Dennis Kennedy, *Granville Barker and the Dream of Theatre* (Cambridge, 1985), p. 136.
39 *Suffragette*, 18 October 1912.
40 Ibid.
41 Ibid.
42 Dennis Kennedy, *Looking at Shakespeare* (Cambridge, 1993), p. 80.
43 Kennedy, *Granville Barker and the Dream of Theatre*, p. 128.
44 *Votes for Women*, 18 October 1912.
45 Ibid.
46 *Evening Standard*, 22 May 1914.
47 *Suffragette*, 29 May 1914.
48 *Evening Standard*, 22 May 1914.
49 *Suffragette*, 19 June 1914.
50 *Suffragette*, 26 June 1914.
51 *Suffragette*, 29 November 1912.
52 See *Theatre and Fashion*, pp. 169–84.
53 *Suffragette*, 6 February 1914.

CHAPTER 9

'A woman of genius': Rebecca West at the theatre

John Stokes

Until quite recently the most widely respected history of the Edwardian period was still George Dangerfield's *The Strange Death of Liberal England* of 1935, which argued that between the years 1910 and 1913 English Liberalism collapsed under the triple assault of Irish politics, the Labour movement, and the activities of the suffragettes. It was a thesis that had held sway for years, and understandably so, because it offered a version of history that was coherent, plausible, internally consistent. In other words, it offered a narrative.

Dangerfield has now been challenged, first by historians who say that there was little or no link between three distinct political movements, and secondly by feminists who object not only to the story that he claims to tell, but to his manner of telling it. Jane Marcus in particular has noticed his habit of denigrating the suffragettes with belittling theatrical metaphors: the Pankhursts are a 'spectacle', according to Dangerfield, their activities a 'comedy'. For Marcus these theatrical metaphors betray an attempt to subordinate the suffrage campaign, which was ultimately successful, to other radical movements which were doomed to partial failure or delayed fruition. A more accurate narrative would reverse these priorities, put the suffragettes in the vanguard and show, says Marcus, how 'Mrs Pankhurst's popular success was due to her embodiment of democratic working-class values'.[1] As Marcus freely admits, the claim fits in well with a common view of our present world where feminism seems to have seized the torch, leaving socialism with the fag-ends of radical idealism.

However, Marcus's new Edwardian narrative would still have to deal with theatricality, because Dangerfield's penchant for the theatrical metaphor is a reflection of the period he writes about. Edwardians habitually resorted to theatrical metaphors themselves to describe the theatricality that was everywhere in their society. Not just in the taste for pageantry that suffragettes shared with royalty,[2] but in the ability to create dramatic events – a talent that Emily Davison shared with Winston Churchill. Theatricality was an Edwardian mode of politics.

Here, for example, is Max Beerbohm describing Christabel Pankhurst's appearance in court in 1908:

> She has all the qualities which an actress needs, and of which so few actresses have any. Her voice is charmingly melodious, and the art with which she manages it seems hardly compatible with its still childish ring. And her face, still childish too, is as vivid and as variable as her voice, whose inflexions have always their parallel in her eyes and mouth. And not there merely. Her whole body is alive with every meaning; and, if you can imagine a very graceful rhythmic dance done by a dancer who moves not her feet, you will have some idea of Miss Pankhurst's method. As she stood there with a rustling sheaf of notes in one hand . . . she was like nothing so much as a little singing bird born in captivity.[3]

Obviously this kind of pseudo-compliment masks deep unease, if not hostility, about its object: Miss Pankhurst is the product of an appreciative male gaze, which at the same moment reduces her to 'a little singing bird'. And, in some ways, it is characteristically Edwardian because of that.

But then consider this: 'Emmeline Pankhurst with all her limitations was glorious. Somehow, in her terse, austere way she was as physically glorious as Ellen Terry or Sarah Bernhardt. She was glorious in her physical courage, in her obstinacy, in her integrity.'[4] That is a female journalist writing in 1933, but remembering the Edwardian period in which she had played her own particular part. That is Rebecca West.

In this essay I argue that it was the profound theatricality of Edwardian politics, in particular the 'physical courage' observed by West, that could make the actual theatre sometimes appear a rather tame rendering of reality. And that this gulf was best appreciated by someone like West who was determined to act (in every sense) in the political drama herself, who allowed no compromise. 'The woman who is acting the principal part in her own ambitious play', said West in 1913, 'is unlikely to weep because she is not playing the principal part in some man's no more ambitious play.'[5]

Born Cicely Isabel Fairfield in 1892 in London, West was a suffragette supporter even in her teens, which she spent in Edinburgh.

Between April 1908 and March 1911 she trained at the Academy of Dramatic Art under Kenneth Barnes, having been spotted in Edinburgh by the actress and drama teacher Rosina Fillipi. The Academy experience was 'brief and unhappy',[6] and she did not complete the course, nor, despite one or two stabs, did she persist with her ambition as an actress. She became first a journalist, then a critic (her book on Henry James was published in 1916), then a writer of fiction (*The Return of the Soldier*, perhaps her most famous early work, was published in 1918), and she maintained all three professions up until her death in 1982.

Her early journalism is a mixture of book reviews, theatre reviews, and polemical sallies to do with contemporary politics – usually on feminist, if not always suffragette, topics. A good deal of it was written for feminist publications such as *The Freewoman* to which West began contributing in 1912, and which later became *The New Freewoman* and, eventually, *The Egoist*. In September, 1912 she moved to Robert Blatchford's socialist paper the *Clarion*. In 1915 she took up literary reviewing for the *Daily News*. And during the same period she published miscellaneous pieces (some of them about the theatre) in the *Daily Herald* (for which she temporarily edited the woman's page in 1912) and other London papers. Later in 1919 West contributed dramatic reviews to the *Outlook* and in 1920 she had, though briefly, a regular theatre column in *Time and Tide*, the weekly founded in 1920 that was owned, managed, and written entirely by women. Much of what West wrote there was retrospective, looking back to the Edwardian period and to her own past.

West belongs, then, with those women who determined to take an active and constructive part in the theatre, not as actresses or as writers, but as critics. In a way, her whole early career was theatrical – because she saw writing as an activity which freed a woman to try on all manner of identities and positions. And of course her choice of pseudonym was theatrical. Why she had to adopt another name she explained on a number of occasions: it was to do with the notoriety of *The Freewoman* (which was controversial even among feminists for the attention it gave to female sexuality) and with her desire not to embarrass her mother.[7] In the early 1980s she was still insisting to Marina Warner that she chose the name, 'not really for any profound reason. It was just to get a pseudonym.'[8] Even so, most people have assumed that the choice of Ibsen's heroine was a deliberate identification with an outspoken and idealistic female character.

Seeing Edwardian theatre through Rebecca West's eyes, the eyes of a feminist socialist, does not mean that we have to find her correct in all her aesthetic judgements. Nor is West necessarily typical or representative of her sex. (How often do we make those claims about the male critics we regularly rely upon for evidence?) In fact I want to emphasize her distinctiveness by making comparisons with another remarkable, but lesser known, woman critic and socialist, Christina Walshe, who also wrote about the theatre in the *Daily Herald* between 1912 and 1913 and who went on to become one of the crusading leaders of the Workers' Theatre Movement of the 1920s.[9]

One of the ways in which Rebecca West identified herself as a feminist theatre critic was by looking back at the recent past and establishing the distance between 'then' and 'now'. For an Edwardian the recent past was, of course, the 1890s: the symbolist world of someone like Florence Farr. When West saw Farr perform at the psaltery in 1912, part of an evening that included Gwen John's violent melodrama *Edge o'Dark*, she was struck by 'the atmosphere of the nineties, full of a calm beauty, perhaps more beautiful because undisturbed by any spiritual upheaval'. 'Miss Farr's art of reciting to the psaltery is typical of her period. It is unimportant from every artistic point of view; yet nothing could be more exquisite than the speech of that lovely, level voice, in which the tears glimmer perpetually, like dewdrops in long grass.'[10]

West thought that it was this nineties taste for the exquisite that had enabled young writers like Gwen John (now better known as a painter) to find a 'tragic beauty' in brutal subjects. There was another kind of nineties theatre, sometimes revived in the Edwardian era, for which she had less patience. It was symbolized by Mrs Patrick Campbell in a revival of *The Second Mrs Tanqueray*. Writing in the 1920s, West was to place Mrs Pat as someone who had fallen 'into the hands of a certain sort of playwright who wanted to talk nonsense about beautiful and passionate women'.[11] Pinero was the representative of a past era, when 'emotional crises were always followed by a geographical displacement'.

If one was jilted by one's fiancée one went and hunted big game in Africa. If one was divorced one took a villa in Florence. Pilgrimage, in fact, became the duty not of the religious but of the amorous enthusiast. Not only were these people of the last generation fettered by incomprehensible conventions, they seemed coldly inhuman in their hearts.[12]

West found her own male contemporaries and acquaintances much more stimulating. After all, they did include Wells, Shaw, Galsworthy, and Bennett, and in a well-known essay she was to link these writers as the four 'Uncles',[13] a typically double-edged tribute that admitted their importance whilst putting four famously vain middle-aged males smartly in their place. West's feminism often had this aspiration, expected access to male power and male opportunities without any loss of female identity.

Where the theatre was concerned, the most important figure for West was not in fact one of the four 'Uncles'. She thought that Granville Barker was the greatest playwright of the time, and in *The Freewoman* in 1912 she wrote a long piece celebrating his talent. It ended with a war-cry inspired by a line from *The Marrying of Ann Leete*: 'He has given us a strong hatred, the best lamp to bear in our hands as we go over the dark places of life, cutting away the dead things men tell us to revere', quoted West admiringly.[14] But Ann's original line had simply been, 'It's great to be a gardener ... to sow seeds and to watch flowers grow and to cut away dead things.'[15] It was West herself who added that emphasis on 'men'.

West's overall enthusiasm for Barker was based on what she saw as his capacity for thought – he went thinking, she said, as other people go hunting – and his war against sterility, his 'reverence for life'. *The Voysey Inheritance* she saw as a play about middle-class dullness:

Certainly the middle classes are unsatisfactory results of crime. For all families such as the Voyseys, whether they have the luck to have a solicitor's business as a lucky-bag, live by the same sort of fraud. If they have to pay their due to the landlord and capitalist, they exploit the workers under them and aim at living on rent and interest. And that is the Voyseys' crime – to be willing to live on the proceeds of theft without running the risks incidental to being a thief... The Voyseys used gold which was sticky with blood and tears to buy black-marble sarcophagus-like fireplaces and to entertain people as dull as themselves. It is an anti-climax.[16]

And, again characteristically, she admired *The Madras House* as much for its condemnation of the middle-class aesthetic consumerism represented by Jessica Madras as for its protest against the exploitation of shop-girls. The department store, she wrote in a review of a book on this quintessentially Edwardian subject, 'is peopled by those strange creatures peculiar to this century, shop assistants, languid, classless beings squeezed into the mould of an unearthly elegance, pallid with the poison of their degrading occupation'.

Any occupation which demands eternal and indiscriminate politeness from man to man is degrading ... The department store is the outward and visible sign, as Granville Barker showed in *The Madras House*, of a woman's movement: not the Feminist Movement, but the last struggle of the women who feel that woman's place is the harem to appeal to the sillier sexual instincts of men ... those gross, animal, middle-class women who spend their mornings in Regent Street and Oxford Street ... [17]

Her favourite Barker play remained *Ann Leete*, on the grounds that it was 'a cry against the fruitlessness of a highly bred class whose energies are diverted into political intrigue'.[18]

So excellent did West consider Barker to be as a playwright, superior even to Shaw, that she thought him to be squandering his time when he put on Shaw's plays. Her review of *Androcles and the Lion*, directed by Barker in 1913, allows that Shaw's oddly religious play is valuable for its portrayal in Androcles of 'the middle-class man who will not practise asceticism, and who has made all revolutions since the begining of time', and, in the figures of Lavinia and Ferrovius, of the soul that must 'be loyal to its own desires ... must abandon itself to its master-passion'. But West is really much more interested in castigating Barker's production (in which characters entered via the stage-box, and Alfred Rothenstein's Futurist décor used cloths in the suffragette colours) for its modish mimicry of Max Reinhardt.[19]

Her extreme sensitivity to physical presence could make her immune to mere visual effect, and she often expressed reservations about Barker's famously innovatory productions. When he staged *The Winter's Tale* in September, 1912 she remained unpersuaded by the production which she found for the most part dull, relenting only for Cathleen Nesbit's Perdita: 'She was trained as one of the Irish Players, who are more in touch with life than any other actors of this day; from their peculiar genius she has absorbed a certain elemental wildness. She plays Perdita like some young animal, graceful, without shame, and fierce.'

Lillah McCarthy (Hermione) had, in severe contrast, betrayed her physical gifts altogether. 'Miss McCarthy enjoys the undoubted advantages of beauty and health, which give her a kind of exciting vitality that makes her animation delightful,' wrote West, 'but in all reflective and dignified parts she becomes nerveless and stolid, mooing her more sonorous lines and acting a little more smugly. When Hermione is unveiled she looks not so much like a statue as like the Marble Arch. Like it she lacks poise and significance. And like it she is out of place.'[20]

Shakespeare no less than any other playwright offered a challenge to the Edwardian feminist. Within a few days, and in the very same paper, Christina Walshe, an equally committed but rather more orthodox socialist, was exhorting her female readership to see Barker's *The Winter's Tale* because 'there is not, in all literature a completer exposition of the humiliation of woman's position as it was yesterday, and is today (more or less), and will not be to-morrow'.[21] Hermione is like a suffragette in that her acceptance of prison is a protest against male tyranny; she is like a modern wife whose feminine qualities are unable to temper her husband's rage, but who has no legal redress either. In Hermione's plight, suggests Walshe, today's women might catch a reflection of their own condition, and react accordingly. For 'this is a play that all women ought to go to, not to learn how to submit, but to learn the dangers of submission'. About the dangers of submission West and Walshe would certainly have been in agreement.

Although Shaw was usually presented as the great Edwardian iconoclast, West's reservations about him were almost always to do with what she saw as his conventionality, his refusal, for all his love of debate, to create a single character 'who infringes the conventions in practice'.[22] This she found particularly frustrating in the case of his women characters.

But other playwrights were worse. West had a little time for Masefield's *Tragedy of Nan*,[23] but no patience at all with anything else that he wrote. Galsworthy she was to remember as a playwright who 'subordinates his characters to his ideas, showing no other facets of their natures save those on which the light of his subject falls',[24] a writer whose 'persistent song' was ' "every nice girl loves a failure" '.[25] Galsworthy was a 'sentimentalist; what he cares for is not discovering the truth about his material but creating with it the greatest possible emotional effect in the audience'.[26]

If these judgements strike a familiar note, seem to chime in with later opinion which has often complained about Galsworthy's 'thin-skinned, tear-in-the-eye, pre-war humanitarianism',[27] we should still beware of simplifying West's criteria. For she was briskly irreverent about plays that have, in even more recent years, come to be much admired. A dedicated supporter of the suffragette cause, a frequent critic of its tactics, she hated suffragette plays, for reasons that may have to do with ideological struggles within the movement, but are revealing about West's sense of the public too. They expose the clash between her advanced aesthetic opinions and her populist politics. This was a problem that Christina Walshe, who enthused equally over the ideas of Gordon Craig, Raymond Duncan, Margaret Morris, Walter Crane, and Ethel Smythe, does not seem to have felt at all. All were progressive artists, enough in itself to link them with the feminist cause.

West was more circumspect. 'I am inclined to agree with the Anti-Suffragists in their opinion that "there are some things which can be safely left to men"', she began a review in *The Freewoman* in 1912. 'Writing bad plays is one of them.' The play in question was Florence Hobson's vegetarian tract *A Modern Crusader*, but West's complaints have a wider reference:

Words are sacred, pen and ink are sacred, because of the noble uses they have been put to by artists, and propagandists who mishandle them ought to be punished for sacrilege. The Pioneer Players and the Actresses' Franchise League are perhaps the most shameless offenders in the way of producing degradations of the drama written by propagandists, who nothing but the fire of Prometheus could make into artists. It is untrue to say that these impertinences towards Art are innocuous by their own ineffectiveness. For the public taste has already been so perverted that dislocated Suffrage speeches, such as Miss Cicely Hamilton's plays, stand the chance of wide popularity.[28]

Nor did she change her opinion about Cicely Hamilton when, in 1913, in one of her few forays onto the professional stage, she had a small part in Hamilton's play *Phyl*, performed at the Brighton West Pier Theatre in March 1913.

When it came to the revolutionary foreigners, Ibsen, Chekhov and Strindberg, West was impressed, but uncrushed. Like other Edwardians she tended to co-opt the continental example for English uses.

At this late date one might have thought that the importance of Ibsen was beyond doubt but, according to West, 'very few middle-class women have ever read Ibsen', and those who had read him still got him wrong. A male anti-suffragist is taken to task because 'he imagines that Nora Helmer left home because she despised motherhood: whereas Ibsen states that she left home because she became conscious that playing lap-dog to a trivial husband had unfitted her for wise motherhood'.[29] West obviously read Ibsen in the light of current debates over motherhood, a dominant topic among Edwardian feminists and anti-feminists alike.

Her views on Chekhov display a fascination with the whole history of Russia that is also typically Edwardian.[30] They belong with the gradual process of education leading to appropriation that was to culminate in Shaw's *Heartbreak House*. She saw *The Cherry Orchard* in the spring of 1911 at the Aldwych, and, in April 1912, *The Seagull* at the Little Theatre. *The Cherry Orchard* she felt to be the greater play:

It is a picture of all Russia. The orchard itself is a symbol of the golden age of Russia, the loveliness created by a wise aristocracy in the good old times... After *The Cherry Orchard* one is filled with the exaltation that always follows the endurance of a tragedy. It brings home to one the sense of one's appalling isolation from every other soul on earth, the indefensible rashness of one's action in being born, and proud consciousness of the splendid and devastating adventures waiting for one in the uncharted sea of life. That is why the audience jeered and tittered: because it feared this knowledge...

The Seagull, in comparison, was more narrowly focused upon the disruptions of capitalism:

The present British thirst for money – a thirst quite as infantile as Nina's desire for limelight – is of course, attributable to the present capitalist muddle, which gives money a fictitious value by withholding it. Nations do not suffer from these sicknesses for nothing. But Tchekhof cannot be bothered with explanations. He throws us his masterpiece, crying: 'Look at this! It's life! Isn't it dirty and stupid and useless and utterly damnable and completely glorious?'[31]

For West *The Cherry Orchard* resembled *The Marrying of Ann Leete* 'both in the fastidious hands it laid on the sterile and sentimental governing classes and its Futurist technique'.[32] Given the chronology this, in effect, was to see Chekhov as an approximation of Barker.[33] When the best new plays came over from the continent, Granville Barker still came out on top.

The Adelphi Play Society staged Strindberg's *The Father* on 23 July 1911, and *Miss Julie* on 28 April 1912. For feminists here was a writer who represented a particular menace,[34] and in 1912 West published two major articles about him. 'Writers on the subject of August Strindberg have hitherto omitted to mention that he could not write', she began. 'His vain face, with the hot, angry eyes, the little lustful mouth, the rumpled forehead and the sharp, peevish chin, proclaims that he had neither the strength nor the humour to become an artist.' Personal slights prefaced weightier complaints:

Strindberg's plays are bad by necessity of his style: one cannot create great drama out of ugly phrases. He tries to paint the battles of emotion between nobility and sensuality, and one cannot paint strong emotions as ugly, because only weakness is ugly. Because he failed to realise this, his plays are unspeakably horrible.[35]

What she meant was that Strindberg could not write beautifully, though he could write brutally. He was torn, she said, because although his great theme was love, the 'religious passion', he could not tolerate the impermanence of sexual desire. Yet 'his style is so grossly material that the mind refuses to recognise the perception of a spiritual truth as the cause of his agony, and seeks for a material explanation'. Then, with one of those rhetorical twists that seem to have come so effortlessly to her, West stages a stunning satirical coup. Strindberg, she claims, is important precisely because his extraordinary, his 'insane' frankness uncovers a psychology all too like that of an ordinary Englishman. The revelation leads to a condemnation of the English divorce laws and of the anti-suffrage orthodoxy which insists that English women should endure life with those 'good men' who are, in fact, the moral equivalents of Strindberg. His works should therefore be made freely available to the English public – an awful warning of what conventional morality can lead to.

As a piece of polemical strategy this is reminiscent of Shaw, but West goes beyond him in her outrage, in her ability to argue to the very end, to follow through the implications for actual practice. In Strindberg she sensed a provocation that simply had to be taken up. And it is striking that it should be in the course of these articles on Strindberg that she should summarize, with particular cogency, her own cornerstone beliefs. 'To submit to unhappiness,' she pronounces, 'is the essence of the surrender of personality, which is sin.' 'Submission to poverty is the unpardonable sin against the body. Submission to unhappiness is the unpardonable sin against the spirit.'[36]

These rules mirror the feminist lessons that Christina Walshe claims to have learned from *The Winter's Tale*, though, in this context at least, they obviously owe a good deal to Nietzsche. In fact, in the figure of Rebecca West we have not just a Nietzschean socialist (a common enough Edwardian phenomenon) but that slightly rarer thing, a Nietzschean socialist feminist. In 1912, when again mounting an attack on the ideal of the meek woman, she cited *Zarathustra*:

Nietzsche says that a man who is aiming at Supermanhood passes through three phases: the camel, the lion and the child. At first the soul becomes mastered by the idea of duty and self-sacrifice. It desires to be a preserver of life. Thus far have women gone ... Let women make haste to become lions, and fearlessly attack the social system. So that together men and women may be transformed for the last time into the child, who, untroubled with the consciousness of material things, is concerned only with love and happiness.[37]

In her comments on the London theatre in the years from 1911 to 1914 the voice of Rebecca West rings out loud and clear; and it is equally clear that commonplace entertainments will never answer its demands. Not only is offstage political history far more dramatic, but most theatre fails to represent the dynamic reality of the lives of ordinary women. 'Domesticity,' she writes, 'is essentially drama, for drama is conflict, and the home compels conflict by its concentration of active personalities in a small area. The real objection to domesticity is that it is too exciting.'[38] What West wants from the theatre, and she is not entirely alone in this (rather similar demands can be found in Titterton's *From Theatre to Music-Hall* and Huntley Carter's *The New Spirit in Drama and Art*, both of 1912) is a display of revolutionary energy, and these needs will not be satisfied by an intellectual writer like Shaw, let alone by Galsworthy. But West differs from the male Nietzscheans in that she expects to find that inspirational energy in women as well as in men, and, specifically, in the female body.

Her response to the phenomenon of the French dancer Gaby Deslys is instructive in precisely this respect. Late in 1912 Deslys's supposedly indecent show at the Palace caused something of a scandal.[39] Writing in *The Clarion* on 27 December, West drew comparisons between Deslys and the wealthy women she saw in Regent Street gazing at shop windows full of wax dummies modelling underclothes:

Recently Mlle Gaby Deslys made a sensation by appearing in a sketch at the Palace in not quite the customary amount of clothing. But there was one excellent point about her performance. She took the full responsibility of the exhibition. She associated herself with the petticoats and faced the attitude of mind which this display provoked. I do not see why the respectable ladies who shop in Regent Street should be allowed to exhibit their clothes in this furtive, anonymous and impersonal manner. If they wish to do provocative things they ought to do them boldly as professionals and not skulking as amateurs.[40]

Shopper or stripper? It is a brilliant exchange between spectator and performer that brings together two familiar Edwardian moral concerns, and places them together within an overall sexual economy.

In the following year, in October, a further scandal erupted when the Bishop of Kensington complained that improper elements had been introduced into Deslys's performance in a show at the Palace. A delegation was sent to inspect the current version. The management of the Palace protested its innocence, as did Gaby Deslys, and a number of dignitaries wrote to *The Times*. Among them was Shaw, who fired off a couple of letters protesting at the bishop's claim to represent public morality.[41]

Again West went to see Gaby Deslys, and again she reported back to the readers of *The Clarion*. By now she had come to recognize in the French dancer an embodiment of the Nietzschean transcendent child:

She is a happy child who dances because she is tingling with life. When she crossed the Palace stage she turned the audience's thoughts to May mornings and ices, and money enough to go where you like. Now if most of us crossed the Palace stage, we would turn the audience's thoughts to November evenings, and cold cocoa ... This is the state of mind that will save the world.[42]

Gaby Deslys obviously had 'physical courage'. But the greatest example of this vital quality was still, even in the Edwardian period, when she was reduced to appearing at the Coliseum, Sarah Bernhardt. West had seen Bernhardt for the first time in Edinburgh in 1902 and by the age of 16 she had seen her four times. She never forgot the actress's 'curious wild grace',[43] and remained faithful in her memories throughout her life. Bernhardt stood for the 'violent events, spillings and stirrings of blood, murders and passions, that in themselves are beautiful'. In the face of such passions there was nothing to do but capitulate to Bernhardt's 'light', to welcome the emotional inspiration she provided. To Bernhardt in *Tosca* West took at least four handkerchiefs:

Laughter directed at her is an impiety ... In the moment of her crises she was like a flame. Burning, flexible, and, as it were, transparent – for every mannerism, every idiosyncrasy was turned away, and there was nothing left but what was necessary for the expression of the passion that governed her. And her effect was immediate and eternal, for, because of its fierceness, her cry struck home to one's heart at once, and, because of its sweetness, it lingered, therefore, for ever memorable ...

Bernhardt had, supremely, 'the prima donna air of being used to the public's stares and liking them'.[44]

Some cultural historians have seen in the Edwardian yearning for images of heroic energy a counterpoint to the surface liberalism of the times,[45] and have sensed an underlying drive for power that could only end in suicidal war. One place for testing that idea might be in responses to the performance of Hardy's *Dynasts*, which was directed by Granville Barker in December 1914. West's long review draws many parallels between the time in which the play is set and the moment of its performance, and ends elegiacally with a sense of loss, above all of what the war would mean for the immediate future of the theatre. As the curtain came down she had 'a rather baulked feeling, as though one had had the most beautiful poem in the world read to one in a mumbling undertone'. Would she ever see it staged on a scale appropriate to Hardy's vision? 'That, one remembered, while the voices crying news of a less merciful war than any of these told one that another ship had gone down and England was the poorer by eight hundred men, will not be an enterprise for this embarrassed country for some years ahead.'[46]

I noted at the start of this essay that Rebecca West claimed to have chosen her pen-name simply because *The Freewoman* was a scandalous paper, and because Ibsen's character could be made to stand as a symbol for all outspoken, idealistic women. In 1919, however, when the war was over, in a review of Ludwig Lewisohn's *The Modern Drama: An Essay in Interpretation*, she wrote this:

Rosmersholm, as everyone ought to know, is one of the greatest plays ever written. It is the *Hamlet* of the revolutionary intellectual movement. It shows how those who battle for freedom against the old evils of slavery and stupidity may be led by war, though it is holy, into curious places where out of contempt for those old evils they do violence to those old sanities and benevolences without which life cannot be lived, and so at the end meet a tarnished and dishonourable defeat, which is yet more honourable than abstinence from such warfare would have been. Its heroine is the one adequate presentation in all literature of a woman of genius.[47]

The heroine of *Rosmersholm* is, of course, Rebecca West. The passage is written with such convoluted awkwardness that it may be an attempt to be especially frank. What Cicely Fairfield seems to be acknowledging is 'Rebecca West' as a possibly heroic, but essentially doomed figure. Of course, in Ibsen's play she had always been that, and it seems strange that no one should have pointed out to her that the heroine destroys herself along with the hero. Or perhaps someone did, or perhaps the knowledge was always there under the surface. And perhaps thoughts of self-destruction were harder to suppress after the trenches. Yet West's word 'warfare' would also seem to refer, in the context of a female Hamlet, beset with father-figures, not only to the war with Germany, but to the Edwardian 'sex-war' itself.

I also began by wondering, along with Jane Marcus, if there was an alternative narrative for the events of the late Edwardian period, a narrative that would be dominated by women. For a socialist woman like Christina Walshe such a narrative would tell of a growing political force reflected in collective theatrical activity, heralded by the radical visions of great artists. Art and politics for her would always remain one.

'The Post Impressionists are in the company of the great Rebels of the World', she had announced in 1913:

In politics the only movements worth considering are Woman Suffrage and Socialism. They are both Post Impressionists in their desire to scrap the old decaying forms and find for themselves a new working ideal. In drama, Craig, Barker, and Bakst, take their place by the side of Van Gogh, Cézanne and Matisse.[48]

In the 1920s Walshe's work for the Workers' Theatre Movement, supported by Huntly Carter and others, was to be deeply influenced by what they knew of Expressionism in Germany and constructivist experiments in Russia.[49]

According to the darkening scenario of Rebecca West, however, the Edwardian narrative would now be marked by confrontation and sacrifice, leading, maybe, or maybe not, to some form of Nietzschean rebirth. That, at any rate, is how she had come to see the ambitious historical play that she believed that she was in, that she saw enacted on the streets, in parliament and in the home, and, latterly, on the battlefields of France, and why she felt as she did about the plays that she saw in theatres.

It might then be said that West's theatrical aesthetic was both diverted and fulfilled by the events of August, 1914: though that is the kind of realization that comes only when it is too late. Correspondingly her feminism, which had involved some real fascination with heroic energy, may have demanded a sacrifice only apparent after the event. Naturally this belated recognition would not lessen her feminist commitment. It would only confirm it, because the basis of the enquiry would now have to be a re-examination of the whole idea of power itself. But somehow, in the course of events, the narrative had undoubtedly turned tragic and 'Rebecca West' – 'a woman of genius' – had by 1919 become a symbol of the tragic heroine, even to herself.

NOTES

1 *Suffrage and the Pankhursts*, ed. Jane Marcus (London, 1987), p. 7. In the research for this essay I have greatly benefited from the advice of Faith Evans, Victoria Glendinning, and Sheila H. Macdonald.
2 See Lisa Tickner, *The Spectacle of Women* (London, 1987).
3 *Last Theatres* (London, 1970), p. 395.
4 'A Reed of Steel' from *The Post-Victorians*, 1933, reprinted in *The Young Rebecca*, ed. Jane Marcus (London, 1982), p. 260. Henceforth referred to as Marcus, this important collection brings together much, but by no means all, of West's early journalism.
5 Victoria Glendinning, *Rebecca West: A Life* (London, 1987), p. 49.
6 *Family Memories*, ed. Faith Evans (London, 1987), p. 196.
7 Marcus, p. 5.
8 *Writers at Work, The Paris Review Interviews*, ed. George Plimpton, 6th series (London, 1985), p. 10.
9 *Theatres of the Left 1880–1935*, ed. Raphael Samuel *et al.* (London, 1985), pp. 34, 87.
10 Marcus, p. 52.
11 *Time and Tide*, 18 June 1920, p. 123.
12 *Time and Tide*, 8 July 1921, p. 649.
13 *The Strange Necessity* (London, 1987), p. 198.
14 Marcus, p. 23.
15 H. Granville Barker, *Three Plays by Granville Barker* (London, 1909), p. 42.
16 *Daily Herald*, 11 September 1912.
17 *The Freewoman*, 30 May 1912, pp. 27–8. Also see Marcus, p. 135.
18 *The Freewoman*, 7 March 1912; Marcus, p. 22.
19 *The New Freewoman*, 15 September 1913; Marcus, p. 24.
20 *Daily Herald*, 23 September 1912.
21 *Daily Herald*, 5 October 1912. For Walshe's mixed views of Granville Barker's *Twelfth Night*, see 'A Post-Impressionist "Twelfth Night"', *Daily Herald*, 18 November 1912.
22 Marcus, p. 20.
23 See *The New Freewoman*, 15 September 1913, p. 128.
24 *Time and Tide*, 28 May 1920, p. 59.
25 *Time and Tide*, 3 June 1921, p. 532.
26 *Ending in Earnest* (New York, 1931), p. 236.
27 George Orwell, *The Road to Wigan Pier* (Harmondsworth, 1962), p. 138.
28 *The New Freewoman*, 23 May 1912, p. 8.
29 Marcus, p. 378.
30 See Samuel Hynes, *The Edwardian Turn of Mind* (Princeton, 1968). One of West's very first reviews, written soon after she had left the Academy, was of Gorky's *Lower Depths* at the Royalty. I have been unable to identify this with certainty, although it may well be the short anonymous notice that appeared in the *Standard* on 4 December 1911.
31 *The Freewoman*, 11 April 1912, pp. 405–6.

32 *The New Freewoman*, 15 September 1913, p. 128.

33 The comparison was made by others. See Allan Wade, *Memories of the London Theatre 1900–1914*, ed. Alan Andrews (London, 1983), p. 5.

34 See, for example, the long obituary by H. F. Rubenstein in *The Freewoman*, 23 May 1912, pp. 5–7.

35 *The Freewoman*, 15 August 1912; Marcus, p. 53.

36 *The Freewoman*, 22 August 1912; Marcus, p. 59.

37 *The Clarion*, 18 October 1912; Marcus, p. 105.

38 Marcus, p. 10.

39 See James Gardiner, *Gaby Deslys. A Fatal Attraction* (London, 1986), chapter 9, and Dave Russell in this volume, pp. 72–3.

40 Marcus, p. 136.

41 See Bernard Shaw, *Agitations, Letters to the Press, 1876–1950*, ed. Dan H. Laurence and James Rambeau (New York, 1985), pp. 153–9.

42 *The Clarion*, 28 November 1913; Marcus, pp. 227–8. Compare Walshe's equally heart-felt, but rather more sombre, report of attempts to unionize chorus girls in 'The Cry of the Chorus Girl', *Daily Herald*, 9 November 1912.

43 *Family Memories*, p. 194.

44 *Time and Tide*, 8 October 1920, pp. 448–9. For a report of Bernhardt's interest in socialism see *Daily Herald*, 6 September 1912, p. 2.

45 See, for example, John Lester, *Journey to Despair* (Princeton, 1968).

46 *The New Republic*, 26 December 1914, pp. 25–6.

47 *Daily News*, 11 August 1919. The comparison between Ibsen's Rebecca West and Hamlet may, in fact, have been well established. It was certainly made by the *Daily Chronicle* in 1891 – see *Ibsen: The Critical Heritage*, ed. Michael Egan (London, 1972), pp. 161–3. At the turn of the century *Rosmersholm* was a deeply problematic play – and for some, among them Sigmund Freud, it was always to remain so.

48 'Post-Impressionism and Suffrage', *Daily Herald*, 25 March 1913. Also see 'The Art World. Post-Impressionism and Socialism', *Daily Herald*, 9 October 1912.

49 Walshe reported regularly on the movement in the *Sunday Worker* between 1925 and 1928.

CHAPTER 10

The East End

Jim Davis

At the turn of this century Walter Besant wrote that 'there is ... no
other city in the world in the least like East London for the
unparalleled magnitude of its meanness and its monotony'. Claiming
that it housed approximately a twentieth part of the population of
Britain, consisting mainly of workers employed locally on weekly
wages, he went on to criticize the East End communities for their lack
of patriotism and for their failure 'to reverence the flag of the country,
as a symbol of their liberties and responsibilities'; 'alone among the
cities of the world', he wrote, 'East London never teaches her children
the meaning of patriotism, the history of their liberties, the pride and
privilege of citizenship in a mighty empire'.[1] Although Besant gives us
a useful account of local trade and industries, he is abruptly dismissive
of local entertainment, writing that 'the theatre and the music hall
claim, and claim successfully, their supporters: concerning the former
one has only to recognise that it may be a school of good manners, as
well as of good sentiments, and also that it is an institution capable of
ruining a whole generation. The pieces given at the theatres of East
London are, so far as I have observed, chiefly melodramas. The
music-halls are places frankly of amusement, and for the most part, I
believe, vulgar enough, but not otherwise mischievous.'[2] This cursory
account hardly reflects the vigorous theatrical life then existing in the
neighbourhood and certainly gives no indication of its many functions
within the community, one of which was arguably providing the
training in patriotic values that Besant felt was lacking. Besant is one
of many commentators, in fact, who succeeded in mythologizing the
East End as a vista of bleak, depressing streets and poverty-stricken
slum dwellings, inhabited by loafers and idlers and the chronically
poor. In fact, as Charles Booth's survey[3] was to show, the East End
was more lively than the myth suggested and poverty, whilst it
existed, was not quite as widespread as supposed. The majority of

East Enders were in regular employment and some areas of the East
End such as Hackney, with its 'well-to-do suburban population',
hardly suffered from poverty at all.[4] Indeed, if the population had
been as chronically poor as the mythical accounts imply, there would
have been little scope for the theatrical activity that actually existed.

If we had visited the East End forty years earlier, in the 1860s, we
would have been struck by how theatrical life focussed on a small
number of large theatres, with seating capacities ranging from just
under 2,000 at the City of London and the Grecian Theatres to
almost 4,000 at the Britannia Theatre. At Shoreditch was located the
Standard Theatre, seating 3,000, and presenting a cosmopolitan
programme that embraced visiting stars and touring companies.
Further north was the Britannia, with a stock company and stock
repertory, catering for the Hoxton public, whilst also to the north was
the Grecian in City Road. At Bishopsgate in Norton Folgate was the
City of London Theatre, whilst in Whitechapel Road were the
Pavilion and, further along towards Stepney, the Effingham (later
renamed the East London Theatre). In Leman Street was the smaller
Garrick Theatre. These theatres operated within identifiable communities and presented repertories that reflected, as far as one can
ascertain, local tastes and interests. However, by the commencement
of Edward VII's reign the City of London, the Grecian, the
Effingham and the Garrick had all disappeared, either through
demolition or through changes in function. Only three of the great
East End theatres survived: the Pavilion, the Britannia, and the
Standard. All three commenced the twentieth century presenting
similar programmes centred on popular melodramas and an annual
pantomime. Yet, by the end of Edward's reign, the Standard had
become a music hall, the Britannia functioned only intermittently as
a theatre, and the Pavilion had become almost entirely associated
with productions of Yiddish plays, staged for the local Jewish
community.

There were several reasons for such changes. One was demographic:
as the city of London expanded and developed, replacing housing
with industrial and commercial premises, so the audiences for the
Standard and Britannia theatres declined, a situation exacerbated by
a decline in prosperity in the vicinity of these theatres. By 1907 it was
generally accepted that the area could only support one theatre the
size of either the Britannia or the Standard.[5] A second cause was
improved communications: it was now much easier to travel into the

West End and, since the East End theatres increasingly drew on West End fare, there was nothing unique to visit locally.[6] Thirdly, the development of the tramways from the mid-1870s and a growth in speculative building led to an outflow of the lower middle classes and respectable working classes from more central districts.[7] As the century drew on, the particularly good provision of service and reduced fares for the working man by the Great Eastern Railway led to further migration eastwards. Businesses in turn began to migrate from the centre, encouraging further demographic shifts. Interestingly, the only increase in population in inner East London by the end of the century was in Whitechapel, largely due to Jewish settlement.

In the meantime a demographic shift to the east and to the north led to the construction of new suburban theatres in such areas as Stratford, Poplar, Stoke Newington and Dalston, thus depriving the larger East End theatres of a potential audience. According to the *Dramatic World* (1 June 1901) playgoers residing in such districts as Tottenham had previously had to make a long journey citywards in quest of dramatic fare; now, however, they could see the best touring companies at the Alexandra, Stoke Newington, or visit the Dalston Theatre, without the need to travel further afield. A further attraction was that some of these new suburban theatres were increasingly used for try-outs; the Borough, Stratford East, for instance, drew both a local audience and a fashionable West End audience, when *Mr Wix of Wickham*, a musical comedy written for Dan Leno, was given its first performances there in June 1902. As well as try-outs, transfers of new plays that had been particularly successful in the provinces were often made directly to the suburban theatres. In general, the repertories, touring companies, and touring actors were interchangeable throughout the suburbs of London, providing popular melodrama, light opera, musical comedy, and the occasional serious drama or Shakespearian performance. *Charley's Aunt, Mrs Dane's Defence, The Prodigal Son, The Belle of New York, The Merry Widow,* and Forbes Robertson in *Hamlet* represent just a few of the pieces toured during the early years of the century. As a result of this development the East End and South London lost their distinctive theatrical traditions and became part of a pattern that prevailed not only throughout the outer reaches of the metropolis but also in the provinces. Other causes of the changes outlined above were the proliferation of music hall entertainment in the inner East End – as early as 1888–9 Charles Booth had commented that music hall entertainment was preferred over the drama by the mass of the population there[8] – and the detrimental effects of the cost of meeting the rigorous safety requirements now demanded by the London County Council, which took over responsibility for licensing the metropolitan theatres in 1888. Inevitably large old theatres in districts suffering economic decline were particularly vulnerable in such a situation.

The inner East End had reverted almost entirely to music hall entertainment by the end of the Edwardian era, whilst the outer suburbs such as Poplar, Stratford, or Dalston supported their own theatre or theatres and often one or more music halls. The siting of these theatres and halls seems to have been supported by the existence of a local population affluent enough to avail themselves regularly of the amusements on offer (in Poplar a weekly visit to the Queen's Music Hall was considered the norm in this period[9]) and by good communications. Both Dalston and Stratford, for instance, were served by major rail links and highways, whilst Poplar was easily reached by the inhabitants of West Ham, Bow, Bromley, Canning Town, Limehouse, and Stepney. Stratford supported two theatres, the Borough, which provided a venue for touring theatre and opera companies, and the Theatre Royal in Angel Lane, given over largely to a repertory of melodrama. Employment in the area was provided by chemical works, the railway (and ancillary industries) and the docks, not to mention a local brewery and the Co-operative Society. Inhabitants ranged from casual labourers to artisans, clerks, railway workers, school teachers, estate agents and shopkeepers, the more well-to-do tending to move further east to Ilford and Romford.[10] From such a community was drawn sufficient support to maintain two theatres and a music hall.

The history of East End entertainment during the Edwardian era is thus, in part, a history that would be equally true of most of the suburbs in the greater London area. There are however several features that were distinct to the East End and it is upon these that the remainder of this paper will focus. First, the increasing use of the Pavilion as a centre for Yiddish drama is worthy of mention. Secondly, the Melville melodramas at the Standard also deserve a place in any survey of East End theatre during the early 1900s, although it is unlikely that the appeal of these annual new autumn melodramas was specifically local. Thirdly, the encroachment of the music halls and the growing threat to the Britannia's and the

Standard's survival as theatres should also be noted. If in 1901 it was still possible to discern some continuity within the East End theatre from the nineteenth into the twentieth century, by 1912 many of the old links had disappeared for ever.

Anthony L. Ellis, writing in *The Pall Mall Gazette* in 1908, states that Whitechapel is 'the home of a unique theatre, in which audience and entertainment are unlike any to be seen elsewhere in this country'.[11] He is referring to the way in which the large Pavilion Theatre had (at least temporarily) become the home of Yiddish drama in East London, catering for the rapidly increasing, foreign-born Jewish population in the area. He describes a typical audience for Yiddish drama, although, to modern ears, his account sounds more like a caricature than an objective report:

The day's work in the tailor's shop or the cap-making factory is over. Presser, machinist and button-hole maker are free to enjoy their precious leisure. Swart and bearded, the signs of excessive labour under unwholesome conditions written in their pallid lips and hollow eyes, these alien-born sons of Israel cast care behind them when the theatre is entered... With them come the daughters of Israel, beautiful sometimes in the flower of their youth, but too often gross and coarse of feature and of figure when once the flower has faded ... of all trades, all ages, and both sexes, the audience pass in, soon filling the house to overflowing. What an audience! Bubbling, effervescent, undisciplined, it is noisy and excitable after the invariable manner of Orientals. When the play begins, however, it follows with rapt attention, yielding to its emotions with the frankness and simplicty of children...

The audience range, according to Ellis, from the poorest to the most prosperous members of the Ghetto, but the fare they enjoy is rather basic. This evening's play is *Holy Sabbath*, 'the quaintest medley of romantic opera, melodrama and sheer farce that can possibly be imagined ... devoid of all the finer shades of artistic perception'. Nevertheless, even if Yiddish drama itself is still at an elementary stage, the power and passion of the actors it produced (such as Jacob Adler, M. D. Waxman, Maurice Axelrad, and Sigmund Feinman) is not in doubt, for 'they are all players of considerable natural power and technical ability. While they are apt, perhaps, to disregard the finer aspects of comedy and tragedy alike, there can be no question about their quite unusual capacity for the expression of emotion, and their unflinching realism in the portrayal of the Jewish character.' Another memorable aspect was the photographic realism with which scenes of 'domestic religious ceremonial' were presented on stage. Equally, the best Yiddish plays arguably raised standards of ideal conduct which could only be a force for good within the Jewish community. From Ellis's English perspective Yiddish theatre also played a part in breaking down the more restrictive Jewish orthodoxies, since the theatre was filled to overflowing every Sabbath Day.

Whitechapel in the nineteenth century was inhabited by Jewish and Irish settlers, dispossessed respectively by persecution and famine. According to Millicent Rose, the Jewish quarter of Whitechapel 'stretched from Goodman's Fields up into the streets around Petticoat Lane, which was regarded as the nucleus of the colony'.[12] The Jewish settlers had gradually usurped the Irish during the last twenty years of Queen Victoria's reign, becoming the main traders in Commercial Road, for example. Unlike other nationalities, who tended to move out of the East End as they prospered, many of the Jews were slow to leave the Ghetto, being 'more interested in food, finery and theatres, than in exchanging their squalid rooms for more spacious quarters'.[13] There had long been a tradition of catering for Jewish entertainment in the East End. The Britannia in Hoxton performed a number of plays on Jewish themes in the mid- to late nineteenth century; the Effingham (or East London Theatre), a little further east than the Pavilion, specialized in Yiddish plays in the late nineteenth century under the name of Wonderland. Mayhew, earlier in the century, had written that 'the City of London Theatre, the Standard Theatre, and other play-houses at the East-end of London, are greatly resorted to by the younger members of the [Jewish] body, who sometimes constitute a rather obstreperous gallery'.[14]

According to a contemporary study, *The Jew in London*, the Jewish community in East London consisted largely of recent immigrants from Germany, Russia, Poland, and other countries in Eastern Europe. Geographically, they could, by 1899, be precisely located, comprising over 50 per cent of the residential population in the immediate vicinity of the Pavilion Theatre, whilst rising to between 75 per cent and 95 per cent of the population in many nearby streets, especially along the high roads such as Whitechapel High Street, Whitechapel Road, and Commercial Road East. The parameters of their territory were tightly defined: they neither expanded eastwards into Mile End nor north into Bethnal Green. Consequently, the Standard and Britannia Theatres on the one hand and the People's Palace on the other were situated outside this area. Although there were small Jewish settlements around Sandringham Park in Dalston and Victoria Park in Hackney, it was generally true that 'the position bounded on the city side by the Minories, Houndsditch and Bishopsgate, north by the Great Eastern Railway and Buxton Street, and south by Cable Street forms the central Jewish area'.[15] The community was expanding all the time and there was pressure for accommodation due to the continued demolition of houses near the city for warehouses, railway extensions, and business premises.

The total Jewish population of London at the turn of the century was estimated at about 110,000, of whom about 100,000 lived in the East End. Approximately 60,000 of these East End Jews had been born overseas. According to *The Jew in London*, which provides these statistics, 'dirt, overcrowding, industry and sobriety may be set down as the most conspicuous features of these foreign settlements'.[16] The author of the study also draws attention to the local provision of entertainment *circa* 1900 in Whitechapel Road, where 'there is a small music-hall called "Wonderland", which is mainly patronised by foreign Jews and supports a company of Yiddish actors; and performances are given on Monday, Friday and Saturday nights and on Saturday afternoons. Similarly, in the Standard Theatre, Shoreditch, Saturday afternoon is commonly selected for the performance of a Yiddish play – presumably as being the likeliest to attract a Jewish audience.'[17] However, the Standard performances were not in fact that frequent and only a small proportion of the overall Jewish population actually attended the theatre on the Sabbath. That the Standard may have relied partly on the local Jewish community for its audiences is implicit, nevertheless, in H. G. Hibbert's later assumption that the annual season by the Turner Opera Company at the Standard was supported 'from the many Jews in the neighbourhood'.[18]

Despite the implication within the *Pall Mall Gazette* article that the Pavilion Theatre had gone over entirely to Yiddish drama, this was not entirely true. Other companies also appeared at the theatre throughout the Edwardian era. The Pavilion presented its fair share of fashionable melodramas (including the 'wicked woman' genre, so popular at the Standard), enjoyed visits from performers such as Dan Leno and also played traditional pantomimes at Christmas. An

account of the theatre published in 1901 gives no indication of a
Jewish audience or of the proximity of the Jewish community.[19] Yet,
even under Isaac Cohen's management in the early years of the
century, the Pavilion was evidently conscious of its local audience. In
1903 James J. Hewson's Russo-Jewish drama *Under the Canopy*
evidently aimed at attracting local interest by drawing for its
subject-matter on the pogroms after the Tsar's assassination in
Russia. Any serious analysis of the Jewish situation is, however,
dispensed with: the play's plot revolves around a wicked Russian
General, his libidinous interest in a beautiful Jewish woman, Naomi,
'the Queen of the Ghetto', and his ruthless persecution of the man
who loves her, Raphael. After opening in Russia, the play's action
moves to London, where Naomi now lives and which the General is
visiting. The play reflects the liberal and patriotic sentiments which
were used to justify the Jewish settlement in the East End by writers
such as the authors of *The Jew in London* (who also point out that
Britain is just about the only European country where Jews are
disadvantaged neither socially nor legally and that 'pride in one's
own country is bound up in it together with a generous feeling
towards foreigners').[20] Despite its appeal to a Jewish audience, *Under
the Canopy* is an English play (although containing a number of
Yiddish expressions and allusions) and was performed by an English
cast.

At the turn of the century the Pavilion also lived up to its
designation as the 'Drury Lane of the East', presenting melodramas
by Arthur Shirley and Benjamin Landeck, Sutton Vane, and George
R. Sims. In other words it presented exactly the same sort of fare as
the two other large surviving theatres in the area, the Britannia and
the Standard. Cohen left the theatre in 1905 and by April 1906
Feinman's Jewish Operatic and Dramatic Company were presenting
a regular repertory of plays in Yiddish, with a change of programme
almost every night. Their repertory, which included *Captain Dreyfus*
and *The Zionist* as well as the plays of Abraham Goldfaden and of
Jacob Gordin, author of *The Jewish King Lear*, largely originated from
the Yiddish theatres of New York. Jacob Adler actually played David
Moscheles, the Jewish King Lear, at the Pavilion, while Sigmund
Feinman, another Yiddish star, played Othello. Adler visited the
theatre in 1906 and again in 1908, when he undertook a fortnight's
engagement. After his final performance in 1908 as Solomon the
Great, he made a speech in which he praised his fellow actors,

commented upon the educational value of Yiddish drama, and called upon the wealthier Jews within the community to support a Yiddish theatre. Then, from late 1908 until at least 1911, the Pavilion largely reverted to traditional pantomimes and stock melodramas such as *Harbour Lights* and *A Girl's Temptations*, relying once again on English performers. In so far as it could be called the home of Yiddish drama, it only fulfilled this function during the Edwardian era on a temporary basis and was more often leased by non-Yiddish companies.

The Pavilion Theatre, like so many other East End theatres, suffered in the early years of the century from the rigorous safety demands made by the LCC. Its management claimed in 1903 that finance for safety improvements required by the Council was particularly difficult to raise for an East End theatre.[21] When the Pavilion was inspected by the LCC in August 1907, it was functioning as a Yiddish theatre; accordingly the Chief Officer of the Fire Brigade recommended that, since the theatre was leased by a syndicate for a number of years and that an exclusively Yiddish audience would be catered for, the Committee might consider the advisability of having all exit and other notices displayed in that language.[22] By 1909 the theatre had again reverted to a non-Yiddish repertory. Although a death by suffocation in the gallery in July of this year was attributed to over-crowding, the management's response to criticism over this incident suggests the theatre had fallen on hard times, claiming that, since 'average receipts for the other evenings of last week ranged from between £3 and £8 for performances, it will be readily gathered that the opportunities for over-crowding in this theatre are very few'.[23]

Even if the use of the Pavilion as the home of Yiddish drama fell into temporary abeyance in the late Edwardian period, Jewish needs and tastes were still catered for. Thus, in August 1909, Jack Woolf of 'Wonderland' fame opened the East London Palace, a Yiddish music-hall, in Field-gate Street, Whitechapel. There had been previous attempts to set up a Yiddish music hall on a less ambitious scale, but these had proved unsuccessful. One short-lived hall had sprung into existence in a room which appeared to be nothing other than an abandoned workshop; a second hall with primitive appointments had appeared in a side-street off Commercial Road. The new hall, which could seat some 800 persons, suffered from none of these defects, for it had complied with all the current regulations stipulated by the LCC and was both commodious and well-decorated.

Yiddish theatre took even longer to find a home. In the late nineteenth and early twentieth centuries, according to Lloyd P. Gartner, 'wandering troupes and celebrated players performed fairly continuously in London and the provinces, but a permanent theatre of a high standard did not evolve'. Gartner maintains that the erection of the Feinman Yiddish People's Theatre, the Temple, in the East End in 1912, was the most ambitious effort to establish a Yiddish theatre, but lack of capital and competition from the re-established programme of Yiddish drama and operetta at the Pavilion led to its demise within a year.[24] The Pavilion itself now re-emerged as an important centre of Yiddish entertainment: in 1913 attention was drawn by J. Rodker to the more adventurous side of its repertoire, which included dramas by Zola, Strindberg, and Tolstoy performed by the Moscovitch company. Rodker was surprised to find plays normally performed only in club theatres for the intelligentsia a regular part of the repertory at Whitechapel. He was also impressed by the fact that lack of funds prevented the engagement of actors who were 'over-refined' and staging that was over-elaborate; that the time of commencement of performances (8.30 p.m.) and the cheapest seat prices (fourpence) allowed the Jewish workers to attend these plays; and by the fact that 'the unconventionality of the audience – which seems at first sight a typically music-hall one busy with oranges and nuts – frees one from all constraints, while in the interval your neighbour will discuss the play with some erudition and much enthusiasm'.[25] Whilst aware that the predominant taste was for melodramas of Jewish life (replete with an atmosphere of deep melancholy and a fatalistic philosophy), Rodker was nevertheless impressed by what he saw and by the fact that Maurice Moscovitch made a point of making an explanatory speech to the audience prior to any play that he considered might be too much above their heads. As a result of Moscovitch's pioneering work and that of the Feinman Operatic and Dramatic Company, the Pavilion continued to function very much as a neighbourhood theatre well into the 1930s.

THE STANDARD THEATRE

Like the Pavilion Theatre, the Standard Theatre also managed to find a unique niche for itself, at least during the early part of the Edwardian era. Under the management of the Melvilles it developed a reputation for its original melodramas, usually premiered during the autumn season. Throughout the rest of the year it hosted touring companies (often performing melodramas), a regular season by the Turner Opera Company and revivals of the most popular Melville melodramas. Its appeal may have been partly local, but according to A. E. Wilson it became fashionable for West End playgoers to visit Shoreditch especially to see the new sensation dramas on their first staging.[26]

Although the Melvilles did not invent the character of the adventuress, she, together with some sensationally realistic effects, seems to have been at the heart of their melodramas. The first of their 'wicked women' melodramas – *The Worst Woman in London* (Walter Melville) – was performed at the Standard Theatre in the autumn season of 1899. In subsequent years Walter Melville wrote a series of autumn melodramas for the Standard, including *The World of Sin* (1900), *That Wretch of a Woman* (1901), *Her Second Time on Earth* (1902), *A Girl's Cross Roads* (1903), *The Girl Who Lost Her Character* (1904), *The Girl Who Took the Wrong Turning* (1906) and *The Girl Who Wrecked His Home* (1907). His brother, Frederick, contributed *In a Woman's Grip* (1901) and *The Beast and the Beauty* (1906). They created similar dramas for the Terriss Theatre, Rotherhithe, which they also owned, and mounted touring productions of these plays, undoubtedly creating a vogue for them during the Edwardian era. Despite their contrived nature, writes H. F. Maltby, who was employed by the Melvilles during this period, 'there was an element of, if not originality, fresh thought about them ... people would sneer at the Melville dramas, but to Walter and Fred they were works of art; they believed every word of them'.[27]

The Melville melodramas typically presented three contrasting sorts of female character: the adventuress, usually unrepentant and irredeemable; the woman who errs but is sometimes redeemed or forgiven (and who is usually treated sympathetically); and the straight heroine, whose virtue and ethics remain unsullied. One wonders to what sort of audience these plays were appealing. The *Era* is ambiguous, referring at times to local popular audiences for the Melville dramas, at others implying a largely middle-class presence in the theatre. Wilson implies that many of the spectators came from the West End, but presumably the growing suburban audiences also felt the plays were worth a special excursion. Prices were certainly reasonable: the gallery cost only fourpence, the back of the pit sixpence, pits, stalls, and back circle 1 shilling, rising to 2 shillings and sixpence and 3 shillings in the orchestra stalls and first circle, whilst boxes cost from 1 to 2 guineas, all of which was about equivalent to what the Pavilion was charging at this time. (The Britannia, under John East's management from 1904 to 1905, was charging less: boxes were 2 shillings and 2 shillings and sixpence, stalls 1 shilling, the circle sixpence, pit fourpence and gallery twopence). The advertisements printed in the Standard's programme for *A Girl's Cross Roads* in 1903 and for an undated revival of *The Worst Woman in London* certainly seem to be targeting an upper working-class and lower middle-class suburban audience. The majority of items advertised are domestic goods or services including vapour baths, electrical wares, pianos, umbrellas, sewing machine repairs, drapers' stores, tailors, polish, cocoa, photography, boots, watches, and matches; not to mention van hire, public houses, and estate agents. Yet such hypotheses are problematic: the Melvilles' own memoirs suggest a less affluent audience. Admittedly, some of their anecdotes date back to the late 1880s and early 1890s: in 1889, for instance, 'gangs of thugs', 'sordid streets' and the menace of Jack the Ripper made it very difficult for the Standard to engage artistes. There are also references to turmoil at the theatre, hissing, a police presence on Saturday nights, fights after the half-price audience had been admitted at 9.00 p.m. and soggy meat pies landing at the feet of distressed and starving heroines. This hardly sounds like the behaviour of a respectable suburban or West End audience. Later mention of tramping the East End with handbills also implies a local audience, as does the rebuff of the Melvilles' attempt to require their male audience to wear collar and tie: 'I am not a ... dog', exclaimed one spectator, when rebuked for his attire.[28]

If the class of spectator attracted to the Standard melodramas is difficult to hypothesize, so equally is the sex. Mario Borsa was certainly struck by the large female audience for the theatre in the early Edwardian period, referring to

the shop-girls, milliners, dressmakers, typists, stenographers, cashiers of large and small houses of business, telegraph and telephone girls, and the thousands of other girls whose place in the social scale is hard to guess or to define; who avail themselves of the liberty allowed by custom, and the coldness of the English masculine temperament, to wander alone at night from one end of London to the other, spending all their money in gadding about, on sixpenny novels, on magazines, and, above all, on the theatre.

Although Borsa is referring to pit and gallery audiences in the West End, he draws on the Standard to support his case:

The British drama ... offers them so much instruction! I once read in the *Daily Telegraph* ... a notice conceived in these terms: 'Who wants a husband? Statistics show that ninety per cent. of women, when they have reached a marriageable age, are only awaiting the first opportunity to get married; yet hundreds remain old maids. Perhaps husbands are scarce! Do you want to know why you do not get one? Go and see *Her Forbidden Marriage* at the Standard Theatre.'[29]

Borsa may be right in his assumption that the plays were aimed at a female audience, although recent discussion of these plays has posited that, since the Melville adventuresses appealed fundamentally as erotic objects of the male gaze, the melodramas may have appealed more specifically to the male spectator.[30] If, however, the female spectator was targeted, the plays were certainly very coercive, in so far as they prescribed a very traditional set of values. Under the title of *In a Woman's Grip* is inscribed in the 1901 programme: 'Woman! Woman! What a willing slave you make yourself to the man you love. No gift is good enough; no burden is too heavy, no sacrifice is too great for the sake of him you love.' In the list of scenes printed in the 1907 programme for *A Girl's Cross Roads* is inscribed under Act I, Scene 3, Epsom: 'Purity of Mind and Conduct is the First Glory of a Woman.' In *The Girl Who Wrecked His Home* Bertha leaves her husband for another man because she feels neglected; in fact, her conduct turns out to be rather heartless, since her husband's long hours at the office are devoted to securing wealth and comfort for both her and his daughter's future. Bertha, soon discarded by the man with whom she commits adultery, learns the bitter truth and declares, 'Blind mad fool that I have been. I have committed a great crime and now comes the punishment. I can never hold my head up again amongst respectable people ... I have sacrificed husband, children, everything that makes life worth living, and for what. To become this man's plaything, his dupe.' Many years later, a beggar and an outcast, Bertha accidentally comes face to face with her husband, who agrees to provide her with a home on his estate, but will initially have nothing else to do with her. Bertha reflects, 'This is my punishment, the bitterest blow of all. He casts me aside and it is all my own doing. Oh, what fools women are. When Heaven blesses them with the love of a good true man, why don't they respect that love.' Bertha is luckier than most: her husband finally relents and takes her back into his home. Worse punishment, however, awaits those women who fall prey to drink: Barbara Wade, trapped in a loveless marriage and clearly an alcoholic, so disgusts her husband by her heavy drinking in

A Girl's Cross Roads that she resolves to leave him. She emerges later in the play, starving and down and out, in several scenes of intense realism, culminating in a scene of delirium tremens to equal Charles Warner's in *Drink*.

A crucial factor in the appeal of the Melville melodramas was their use of realistic and elaborate settings and of some very spectacular climaxes. At the conclusion of *That Wretch of a Woman* the adventuress will stop at nothing to have her way: having slapped the face of the heroine, Grace, who is being held prisoner, she mortally wounds a small boy, Dick, and then departs, having set the building on fire. The wounded Dick now crawls across the floor and unties the ropes binding Grace, who then makes a sensational escape across a burning rafter, carrying the dying boy in her arms. Equally sensational was the escape of the heroine from a similar adversary in *The Worst Woman in London* by sliding down a telegraph wire which she reached from the top floor window of a house engulfed in flames. The lurid and the realistic seemed popular features of these plays, which were often praised for the quality of their scenery. Rarely, however, was setting specific to the East End: gone are the local scenes familiar to a Shoreditch audience which had been a highlight of Walter Melville's and George Lander's *The Great World of London*, staged in 1898. The choice of settings in general suggests the plays were obviously manufactured with an eye to their provincial and suburban tours.

The Standard melodramas proved enormously successful, enjoying an East End run of six to eight weeks every autumn, before touring. Yet in 1907 the Melvilles sold the Standard Theatre and shortly afterwards sold their interest in the Rotherhithe theatre; within three years they had moved to the West End, where they undertook management of the Lyceum Theatre from 1910 and opened the Prince's Theatre in 1911. They also continued to run touring companies and retained an interest in a number of provincial theatres. 'They were undoubtedly excellent businessmen', wrote H. F. Maltby of the frugally-minded, teetotal brothers, 'but they got less out of life than anyone I had ever met.'[31]

THE DEMISE OF THE BRITANNIA AND STANDARD THEATRES

The departure of the Melvilles from the Standard Theatre may, in part, be linked to the intervention of the LCC. Several years earlier the Crauford brothers had ceased active participation in the management of the Britannia Theatre. In order to satisfy the LCC's safety regulations and ensure the renewal of the theatre's licence, expenditure in the region of £8,000 was demanded.[32] Although such expenditure would have been within the Craufords' means,[33] a marked decline in the neighbourhood of Hoxton probably no longer justified such investment in the theatre. George R. Sims, writing in 1905, when the Britannia was functioning as a variety house, asserted that 'it is generally admitted that Hoxton is getting poorer. People with a little money move out of it, while demolitions on the city border are constantly driving into it the lowest class of evicted tenant, thus further congesting its over-crowded ovens of crime and poverty.'[34] If this was the case, the Craufords may well have heeded the view expressed by the former manager of the New East London Theatre, Morris Abrahams, when he claimed that the improvements demanded by the LCC (which invariably required alterations in seating and restrictions on numbers) could only be covered by a rise in prices, but if prices were raised, the clientele disappeared.[35] The Craufords may have felt that the capital expenditure required was not worth the likely reduction in profit that would result from compliance with the 150-odd improvements demanded by the LCC.

The Melvilles left the Standard just after they had been confronted with a similar set of demands. Although the theatre had been rebuilt just prior to Christmas 1897 and electricity replaced gas in 1904, problems emerged during each annual inspection by the LCC, culminating in the 1907 demand that forty-five points be attended to. The Melvilles' memoirs make it clear that by June 1907 they definitely wanted a West End theatre: it may be that, when Walter Gibbons offered them £80,000 for the purchase of Terriss's and the Standard, it was an offer they could not refuse and that the LCC's demands were merely a secondary factor in their decision. There was quite a degree of local concern, however, when it was learnt that Walter Gibbons had purchased the Standard and wished to turn it into a music hall. The Shoreditch Trades and Labour Council, the Actors' Union, the Amalgamated Musicians' Union and the General Staff Branch (London) of the National Association of Theatre Employees all opposed him on grounds that there were already twelve music halls within a radius of the Standard Theatre, three of which were within a quarter of a mile; secondly, the Standard Theatre's success proved that there was a need for a legitimate theatre to supply the needs of a vast number of local residents; thirdly, that it provided employment for members of the musical and dramatic profession.[36] Nevertheless, Gibbons received the licence.

The LCC certainly inspected the music halls regularly, paying attention to safety regulations, to audience behaviour and to the content of programmes presented. Thus the Bow Music Hall, which generally appeared to be unexceptional, almost lost its licence in 1901 when a comedian called Bentley, dressed as a policeman, sang an indecent song accompanied by indecent gestures. In 1903 a police action was brought against the hall on the grounds that boys under the age of 14 were being sold intoxicating liquors.[37] In the same year the Bow Music Hall was cited, along with the Foresters' Music Hall and Sadler's Wells Theatre, as 'a rendezvous for the meeting of the low music hall crowd, their associates of the betting fraternity, book makers, prize ring fighters and the roughest element of East London'.[38] The complainant, an employee of the Foresters' Music Hall (in Bethnal Green), claimed it to be 'the greatest inducement to vice and immorality that possibly could be permitted'. A married man with grown-up daughters and sons, he was particularly anxious that inspectors (preferably in disguise) should visit the Foresters' Music Hall,

where every license is permitted for gentlemen friends of the management, to go on the side of the stage while the lady artistes are performing; visit them while they change their dresses on the side, without the slightest attempt [by the management] to provide a proper change[ing] room, which they should have, as frequently they, the ladies, in changing, are in a half nude state, and the crowd of men in the immediate vicinity [are] gazing on the ladies in a most objectionable and disgusting manner; this is occurring nightly at the present time...

The anonymous complainant also draws attention to the fact that certain gentlemen were importuning all the younger and more decent lady artistes. Yet LCC inspectors rarely noticed anything untoward at the East End music halls. There were no improprieties observable at the Bow in 1903, the audience being 'orderly and quiet, no shouting or whistling to speak of'.[39] As for the Royal Cambridge, reports at the beginning of the century state that its programme is 'inoffensive' and 'free from vulgarity', whilst the audience was generally orderly apart from the crush to get into the gallery. The bars were not extensively patronized and 'no women of questionable character' were in evidence.[40]

Charles Booth had commented towards the end of the nineteenth century on the general propriety of music hall audiences in the East

End.[41] He had also affirmed that the halls were more popular than the theatres. Thus the fate of the Standard was perhaps inevitable: it became the Shoreditch Olympia. The Britannia, meanwhile, struggled on throughout the period, used sometimes as a theatre, sometimes as a music hall, and sometimes as a venue for sporting events. Yet its popular, local identity had disappeared, along with its former reputation. Only the Pavilion was to survive intact as a theatre, largely because it served a particular need within a particular community. Otherwise the inner East End was claimed by the music hall, whilst further north and further east a ring of suburban theatres provided a bland medley of entertainment which, rather than identify and exploit what was specific to local communities, ensured that they grew more and more like each other as they supported a product which was no longer organic but imposed upon them.[42]

NOTES

1 *East London* (London, 1901), pp. 14–15.
2 Ibid. p. 313. Among the trades to which Besant refers are clothes in Whitechapel, furniture and woodwork in Bethnal Green and Shoreditch, the docks by the riverside, boot-making in Mile End/Old Town and Old Ford, the silk trade in Spitalfields and Bethnal Green and small industries such as fur and feather dressing at Hoxton.
3 *Life and Labour of the People in London: East London* (London, 1889–91), p. 11.
4 See P. J. Keating, 'Fact and Fiction in the East End' in H. J. Dyos and Michael Wolff, *The Victorian City: Images and Realities* (London, 1973), vol. II, pp. 585–602, for a fuller discussion of this problem.
5 Clive Barker argues for a decline in the Britannia audience in 'The Audiences of the Britannia Theatre, Hoxton', *Theatre Quarterly*, 9:34 (1979), pp. 27–41. See also Theatres and Music Halls Committee of the LCC, *Presented Papers*, Standard Theatre, October 1907.
6 H. G. Hibbert, *Fifty Years of a Londoner's Life* (London, 1916), p. 63, laments the passing of the distinct theatrical forms of East and South London. 'The East-ender or Surrey-sider comes west, or indulges the picture palace habit, with an occasional divigation to a suburban empire.'
7 Gareth Stedman Jones, *Outcast London: A Study in the Relationship between Classes in Victorian Society* (Oxford, 1971), pp. 207, 323–5.
8 *Life and Labour*, p. 116.
9 J. Blake, *Memories of Old Poplar* (London, 1977), p. 28.
10 Full details of the Stratford community at this period can be found in Edward G. Howarth and Mona Wilson, *West Ham: A Study in Social and Industrial Problems* (London, 1907), pp. 33–40.
11 'The East End Jew at his Playhouse', *The Pall Mall Gazette*, NS 41:78 (February 1908), pp. 174–9.

12 *The East End of London* (London, 1951), p. 202.

13 Ibid. p. 207. Rose's source is the novelist, Israel Zangwill.

14 Ibid. p. 225.

15 C. Russell and H. S. Lewis, *The Jew in London, a Study of Racial Character and Present-Day Conditions* (London, 1900), p. xxxvii.

16 Ibid. p. 13.

17 Ibid. p. 225.

18 *Fifty Years of a Londoner's Life*, p. 69.

19 *Living London*, ed. George R. Sims, 3 vols. (London, 1901), quoted in *Victorian Theatre*, ed. Russell Jackson (London, 1989), pp. 75–6.

20 Russell and Lewis, *The Jew in London*, p. 88. However, it should be noted that, despite such sentiments, anti-Semitism and criticism of England's immigration policy were also rife, culminating in the Alien's Act of 1905.

21 *Presented Papers*, Pavilion Theatre, letter dated 24 November 1903.

22 Ibid. report dated 26 August 1907.

23 Ibid. letter dated July 1909.

24 *The Jewish Immigrant in England 1870–1914* (London, 1960), pp. 260–1. This source gives 1,500 as the theatre's seating capacity. However, David Mazower, *The Yiddish Theatre in London* (London, 1987), p. 67, gives the figure as 900.

25 'The Theatre in Whitechapel', *Poetry and Drama*, 1 (1913), p. 43.

26 *East End Entertainment* (London, 1954), p. 134.

27 *Ring Up the Curtain* (London, 1950), pp. 104–5.

28 Melville Manuscript, University of Kent. I am grateful to Louis James and Jan Shepherd for making these details available to me.

29 *The English Stage of To-day* (London, 1908), pp. 4–5.

30 Elaine Aston and Ian Clarke, 'The Dangerous Woman of Melvillean Melodrama', unpublished paper presented at 'Melodrama: Stage, Picture, Screen', British Film Institute Conference, July 1992.

31 *Ring Up the Curtain*, p. 105. However, Maltby claims that the Melvilles 'always mounted their melodramas well; plenty of colour and light and uniforms they loved'.

32 John M. East, *'Neath the Mask: The Story of the East Family* (London, 1967), p. 203; *Presented Papers*, Britannia Theatre, Hoxton, 1888–1909.

33 Sarah Lane, the manager of the Britannia Theatre, had left £126,000 on her death in 1899.

34 'In the Heart of Hoxton', no. 6 of 'Trips about Town' in *Strand Magazine*, 30: 177 (1905), p. 331.

35 Penny Summerfield, 'The Effingham Arms and the Empire: Deliberate Selection in the Evolution of the Music Hall in London', in *Popular Culture and Class Conflict 1590–1914: Explorations in the History of Labour and Leisure*, ed. Eileen and Stephen Yeo (Sussex, 1981), p. 240.

36 *Presented Papers*, Standard Theatre, 1907.

37 *Presented Papers*, Bow Music Hall, letter dated 15 July 1903. The author of the letter, the clerk of the managers of the School Board, claimed 'I have

since visited these Music Halls and consider it disgraceful that intoxicating liquors should be supplied to mere boys. I suggest that a recommendation should be forwarded to the LCC asking for the abolition of drinking facilities at the early performance which is frequented mainly by boys under the age of sixteen.' The 1901 report is dated 2 November.

38 Ibid. letter dated 30 September 1903.

39 Ibid. report dated 23 October 1903.

40 Ibid., Royal Cambridge Music Hall, Reports, 20 July 1901, and 5 August 1902.

41 *Life and Labour*, pp. 116–17.

42 Hibbert, *Fifty Years of a Londoner's Life*, p. 73, states that 'of the thirty suburban theatres that suddenly encircled London, half were soon in financial difficulties, and now are music halls or picture palaces, or anything'. Hibbert felt that far too many suburban theatres were built to accommodate the touring companies that had been formed, originally, to visit the provinces.

Changing horses in mid-ocean: 'The Whip' in Britain and America

David Mayer

Some papers in this volume celebrate the changes and characteristics which transformed the Victorian theatre into entertainments different enough to be labelled 'Edwardian'. Others identify the events and developments and innovations which help to distinguish entertainments of the early twentieth century from their immediate predecessors and which can be identified as the 'New Drama'. One of these developments has to be the arrival and commercial success of motion pictures. In 1900 this arrival is barely discernible, little more than the making and viewing of 'actuality' films and a very few and very brief dramatic narratives. The commercial success of these earliest films is limited to what they can command as a turn in the music halls or variety houses which have invested in rudimentary projection equipment and screens. A dozen years later – perhaps less – movies are watched by millions of people and are arguably the most significant art medium of the young century.

Whilst we can discern and describe change in this period, we must also recognize the phenomenon which Thomas Kuhn observes[1] when an older paradigm, a model or description of reality – or, for our purposes, theatrical representations of human experience and the world – is challenged by a newer one. The old paradigm does not vanish. Rather, its proponents try with renewed vigour to prove its validity and viability. For some time, perhaps for decades, it may coexist alongside the newer model. So it is with drama in the Edwardian era. The Victorian popular stage does not melt away; it coexists with the New Drama and with the Edwardians' own spectacular stage and is adorned and refurbished by its adherents and practitioners who give little ground, and then only grudgingly, to an artistically respectable avant garde. Nowhere is this phenomenon more evident than in the development of motion pictures and cinema's co-existence with the 'live' stage. Even as film technology and marketing and distribution, reflected in developing techniques and enlarging audiences, grow and become more sophisticated, there is a retrogressive step. Filmmakers themselves hold up the stage as a worthy and respectable medium, while cinema, they declare, is neither worthy nor respectable. Motion pictures thus pause in the development of their own vocabularies and techniques and choose as subject-matter the material of the popular Victorian stage.

That is the subject of this essay: an examination of some of the interstices between stage and film. My conclusion is that there is no conclusion. My observations instead recognize an assortment of discontinuous and overlapping events and developments which begin at the points when the Victorian theatre and the music hall are at their most opulently spectacular, and commercial motion pictures (which for all practical purposes begin in 1895) start their transformation from the 'pre-industrial' phase. This phase is roughly characterized by the use of a variety of film technologies – for example, non-standard film/camera/projector sizes, by film exhibition at fairground booths and storefront 'nickelodeons' not dissimilar to penny-gaffs, and by largely anonymous performers appearing in anonymously written and directed motion pictures which rarely exceed a running-time of 30 minutes and, more often, run for under 15 minutes. Within the same period, perhaps from 1908 onward, the 'industrial' phase of cinema begins, and motion pictures are changed by the acceptance of industry-standard (35 mm) camera and film size, thereby allowing films produced by any maker to be exhibited in any venue. It finds the emergence of film acting as distinct from stage acting and recognition for actors and directors with remuneration, fame, and star status. The industrial phase is signalled by the advent of 'picture palaces' and by attendance at films by a full spectrum of national populations. It further finds films growing in length from 30 minutes duration to what we now recognize as feature-length. It begins to see the growth of the 'studio system', first in Paris, London, Rome, and on the Eastern North American seaboard and, subsequently, in Hollywood. The period in question continues past the end of the First World War and to the virtual expiration of labour-intensive Victorian and Edwardian stage practices and the relinquishing of elaborate stage effects to the province of the cinema.

In considering the inter-relationships between the late Victorian and Edwardian stage and early motion pictures, I find that my observations contradict A. N. Vardac and other historians of early cinema[2] who describe a stage which, unable to cope with a growing demand for the realistic – or even naturalistic – effects required by nineteenth-century audiences, aspired to the graphic explicitness of motion pictures. Film's arrival, these scholars declare, was the natural outcome of this aspiration. I find no evidence to support their deterministic teleology and, instead, describe stage authors, artisans, and audiences who, for at least fifteen years after the appearance of commercial films, regarded motion pictures as an inferior medium of entertainment. To some extent, but only to some, that same attitude was shared by filmmakers who envied the stage for its apparent legitimacy and for the breadth and loyalty of its middle-class audience. At the same time, there are pressures on the late Victorian and Edwardian stage to address modern issues; there are pressures, too, to change theatrical work methods and practices. Costs of theatrical production are rising. Labour is still cheap, but machinery is becoming cheaper than labour. There will be sound economic reasons why the film industry – when it becomes an industry – will be more cost-effective and profitable than the theatrical profession. The consequence of these conflicting views and pressures was to create, between 1908 and 1919, a climate of uncertainty about the comparative merits and technologies of each medium. My narrative dwells upon some of these uncertainties.

At the core of my essay, and as an example of the tensions and the sequence of somewhat confusing events, is the Drury Lane autumn melodrama of 1909, *The Whip*. *The Whip* was a particular sort of stage play which was seen yearly – every September through November – at what was then advertised as Britain's 'National Theatre', the Theatre Royal, Drury Lane. Such melodrama, which audiences began to see from as early as 1880 until the start of the First World War, was called 'autumn drama', and *The Whip* is both the best known of this species of play and, at least for the present, our only example of Drury Lane autumn drama adapted for the screen to survive. Bringing *The Whip* from stage to motion pictures will be seen to be a part of a process which, while furthering some of the intentions of filmmakers, in other respects reflects a conservatism which arrested the development of motion pictures even as it preserved, on film, views of the Victorian and Edwardian stage.

Drury Lane's autumn dramas, as well as comparable pieces launched with less frequency and success from other playhouse managements, belong to a larger category of Victorian and Edwardian stage melodramas called 'sensation dramas'. Sensation dramas are plays of adventure, romance, and intrigue, of treachery, bravery, and thoroughly identifiable good and evil locked in endless conflict. In a very real sense, the Drury Lane autumn dramas extended the Victorian age of theatre for nearly two decades after Queen Victoria's death. While the so-called New Drama is fragmenting theatregoing and claiming audiences for Pinero, Jones, and Shaw and for Ibsen and Strindberg in English, the popular audience – great-grandparents of today's mass cinema audience – continued in their preference for the excitements of autumn drama and then for the cinema that eventually supplanted and replaced it.

Many such autumn pieces chronicle the international rivalries accompanying the expansion and consolidation of the British empire. Others – and *The Whip* is one of these, a racing or 'sporting' melodrama (The Whip is the name of a racehorse) – feed the Victorian delight in new spectator sports and attendent betting. They also nourish other preoccupations: the interactions of social class in public institutions such as the military or the church, in work and career, in sport, in marriage, the advent and impact of the 'New Woman' (the film discards an important stage representation of the New Woman, but in the Americanized character of Diana Beverley nominates a cinematic version); and still other concerns – speed, the still-novel automobile, and the ever-dangerous urban landscape.

Although unpublished and rarely read, Henry Hamilton's and Cecil Raleigh's *The Whip* is widely known to theatre historians through a series of photographs originally published in *The Play Pictorial* in 1909[3] (see plate 13). The instant and continuing popularity of *The Whip* assured its revival in 1910 for a second season at Drury Lane; then it toured widely throughout Britain until the First World War. Meanwhile, in 1912, this piece was staged in a replica production in New York by the Shubert management with the elaborate scenery of the 1899 *Ben Hur* taken from storage to assist the climactic Newmarket Race scene. Here *The Whip* was seen by Maurice Tourneur (1876–1961), one of the more innovative film-makers of the second and third decades of this century. Impressed by the filmic possibilities of *The Whip*, Tourneur was engaged by the Shubert management to direct three Drury Lane autumn sensation melodramas by Hamilton and Raleigh. In addition to acquiring film rights to *The Whip*, the Shuberts bought *The White Heather* (1897), and *The Great Ruby* (1898).[4] Tourneur's version of *The Whip*,

13 *The Whip* on stage. Drury Lane 1909 (*Play Pictorial* 1909)

translated from England to America, was released in 1916. Identified
in the film's inter-titles as 'The Great Drury Lane Drama', it was
exhibited in both America and Britain. In 1920 it was reissued in an
abridged version and was exhibited for a further half-decade.
Meanwhile, in 1917, *The Whip* was the subject of a film parody which
lampooned both the stage and the original film versions.[5] Thus, while
I intend to draw the reader's attention to *The Whip* as one of the first
attempts to adapt a full-length Edwardian (or late-Victorian) stage
play as a motion picture and to preserve the production values of that
play, I intend as well to explore the tensions between older and newer
forms of entertainment and the conservatism which fostered this
filmic adaptation.

The Whip enacts the attempts by the villain, Captain Greville
Sartorys, and his henchwoman and sometime mistress, Mrs D'Aquila,
to disrupt the courtship of Lady Diana Sartorys, daughter of the
Marquis of Beverley, and Hubert, Earl of Brancaster. It is Sartorys's
purpose, in alienating the high-born couple, to insinuate himself into
Lady Diana's favour and thereby marry into the Beverley wealth. To
this end Sartorys must eliminate Brancaster, first by sabotaging the
Earl's car and causing a nearly fatal crash, next by claiming falsely
that Brancaster had already secretly married Mrs D'Aquila, and,
when these stratagems fail, by bankrupting the young lord, whose
financial solvency is wholly contingent upon his horse, The Whip,
winning the 2000 Guineas race at Newmarket. Although Sartorys has
blackmailed Brancaster's jockey and attempts to prevent the horse
reaching the race meeting, he is unsuccessful. The horse reaches the
track, the race is won by The Whip (both blackmail and rescue of The
Whip are handled differently in play and film), and the couple are
united. The play, as is characteristic of Drury Lane autumn drama, is
dependent upon a sequence of set-piece episodes which draw upon
the resources of the labour-intensive late-Victorian stage: an on-stage
fox hunt, a car smash, weekend confinement in the Chamber of
Horrors at Madame Tussaud's, and a car chase to rescue The Whip
from the railway line, where he has been stalled in a boxcar horse-van
in the path of an oncoming express train. Only just in time The Whip
is rescued, but the horse-van is demolished and the locomotive
derailed. Finally, there is the 2000 Guineas race.

There are key elements of the plot which will be seized upon and
changed or parodied in subsequent versions: the Drury Lane text
makes much of a growing romantic attachment between Diana

Sartorys's cousin, the Hon. Mrs Beamish, and The Whip's working-class trainer, Tom Lambert. In contrast to the romance between Diana Sartorys and Hubert Brancaster, Hamilton and Raleigh exploit the melodrama's traditional comic pairing to highlight a love affair across class divisions. It is the trainer Tom Lambert who is locked in Tussaud's and Mrs Beamish who is driven at high speeds to rescue The Whip from the stranded horse-van. At the Newmarket meeting Sartorys makes his last attempt to defeat Brancaster. His stratagem is to have The Whip's jockey arrested and taken into police custody moments before the race is to begin. Here the race-loving British sporting public intervenes, rescuing the jockey from the police and placing him upon The Whip's back.

In the 1909–10 Drury Lane production, the set-piece episodes are the result of the scenic designers' ingenuity and craftsmanship. What particularly characterized Drury Lane autumn melodrama was the attention paid to elaborately realistic sets and to illusions of apparent reality and great danger. It probably is not too much of an exaggeration to insist that however good the scripts may have been – by such dramatists as Augustus Harris, Arthur Shirley, Arthur Collins, Henry Hamilton, and Cecil Raleigh – each drama was in reality a collaboration between various combinations of these playwrights, the clever orchestra conductor and composer Jimmy Glover who devised incidental music for these pieces, and Drury Lane's scenic staff, in particular Harry Emden, and the Lane's leading designer, Bruce Smith, otherwise known – for obvious reasons – as 'Sensation Smith'.

'Sensation Smith' was well established as a London scenic designer[6] and had already earned his nickname many times over when, in 1902, he came under the influence of an American stage production, Klaw and Erlanger's 1899 adaptation of General Lew Wallace's novel *Ben Hur*. American theatres had previously tried out and had described the technology at the centre of *Ben Hur*, the fifth-act chariot race in which 30 tons of horses and chariots galloped and wheeled before a moving backcloth of the Circus Maximus at Antioch. When the production crossed to Drury Lane three years later, the staging of this race was managed by American technicians who operated imported American equipment and who did their best to prevent British stage technicians from copying their effects. Smith was assigned the lesser task of creating the effect of the galley – in which Ben Hur is unjustly kept a prisoner – rammed and sunk by a pirate vessel. Smith let the Americans get on with their work of assembling and operating the chariot race, while he devised the trickwork for the sinking ship. But he kept his eyes open and learned.

Bruce Smith's and Harry Emden's settings were elaborately fleshed out with appropriate furniture and equally elaborate living properties – properties who were well-dressed and well-drilled supernumeraries or, when required, live animals. Whereas today's theatre programmes carry acknowledgements that laundry-care is by Persil and that the theatre is disinfected by Jeyes Fluid and sells Lyons' icecreams, the Drury Lane programme for *The Whip* informs us that Spratt's Patented Dog Food was fed to the pack of hounds used in the on-stage fox-hunt and that Molassine Meal was supplied to the six or eight horses hired from T. G. Hales that appeared first in the hunt and later in the 2000 Guineas Newmarket race.

Photographs of *The Whip* may mislead the modern viewer who is unprepared to consider that in 1909, the year of *The Whip*, theatre photography required further extensive lighting to supplement conventional stage lights. The result is that we see Bruce Smith's sets, [7] not as Drury Lane's and provincial and New York audiences saw them, but washed-out and somewhat faded and, to our eyes, a bit obvious.

What moves this essay from a reflection on late-Victorian stage practice into an exploration of the dilemmas and solutions of a fractionally later era is the advent and immediate success of motion pictures. In 1895 the Lumière Brothers had exhibited motion pictures as a turn in New York and London variety houses. Later that year, the Epsom Derby was filmed by cameramen at the racecourse and the finished film was shown at the Empire Music Hall on the following day. Motion pictures, usually a few minutes in duration and projected in clusters, became a regular feature of Edwardian music hall entertainment. Audiences became accustomed to viewing films in close proximity to dramatic sketches offered under the '18-minute rule' which bound dramatic material in these venues to short pieces performed by a few actors and accompanied by music – a practice not altogether dissimilar to silent film of the period.[8] Thus, a 1905 programme at the London Coliseum can be described in a review which, in consecutive paragraphs, embraces both film and the dramatic sketch.

The American Bioscope is responsible for a humorous series of pictures entitled 'A False Alarm', in which a drunken traveller, setting fire to his Gladstone bag, sounds the fire alarm and brings a posse of engines. The brigade men turn their hoses on the delinquent to whom no mercy is shown. An interesting domestic story is told in 'Found by Rover', in which a fine collie is the means of discovering and restoring to its parents a stolen infant.

The Charioteers, the sensational dramatic, and musical wordless spectacle, which we have already noticed in these columns, concludes the programme, one of the most remarkable that has been given at this very fine house.[9]

Concurrently, small picturehouses (in America, 'nickelodeons') offering audiences a programme of short films at cheap prices sprang up in most urban centres of Europe and North America where there were ample working-class populations and, in Canada and America, immigrant populations who spoke no English and who therefore were unlikely to attend stage plays.

Another three years elapsed before American filmmakers found the means to attract new middle-class audiences to new venues which assured comfort and respectability for motion-picture viewing. Theirs was a solution which brought *The Whip* to the screen but was, nonetheless, a regressive step because it directly inhibited the techniques and processes of making original films. In 1912 the film producer Jesse Lasky formed the Famous Players – Lasky Company with the declared purpose of bringing to the screen noted actors in established dramas. Each film was to be in excess of six reels (approximately an hour's viewing time) and to emulate, within the limits of a silent medium which required dialogue presented in inter-titles, the original stage production. In short, motion pictures were to forsake original film methods and narrative means and were, instead, to emulate theatrical techniques and aspire to the theatre's cultural respectability.

Lasky's surviving productions from the early phase of this project include Sarah Bernhardt in *Queen Elizabeth* (1912)[10] and James O'Neill in *Monte Cristo* (1912–13).[11] *Monte Cristo* exemplifies the retrograde approach to this phase of filmmaking: an over-age and conspicuously overweight actor, well-schooled in the ample gestures appropriate to the stage where he had followed his long career, speaking lengthy passages of dialogue which are only partly summarized in the inter-titles, action set against painted theatre sets – presumably those from the stage *Monte Cristo* – occasionally intermingled with a handful of outdoor shots which contribute little to the forward movement of the drama and which expose the differences between scenery painted to be photographed and stage scenery. The filmmaker's rhetoric of camera shots and intercutting, developed by practitioners such as Edwin Porter as early as 1903, is abandoned. *Monte Cristo* is an invaluable source for studying the late-Victorian stage, but it is a wretchedly bad film.

As other filmmakers begin to adapt stage plays for motion pictures and for the new audiences who viewed these films in the opulence of the new 'picture palaces', there is evidence that their directors are increasingly sensitive to the need to construct and dress appropriate settings, and they appear willing to use the camera's mobility to show their performers in close-ups and medium shots.[12] Too often, however, the chief actors are the stars of West End and Broadway stages and perform with movements and gestures which have been accustomed to reach the farthest rows of large theatres. Thus the performances of Herbert Beerbohm Tree in *Trilby* (1913),[13] William Farnum in *The Sign of the Cross* (1914),[14] and H. B. Irving and Nancy Price in *The Lyons Mail* (1917)[15] reveal minimal recognition of developed film technique, even as they preserve the visual rhetorical vocabularies of the Victorian and Edwardian stage. For these stage actors the camera occupies the position of a privileged spectator. It is addressed, gazed at, nudged knowingly and conspiratorially. The performances of these actors are oversized, but they are powerful and eye-catching. By contrast, younger actors employed in these productions treat the camera as if it were another actor on stage with them. These actors show an awareness that movements can be simplified and diminished in size for maximum effectiveness on the screen, that a nod will tell as well as a grimace, that the movement of a finger informs as much as the sweep of an arm. But at this early date there is also the older repertory actor in a supporting role whose robust movements remind us that stage and film acting are distinct and sometime incompatible arts.

Maurice Tourneur's adaptation of *The Whip* is, mostly, a free-standing motion picture, but at moments it still acknowledges its stage origins. Some of the freedom comes with changes in locale and identity. Whereas the original Hamilton and Raleigh melodrama is set entirely in England, the film locates all but the first reel in socialite New York State. Both dramas enact the predations upon the Beverley family of the villainous Captain Sartoris (the spelling of his surname has been altered in the American intertitles) and his accomplice the 'adventuress', Mrs D'Aquila. Both Sartoris and Mrs D'Aquila, whose origins and connections with the Beverley family are now obscure, seek wealth in the New World. Sartoris hopes to win Diana and unsuccessfully dangles Mrs D'Aquila before young Hubert Brancaster – in film, already the democratic idiom of America – plain Mr Brancaster. Relocating *The Whip* in an American setting requires ingenuity, and Tourneur has devised an opening aboard an ocean liner. Briefly, thereafter, Tourneur's directorial hand falters as he starts the action of the play at the Beverley country estate. Characters have been eliminated or their status changed. Brancaster will lose only a modest fraction of his wealth if The Whip is beaten. The Marquis of Beverley has been demoted to a judge, and his daughter Diana is similarly without an aristocratic title. The Hon. Mrs Beamish has been replaced by Diana's friend Myrtle Anson, and, with the former's disappearance, there is no sanctioned romance across class boundaries, nor does Tourneur's nominee for the New Woman race in a chauffeur-driven car to halt a threatening express train.

Both dramas operate in worlds of luxury and money, but Tourneur's characters have greater mobility and are less bound by restrictions of class and etiquette. In the film Diana Beverley and Myrtle Anson, rather than Tom Lambert, The Whip's trainer, are locked for a terrifying weekend in the Chamber of Horrors of the Eden Museé,[16] New York City's version of Madame Tussaud's. The effect is to shift action and decision-making from the play's low comics to the film's modern American females who, concurrently, can be amusingly frightened, but ultimately intelligent enough to detect villainy and decisive in preventing the racehorse's death. Yet there is also something lost from the British model, because when Lambert gets free, the forward-looking, independent Mrs Beamish races the locomotive and, choosing the trainer, can marry beneath her class.

The film's most notable advances on the stage play are in Tourneur's handling of key sensation sequences. With Edwin Porter's *The Life of an American Fireman* (1903), which innovatively intercut scenes of a woman trapped in a burning house and a fire company racing to save her, motion pictures had learned to dramatize the concept of 'meanwhile' and to depict separate-but-related simultaneous events. However, there is no 'meanwhile' in the Drury Lane text. Sartorys's attempt to destroy The Whip is shown in a linear sequence of animated tableaux. In two swift scenes which require little stage depth and are uninterrupted by the close of stage curtains, The Whip is loaded into his horse-box; the watching grooms and waving supporters are drawn off, as a moving backcloth behind the horsebox and profile railway coaches inform us that the train is in motion. Now Sartorys, who has surreptitiously boarded the train, disconnects the horse-box from the moving train. Losing speed, the horse-box glides on to the final, full-stage, setting and comes to a stop. In the silence of the deserted countryside the audience begin to hear the ominous rumble of an approaching locomotive. A car's horn is sounded. Moments later Mrs Beamish appears.

Mrs BEAMISH [Speaking from a bridge that apparently runs above the top of the tunnel] Harry – Harry Anson [The Whip's jockey, now travelling in the van] – Harry – he can't hear us – Harry – Harry for your life – this way,
     quick, both of you – on to the line.
(Mrs B. is seen scrambling down alongside the tunnel R.C. followed by the CHAUFFEUR and a STABLE LAD.[17] [The van door is forced open,[18] Harry Anson and the Stable Lad throw down a ramp, and Anson leads The Whip down the ramp to safety. As horse and jockey get clear of the van, the express locomotive enters R, demolishes the van, and, amidst clouds of escaping steam, falls upstage.]

In Tourneur's *The Whip* concurrent events are skilfully and suspensefully intercut. We watch as the racehorse and jockey are loaded into a boxcar, while Sartoris secretly boards a passenger coach at the same stop. As the train pulls from the siding, the film then cuts to the women still shut in the Eden Museé, to Brancaster innocently motoring towards the race meeting at Saratoga, then to Sartoris patiently seated in the coach, consulting his watch. The film continues to intercut at an accelerating tempo as the train proceeds, as Diana frees herself from the Museé, as Brancaster settles to a comfortable dinner in an upstate New York inn, as Sartoris rises, leaves the coach and climbs to the train roof to disconnect the boxcar – which then slides away from the moving train and stops on an isolated section of track.[19] The long sequence continues as Diana, telephoning, interrupts Brancaster's meal, as the express train rushes towards the stranded boxcar, as Brancaster, in consternation, puts down the telephone, runs to his car and heads to intercept the express, as the train rushes onward, as Brancaster is forced to wait at a level crossing as the train rushes past, and, finally, as Brancaster overtakes the express train and, only just in time, frees both horse and jockey

14a & b *The Whip* on film. 1916.

from the boxcar before the locomotive hits the boxcar and both are demolished.[20] Coincidentally, perhaps because these episodes are some of the more emotionally charged of the film, restrained film-acting yields to the enlarged gestures of the earlier stage. Although Tourneur seems concerned to catch the psychological moment of the impact and to convey to his audience the horror of the event through Brancaster's eyes, he resorts to belt-and-braces direction which, through excess, undermines his intent. Irving Cummings, playing an aghast Brancaster, registers the event in medium close-up through his facial expression, but this moment is followed by stage gesticulations of dismay and horror which involve throwing fisted arms upward, then twisting laterally and bending elbows over his bowing head.

Tourneur's handling of 'meanwhile' is again skilled as the climactic horse-race unfolds. We watch in dismay as the jockey Anson is arrested and led away. There is no sporting crowd to snatch him from the police and place him in The Whip's saddle. Again, in a sequence which gathers momentum, we see Sartoris and his co-conspirators jubilant, then Brancaster and Judge Beverley walking disconsolately to the rail at the edge of the racetrack, thence to a bugler calling the race, to the lineup, to the start, back to conspirators, again to Brancaster and Beverley, then to the race and the anonymous bunched horses, then to the crowd shouting, the inter-title informs us, 'The Whip! The Whip!', and then to the film's *coup de théâtre*: Diana Beverley has dressed herself in the detained jockey's racing silks and is riding The Whip to victory. Rapid intercutting continues to the race's and film's end where the owner of the winning horse embraces an American version of the New Woman.

Provincial stage tours of *The Whip* continued into the 1920s. Tourneur's film was reissued by Paragon Films in 1920. Sensation melodrama, exiled to motion pictures, flourishes today. The Monster Melodrama will neither die nor stay confined to the historical period with which it is most closely associated. *The Whip* is only one melodrama among dozens to have a life well past the period whose nominal dates determine the contents of this volume. We can easily observe a similar theatrical longevity for such 1880s and 1890s favourites as *The Silver King*, *The Still Alarm*, *The Lights o' London*, *Tommy Atkins*, *The Sign of the Cross*, and *The Only Way*. Our problem, in part, is that we have accepted a taxonomy for theatrical forms, practices, and technologies which gathers these elements under the names of reigning British sovereigns. King Edward VII reigned a scant nine years. If, nonetheless, we seek evidence that sensation melodrama could not survive, we may offer Vardac's rationale and observe the genre comfortably established in motion pictures. The fault, he claims, was not sensation melodrama's but the palpable inadequacies of stage illusion and theatrical technologies. Audience preferences for melodrama are undiminished. *Die Hard* and *Jurassic Park* are here to prove the point.

On the other hand, illusion may not be the problem, and it is worth looking at such other factors as theatrical economics. *The Whip* at Drury Lane or New York and on tour required a cast of twenty-three salaried actors and an unspecified number of supernumeraries.[21] Full production required a minimum of eleven separate scenes. Other autumn and sensation melodramas made similar demands on cast size and scenic requirements. As labour costs rose in the twentieth century, the cost of theatrical wages alone was cause enough to make managements reconsider what they offered and to seek cheaper alternatives. Only the motion picture industry, able to print and circulate numerous copies of a single film, could meet such prodigal expenses. It is therefore the very lavishness of autumn melodrama's spectacle which contributes to its extinction. In that sense, to the degree that *The Whip* is emblematic of a lavish era destined to succumb in a colder economic climate, Drury Lane's 1909 autumn piece is a striking example of Edwardian theatre. Tourneur's *The Whip*, in its turn, celebrates that autumnal theatrical extravagance before winter sets in.

NOTES

1 Thomas Kuhn, *The Structure of Scientific Revolutions*, 2nd edn, rev. (Chicago, 1970), pp. 160–73.
2 A. N. Vardac, *Stage to Screen* (New York, 1987); John Fell, *Film and the Narrative Tradition* (Berkeley, 1986).
3 *The Play Pictorial*, 14:87, 1909.
4 I have found enough segments of Tourneur's *The Whip* in the Library of Congress's archives (FAB 1898, FEA 5902-FEA 5906, FDA 2302, reels 4–8) to have been able to assemble and exhibit an almost complete print. This film, with a score by Matthew Scott, was shown at the National Film Theatre in May 1990, and a year later at the Mary Pickford Theatre of the Library of Congress. It was shown, with a different score, at the Edwardian Theatre Conference which gave rise to this present volume. I am still searching for prints of *The White Heather* and *The Great Ruby*, neither of which is listed in filmographies of Maurice Tourneur's work but which have copyright and release dates.

5 *Pimple's 'The Whip'*, produced by Fred Evans (1889–1951) and Joe Evans (1891–1967), print in National Film Archive (UK).

6 Denis Castle, *Sensation Smith of Drury Lane* (London, 1984).

7 The remarkable flying system and below-stage machinery that enabled Emden and Smith to manage some of these Edwardian stage effects still exist and can be seen at Drury Lane.

8 For a discussion of this practice and the parallel conventions of the music hall dramatic sketch and early motion pictures, see my *Playing Out the Empire: Ben Hur and other 'Toga' Plays and Films, 1883–1908* (Oxford, 1994).

9 *The Era*, 23 December 1905.

10 Library of Congress Paper Print Collection, FLA 5941.

11 Library of Congress Paper Print Collection, FLA 5924–5925.

12 Some of D. W. Griffith's most admired films, including *Way Down East* (1921) and *Orphans of the Storm* (1922) are a part of the same impetus to adapt stage plays for the screen. Such is the uniqueness of Griffith's film technique that his films are rarely recognized as filmed stage pieces.

13 National Film Archive (UK).

14 Library of Congress, American Institute Collection, FEA 4192–4193 (latter half only).

15 Library of Congress, FLA 489.

16 Dr Patrick Loughney of the Motion Picture Division of the Library of Congress has remarked on the appropriateness of this setting because the Eden Museé became one of the first public venues in America to be turned into a picture-house.

17 Cecil Raleigh and Henry Hamilton, *The Whip*, Act III, sc. 5, Lord Chamberlain's Plays (1909), British Library.

18 The scene and stage directions end with the previous sentence. Stage directions in square brackets are inferred from the sequence of photographs published in *The Play Pictorial*. See note 3.

19 I am informed by indignant British and American railroad employees that Sartoris's crime was technically impossible. If a single horse-box were to be detached, current safety mechanisms would have brought the entire train to a halt.

20 The undated pressbook for the film of *The Whip* describes the filming of the train crash in Maryland. The book claims that 'The train wreck in *The Whip* ... is absolutely the most realistic ever staged for the movies and is also the most costly single scene ever staged for a screen production. The cost was over $25,000 ...' The earliest train crash to be filmed was at Brighton Beach Race Track, New York, on 4 July 1906. There, before a crowd numbering in excess of 35,000 spectators, promoters staged a head-on crash between two obsolete locomotives. Film of the event was shown in American variety theatres. Library of Congress Paper Print Collection, FLA 5424.

21 A single benefit performance of *The Whip* at the Metropolitan Theatre, London, in May 1962, used in excess of thirty-five supernumeraries.

Index

Page numbers in **bold** type refer to illustrations.